JESU
the Sorcerer

SATOR
AREPO
TENET
OPERA
ROTAS

JESUS the Sorcerer

Exorcist, Prophet of the Apocalypse

Robert Conner

Published by
Mandrake of Oxford
PO Box 250
OXFORD
OX1 1AP (UK)

A CIP catalogue record for this book is available from the British Library and the US Library of Congress.

1869928854

Contents

Acknowlegements and dedication

To Christopher Cochran, hierophant and healer, an immense debt of gratitude. Without his influence, this book would never have been contemplated, much less written.

To Mogg Morgan, who took this book in from the cold and brought wisdom, patience and perseverance to the work of hammering into shape, my deepest thanks.

And finally, to the staff of the theological libraries at the University of Chicago, Harvard, and Yale, my thanks for your courtesy and patient direction.

Robert Conner

Preface

The very notion of Jesus being a *sorcerer* runs so against the grain of the Western cultural myth that even non-Christians are likely to find it far-fetched or even vaguely disturbing. Nevertheless, scholars steadily accumulated evidence for magical practices in the New Testament throughout much of the 20th century —in the 1920s occasional articles on the subject began to appear in specialty journals and by the 1970s books setting out the evidence for magic in primitive Christianity were published. In the final decades of the past century academic interest in magic in the Greco-Roman world increased dramatically, with the result that further connections between Christian and pagan magic were documented.[1] It is that ever expanding body of knowledge that has made this book possible.

The present work will not attempt a detailed historical reconstruction of the brief career of Jesus of Nazareth. That project has been done often poorly and occasionally very well by such writers as E. P. Sanders and Bart Ehrman whose books are enthusiastically recommended.

Instead, this book examines the following topics which I believe to be of particular importance to a modern non-sectarian understanding of Christian origins:

♦ The nature of the earliest Christian documents, the defects of their transmission, and the evidence for the suppression of descriptions of magical acts.

♦ The closely related problem of the New Testament accounts as historical sources.

♦ The radically apocalyptic nature of Jesus' message and the expectations of the early church.

♦ The failure of the apocalypse to occur and the theological reaction to that failure.

♦ The role of magic and mystery religion in early Christianity.

♦ A revisiting of the story of the "beloved disciple" and what it may tell us about Jesus and suppression of evidence about his life. *all Supposition .*

A particular emphasis has been placed on the role of magic and exorcism in the careers of Jesus and of his earliest disciples. Even so, the evidence for magical practice by Jesus and the early church is so variable and extensive that the presentation given herein may be regarded as a summation of the most salient arguments for the case.

Several additional points remain to be made. This work assumes that Jesus was a real person. Although it has been argued for several hundred years that Jesus of Nazareth never existed and that the gospels are a complete fabrication, a recent summary of the evidence for such claims concludes, "The theory of Jesus' non-existence is now effectively dead as a scholarly question."[2] Jesus is scarcely mentioned outside the New Testament because he was unimportant, not because he was fictional. *o* The emergence and survival of Christianity is an example of the sort

He never claimed to be unimportant or the Son of God . quote Joseph.

9

of trivial coincidence on which human history so often seems to turn.

This book has not been written to disabuse Christian believers. Christians are in a paradoxical situation: many feel committed by faith to the belief that the Bible has all the answers that matter, but pick and choose among those answers, ignoring whatever makes them feel uncomfortable. Although most profess to want a church that operates "by the book," they dispute endlessly over what their book means and disregard the clear implications of its text whenever it suits them. Many argue that behavior —particularly sexual behavior— they find objectionable is "contrary to nature," but in the next breath claim that nature is "fallen." When it comes to issues of religion or science, many are unable to discern the difference between explaining and explaining away, or between ideas and ideologies.

I make no pretense of having written a book sufficient for the needs of these confused and conflicted souls, and unlike some modern authors I do not advocate a *rapprochement* between secular pagans and Christians.³ In point of fact, pagan critics of antiquity noted some of the many logical inconsistencies posed by Christian preaching and even pointed to discrepancies between the various gospel accounts.⁴

There are many non-biblical documents that are potentially relevant to an understanding of the formation of Christianity, not the least of which are the Greek magical papyri which illustrate numerous similarities between ancient magicians and Jesus of Nazareth. The pre-Nicene church fathers are another important —although obviously biased— source of information about the religions of antiquity as well as some of the earliest Christian sects, and even though I've drawn

10

on those documents, I have focused primarily on the text of the New Testament. That decision was motivated in part by the fact that most Christians, and hence most of us born into the Christian culture, are conditioned to see this collection of books as a "Bible," a closed, self-referential system, a *canon*. As is well known, fundamentalist sects typically ignore the evidence of extracanonical works they deem to be uninspired, which is, in the end, a happy coincidence: we will not need to stray far beyond the limits of the Old and New Testaments to establish the points I care to make.

This book entirely dispenses with the pleasant pretext that the *life* of Jesus is or ever was truly relevant to much of anything. Christianity began as an obscure apocalyptic sect of Palestinian Judaism. Its "founder" thought the world would end in his lifetime. It is certainly fair to say that Jesus was personally unknown to the majority of Christians who could have been his contemporaries. Indeed it appears that he was personally unknown even to Saul of Tarsus who, writing as the apostle Paul, became Christianity's chief spokesman. During the first centuries of its existence, a person would have been hard pressed to name more than two or three ideas that were uniquely Christian. There were, as the New Testament itself informs us, conflicting interpretations of Jesus —many "gospels"— and the preachers of those gospels were at each others' throats from the very beginning. Not even Jesus' closest associates were sure what to believe.

Jesus-in-the-mind-of-believers, on the other hand, is another matter entirely. Both by virtue of its number of adherents, estimated at more than two billion, as well as the ideology of its leadership, Christianity is a formidable cultural force and humanity, both those who believe and

11

those of us who don't, will live in its shadow for a long time to come.

Before moving into the body of the work, several additional comments about presentation and methodology are in order. Endnotes have been generously employed, particularly for such details as citations of supporting references and remarks about the vocabulary of the original documents. I have tried to make the evidence for my conclusions and the process by which I have arrived at them as transparent as possible. To some extent this results in parallel texts: the body of the book can be read without recourse to the notes, whereas for those who are interested, the notes present a wealth of related data I considered too technical or too extensive to be comfortably incorporated into the main text.

The translations of the Greek New Testament and other sources in Greek are my own. Translation, however, is a two-edged sword. On one hand, it enables comprehension by rendering texts into a familiar language, but on the other, it inevitably loses the rich field of association that every word has in its own language. To partially address this problem, I have reproduced the details of numerous passages in the notes and have attached comments on the vocabulary.

The approach of authorities I favor is generally historical, which means they tend to take no overt position up or down on the reality of the miraculous or uncanny, support particular doctrinal positions, or argue for the inherent truth of Christianity. Their conclusions are therefore objectionable to many believers and I trust my own conclusions will be doubly so.

The late Morton Smith, who is referenced in this book, was subjected to a variety of ad hominem attacks, including accusations of mental instability. It is my conviction that all conclusions, regardless of who arrives at them, should stand or fall on their own merits, but as Smith's case illustrates, this is not often the way business is conducted in the great gray factories of higher learning. Within each discipline there are certain topics that cannot be safely written about and questions that are dangerous to ask, and nowhere —or so it would appear— is this more true than in the field of New Testament studies. The notion that academics are free to follow the evidence wherever it may lead is simplistic and mostly false.

Shawn Eyer has likely put his finger directly into the wound that Smith opened up in the side of Jesus studies, noting that he "took the Gospels as more firmly rooted in history than in the imagination of the early church," that he "refused to operate with an artificially thick barrier between pagan and Christian," and that he published his theories "in plain, understandable and all-too-clear language," sins the present writer can only hope to emulate. [5]

It is my expectation that the readers for whom this book has been written will easily rise above disputes about personalities and credentialism, and judge the arguments made herein on their factual merits. Few of the broad conclusions of mainstream New Testament scholarship will be rehashed here. Those who are interested in the details of these larger questions will find them adequately covered in the references I cite, and in most cases will be able to find extensive additional data available on the world wide web by doing simple subject searches.

Notes:

1 Notably with Campbell Bonner (1927) and P. Samain (1932). Samain's article stands as one of the most completely documented and tightly reasoned summaries in the literature. Among the book length treatments are John Hull's *Hellenistic Magic and the Synoptic Tradition* (1974) and Morton Smith's *Jesus the Magician* (1978). More recent works include Hans-Josef Klauck's *Magic and Paganism in Early Christianity*, first published in German in 1996, and Naomi Janowitz' *Magic in the Roman World: Pagans, Jews and Christians* (2001).

2 *Jesus Outside the New Testament*, 14.

3 Gus diZerega's *Pagans and Christians: The Personal Spiritual Experience*, for example. Although his book is an excellent presentation of modern pagan spirituality, I will argue that Christianity is at its core radically apocalyptic, dualistic, and totalitarian. I cannot imagine what modern pagans hope to gain by a dialogue with believers in such a system.

4 See particularly Hoffman's *Celsus On the True Doctrine* and *Julian's Against the Galileans*.

5 *Alexandria: The Journal for the Western Cosmological Tradition* 3:103-129. For those interested in the *Secret Gospel of Mark*, discussed in a subsequent chapter, Eyer's article is essential reading.

Chapter One:
The Documentary Evidence

For all practical purposes, the reconstruction of Jesus' life and teaching is based entirely on the documents of the New Testament. There are, of course, other sources, but their testimony is either so slight or so distorted by time and fabulist tendencies that their value is nil.[1] *Supposition.*

For reasons I will begin to discuss in a subsequent chapter, it is unlikely that Jesus' followers even considered a written record of his teachings *?* to be of much importance until long after his death. Be that as it may, the fact remains that were it not for the gospels of the New Testament, Jesus would have long since faded into oblivion, so it is with a brief examination of the gospels and their formation that we must begin.

not true.

The oral tradition.

In daily conversation Jesus and his disciples spoke a dialect of Palestinian Aramaic, a Semitic language closely related to Hebrew. In a few places the writer of the gospel of Mark records Aramaic words or phrases and provides a Greek translation, particularly when the words in question are "words of power" that accompany the performance of miracles and exorcisms.[2]

Of course the official language of Rome and the Italian peninsula was Latin, but in most of the eastern Roman territories of Jesus' time the language most commonly used from day to day was not Latin, but Greek. The New Testament is therefore written in Greek, but not in the polished language of the rhetoricians of classical literature:

> As we study the New Testament…the first great impression we receive is that the language to which we are accustomed in the New Testament is on the whole just the kind of Greek that simple, unlearned folk of the Roman Imperial period were in the habit of using.[3]

Whether Jesus spoke any language other than Aramaic or was even able to read has been the subject of some debate. Modern societies expend enormous resources to educate their populations, but pre-industrial societies had neither the resources nor the motivation to teach many people to read and write. Reading was simply not necessary for the types of work that the majority of people performed. It has been estimated that about 90% of the population in the 1st century was completely illiterate and the New Testament specifically states of Peter and John that they were αγραμματος (agrammatos), "without letters," unable to read or write. [4] Since Jesus' closest disciples were predominantly men who worked with their hands, an inability to read or write would have been completely in keeping with their times and their station in life.

All the gospels agree that Jesus taught in synagogues. On one such occasion the gospel of Luke has Jesus being handed a scroll from which he reads a passage from Isaiah, [5] but the historical authenticity of this account is questionable. Regarding the reaction to Jesus' teaching, John says, "Consequently the Jews were amazed, saying, 'How does this man know letters when he has not been taught?'" The clear implication is that Jesus himself was "without letters." [6]

Jesus is sometimes referred to as "rabbi," which means "teacher." However, just what the speakers meant by this title is unclear. In Mark 9:5, for instance, Jesus is so addressed after Peter, James, and John witness the transfiguration. In John 3:2, Nicodemus also calls Jesus "rabbi," but appears to do so in recognition of his miraculous signs. In other words, it is not Jesus' remarkable erudition that calls forth this title of respect, but rather the visions and miracles associated with him. *AS A MASTER*

The villagers of Nazareth ask concerning Jesus, "Isn't this the laborer, the son of Mary and the brother of James and Joses and Judas and Simon, and aren't his sisters here among us?" [7] In this passage, the word τεκτων (tektôn), "laborer," refers to a person who works with wood or stone, a person who in Jesus' times could hardly have been expected to be literate. *all the more wonderful*

Might Jesus have spoken Greek or at least understood it to some degree? The idea derives some support from the fact that a Hellenistic enclave, Sepphoris, lay a mere four miles from Jesus' boyhood home of Nazareth. It has been claimed by some that Jesus might have spent part of his youth working in Sepphoris as a carpenter and may have

17

thus acquired some familiarity with Greek language and culture. However, there is no evidence in the gospels that Jesus spent any time in any pro-Roman city of his day. To the contrary, Jesus may have actually avoided contact with major towns and cities, and his disciples were specifically instructed not to enter Gentile or Samaritan cities. [8] Absent other evidence, the proximity of Hellenistic colonies is not proof that Jesus had enough dealings with speakers of Greek to have acquired proficiency in the language. It is also to be expected that Greek language skills dropped off dramatically as one moved from city to village, and from all indications Jesus taught primarily in villages and rural settings.

There is no evidence that Jesus wrote down any of his teachings. Based on careful study of the surviving gospels, it is certain that Jesus' sayings circulated in oral form, probably for as long as several decades, before any were written down. Moreover, if the earliest Christian documents were written in Aramaic, no trace of them remains. [9] All of the earliest surviving Christian writings are in Greek.

At some point, likely decades after Jesus' death, the teachings that had been passed on orally were committed to writing. Some scholars envision this process to have involved compilations of lists of sayings and lists of miracles which were only later put into the context of a narrative. [10] In fact there exists a collection of dicta called the *Gospel of Thomas*, a Coptic translation of a Greek original, which consists of nothing but isolated sayings unconnected by any narrative.[11] It is not hard to imagine various sayings uttered at different points of Jesus' career being collected into "sermons." In any case, it is nearly certain that the context of much of what Jesus said was lost or confused in the decades between the earliest oral tradition and the writing of the first documents.

The autographs

A printing press with moveable type was invented by Johannes Gutenberg approximately 40 years before Columbus sailed on his first voyage of exploration. The Latin Bible, printed between the years 1452 and 1456, was the first major project to issue from Gutenberg's press. A few dozen copies of this Bible survive, each valued in the millions of dollars.

Before the invention of the press, every document was handwritten and every copy made by hand. In the event an original wore out from use or was lost or destroyed, subsequent readers would have to rely on copies or even copies of copies. The process of reproduction by hand was laborious, time-consuming, and expensive, and abundant mistakes crept into handwritten copies. Besides unwitting errors, the possibility existed that the text might be deliberately changed at the whim of a copyist, or that the text might even be merely paraphrased. The earliest copies of New Testament manuscripts often exhibit the handwriting of unprofessional scribes, and the text reproduced by some of them is charitably described as "free." Of one such early copyist it has been observed that "he worked at reproducing what he imagined to be the thought of each phrase...he transposed and omitted many words and deleted several phrases." [12]

When textual scholars speak of an *autograph*, they are referring to the original document as it came fresh from the pen of the author. *It is universally conceded that none of the autographs of the New Testament books survive.* All the documentary evidence known to exist consists of copies of copies of copies of the autographs.

There is abundant evidence that the books of our present-day New Testament were not the only documents, nor were they necessarily the first. [13] The majority of scholars accept that the writers of the gospels of Matthew and Luke used the gospel of Mark and an additional early gospel, called *Q* (from the German *Quelle,* "source"), as their primary sources of information. Both Matthew and Luke also incorporated material peculiar to each of them from other sources. The gospels of Matthew and Luke therefore contain material from *at least* four different sources: quotations from Mark, quotations from Q, material peculiar to Matthew (i.e., not from Mark, Q, or Luke), and material peculiar to Luke (i.e., not from Mark, Q, or Matthew). In New Testament studies this is known as the *four source hypothesis.* [14]

The extensive borrowing from primary sources explains why we often see near verbatim agreement among the gospels Matthew, Mark, and Luke. The first three gospels, because of their close similarities of viewpoint, are known as the *synoptic* ("seen together") gospels. The gospel Q, sometimes called the *Synoptic Sayings Source,* which obviously antedated Matthew and Luke since they quote from it, is now lost to us although textual scholarship has managed to reconstruct it at least in part based on comparisons between the texts of Matthew and Luke.

The most important point to understand is that *the writers of the gospels were not eyewitnesses of the events they describe.* If they had been eyewitnesses, there would be little reason for them to have relied so extensively on other, previously written, accounts. The complex question of unnamed

20

sources is summarized by Van Voort, who notes regarding them, "No manuscript evidence has survived, and no ancient Christian author mentions them...the communities that used and copied them also disappeared, most likely into the churches that used the fuller Gospels."[15]

Even the question of an autograph itself is not necessarily as straightforward as we might at first suppose. If a writer produced more than one edition of his text, which should be considered the real autograph, the first document or a subsequent variation, both presumably by the same hand?

Additionally, it is now widely recognized that the names attached to the gospels and most of the other New Testament books are not the names of the actual authors. Among the letters attributed to Paul, only Romans, the letters to the Corinthians, Galatians, Philippians, 1 Thessalonians and Philemon are considered with any degree of certainty to be authentic. Attribution of the gospel which bears Matthew's name does not occur until the 2nd century, and even then it is not clear that the reference is to the canonical gospel of Matthew.

Ancient writers often attributed their writings to more famous personages. These documents, produced under false names, are called *pseudepigrapha*, an elegant term for *forgeries*. There is virtually no doubt that the majority of New Testament books, including the gospels, the pastoral epistles (1 and 2 Timothy and Titus), and Revelation, are pseudonymous. As Lane Fox observes, "By withholding his name, the writer lent authority to texts which had none...However we try to justify the authors' practice, at bottom they used the same device: falsehood."[16]

The transmission of the text.

The study of texts which have come down to us in multiple handwritten copies is quite complex and the details of such study are far beyond the scope of this book. Nevertheless, the principle obstacles to the reconstruction of a lost original from imperfect copies are easy enough to understand.

1. If the original of a document is lost and only imperfect copies survive, the reading of any given portion of the text of the original can still be established *assuming that at least one of the imperfect copies preserves the correct reading of that particular portion of the original.* [17]

2. If the original text contained a reading that seemed inadequate to the copyist and the copyist "improved" it, and all surviving copies contain that "improvement," then the original reading is lost.[18]

3. If a copy of the original text contained a corrupted reading, and all surviving copies are descended from that corrupted copy, then the original reading is lost —textual critics call this "primitive error."

4. If, on comparison, copies judged to be of equally probable authority are found to preserve conflicting readings, and one of those readings is assumed to be the original, then in principle it is still not possible to establish the original text with absolute certainty.

Knowing that there are well over 5000 manuscripts of the Greek New Testament which have been compared one to another, and that *none of them contain identical readings*, the perceptive reader will immediately get some sense of the enormity of the problem of establishing the original wording of the New Testament.

Given the humble origins of the earliest Christians, it is unlikely that professional scribes were employed to copy their texts until around the middle of the 4th century. On the contrary, based on study of the handwriting of the earliest copies of the New Testament books, it seems clear that most copies were produced ad hoc by literate amateurs, with the result that the surviving copies are known to contain "far more variants than there are words in the New Testament." [19]

Like Christianity today, early Christianity encompassed a very diverse set of interpretations of the gospels and epistles. After the Roman emperor Constantine declared Christianity to be the official religion of the Empire in the 4th century, the question of whose interpretation of Jesus' teachings represented Christian truth suddenly assumed greater importance. Under pressure from the Roman state and motivated by personal antagonism, bishops in the major cities met to formulate an official —"orthodox"— Christian theology and began to actively suppress the many unofficial interpretations which were declared to be heretical.

For a very long time it was assumed by scholars that only the "heretical" sects sought to change the text of the New Testament. However, recent attention to the evidence has demolished that comfortable position. There are abundant indications that the suppression of the many early forms of Christianity that diverged from the orthodox position also entailed making "refinements" of the New Testament text. [20] Even after several centuries of exacting study of thousands of manuscripts, the text of the New Testament remains to some extent unsure, a situation which has led one textual critic to ask, "Why is almost no one…willing to claim, at least with any substantial degree of confidence, that with our current critical texts we have recovered the N[ew] T[estament] in the original Greek?" [21]

Some conclusions

The overwhelming majority of people who take a Bible from the shelf assume that the words of the books therein are the words of single authors. This is a naïve —and yet rational— assumption. Books have authors and, once printed, their words don't disappear or rearrange themselves, popping up in odd places. Because modern Bibles are printed, it is natural to assume that the books therein follow the rules of other printed books with which we are familiar. Unfortunately, the text of each New Testament gospel is known to have a complex, multi-layered —to say nothing of an additional *unknown* and *unverifiable*— history that requires a level of sophistication unnecessary for the reading of most modern books. The text of the gospels is in a very real sense a trap for the unwary and uninformed. In all fairness it must be pointed out that New Testament scholars have written books in an attempt to disseminate their understanding of these complexities, yet the majority of Christians remain blissfully ignorant of controversies that are common knowledge in the field of New Testament studies.

In subsequent chapters we will examine various examples of textual alteration, particularly in the ways in which Matthew and Luke treated potentially embarrassing material in the gospel of Mark. Although it is customary for scholars to refer to such manipulation as "editing," it is in fact an early example of "spin," of tweaking the text, recasting it to make it say something rather different, or more commonly, evading problematic topics by saying nothing at all. However, a subject raised by one author that is met with thundering silence by a subsequent "editor" is often just as revealing as what is openly acknowledged.

Most importantly, the extensive use of sources reveals that the gospels were not written by eyewitnesses. It is inconceivable that an eyewitness would not have used his own recollections. According to Christian apologists, Jesus' life was the most important life ever lived, and yet amazingly none of our surviving documents appear to contain the direct personal account of anyone who actually saw it. *Jos ph*

Notes

1   A clear and accessible account of the apocrypha can be found in Ehrman's *Lost Christianities: The Battle for Scripture and the Faiths We Never Knew*.

2   Such as ταλιθα κουμ (talitha koum): "get up, little girl" (Mark 5:41), or εφφαθα (ephphatha): "be opened" (Mark 7:34). John Hull: "Foreign words are a very familiar feature of magic spells and the papyri are full of examples…In the Coptic magical papyri Greek appears as the strange and forbiddingly authentic sound, while in the Greek magical world Jewish names and words had special prestige…The foreign expressions are sometimes translated into Greek for the professional use of healers and exorcists…The continued use of Ephphatha in the baptismal ritual of the church (which was also exorcism) can hardly be accounted for except by the supposition that the word was believed in itself to possess remarkable power." *Hellenistic Magic and the Synoptic Tradition*, 85-86.

On the words of power used in Mark 5:41, Smith noted of the formula used by Peter to raise a dead woman (Acts 9:40) —

Ταβιθα αναστηθι: "Tabitha, get up"– "*Tabitha* is a mispronunciation of *talitha*, which the storyteller mistook for a proper name." *Jesus the Magician*, 95.

In the technical literature, a "word of power" is often called a *vox magica* (plural: *voces magicae*).

3   *Light from the Ancient East*, 62.

4   Acts 4:13. Early Christian converts were most frequently women, slaves, soldiers, and laborers, i.e., members of groups with very low rates of literacy.

The low social status of the early Christians reflects a bitter reality of the ancient world generally. Lane Fox: "The social pyramid tapered much more steeply than we might now imagine when first surveying the monuments and extent of the major surviving cities. By itself, a specialized ability in a craft was not a source of upward mobility. Its adepts were often slaves themselves, and even if they were not, they were competing with slave labour, which kept the price of their own labour low. The most upwardly-mobile figures were the veteran soldier, the athlete, the retired gladiator and perhaps (if we knew more) the traders in slaves themselves." *Pagans and Christians*, 59.

5   Luke 4:16-20.

6   John 7:15. "Letters," γραμματα (grammata), i.e., *reading and writing*. The villagers of Nazareth raise the same question according to Matthew 13:34-38. Joseph Hoffman: "…even the members of the synagogue in Nazareth, not the most cultivated of towns (see John 1:46), were offended at the sight of someone with this background teaching in public." *Jesus Outside the Gospels*, 29.

Making a virtue of necessity, Paul openly acknowledges Christianity's appeal to the humble and disenfranchised (1 Corinthians 1:26-29).

7   Mark 6:3. ουκ ουτος εστιν **ο τεκτων**: "Isn't this **the laborer**…?" Matthew, on the other hand, rephrases the question to avoid making Jesus out to be a mere laborer: ουκ ουτος εστιν ο **του τεκτονος** υιος: "Is this not the son **of the laborer**…?" (Matthew

13:55). Luke and John simply omit any reference to Jesus' day job.

Modern sociologists place 1st century artisans such as carpenters below agricultural workers in the social hierarchy. *The Historical Jesus*, 46.

8   Matthew 10:5.

Ehrman also notes Jesus' avoidance of cities: "When Jesus engages in his ministry, according to our Gospels, he *avoids* all major cities but spends his time in small villages and remote rural areas, until his final trek to Jerusalem to celebrate Passover." *The New Testament: A Historical Introduction to the Early Christian Writings*, 254.

Of an apparently long-standing antipathy Crossan notes: "Peasant hatred for administrative centers such as Sepphoris and Tiberias...points toward social revolution or...at least toward social insurrection. The Galilean peasants might not have been able to imagine a new social order, but they could well imagine a world with certain administrative centers razed to the ground." *The Historical Jesus*, 193.

9   "The Christian missionaries with an Aramaic book of gospels in their hands would have been powerless to make propaganda in what was in fact a Greek or rather Hellenized world. An Aramaic gospel-book would have condemned Christianity to remain a Palestinian sect." *Light from the Ancient East*, 65

10   "...the first of his signs...the second sign...many other signs not written in this book..." is probably part of the surviving framework of just such a list (John 2:11, 4:54, 20:30). It has been proposed that a more primitive source, tentatively designated the *Gospel of Signs*, lies somewhere behind the present-day gospel of John.

11   "The Gospel of Thomas has no christological titles, no narrative material, and no reference within its sayings to any action of Jesus or any event in his life." *Jesus Outside the New Testament*, 189.

12   *The Text of the Earliest New Testament Manuscripts*, 161.

13   Papyrus Egerton 2, for example, dated from the early 2nd century, consists of four fragmentary pages of a gospel with similarities to parts of Mark and John. The text, first published in 1935, is widely believed to represent an early lost gospel. *Ancient Christian Gospels*, 205-216.

In addition to those gospels for which we have some fragmentary evidence, other lost gospels such as *The Gospel of the Twelve Apostles*, a *Gospel of the Egyptians*, the *Gospel of Basilides*, the *Gospel According to the Hebrews*, and a *Gospel of Matthias* are mentioned by early Christian writers. There were also numerous forged epistles, Acts, and apocalypses.

14   That the gospel of John does not share the viewpoint of the synoptic gospels is obvious even to the most casual reader. Nevertheless, that there is a close relationship between the gospel of Mark and the gospel of John is also self-evident to most scholars. Regarding the "Semeia Source," the list of miracle stories used by the author of John, Helmut Koester observes: "The stories of the Markan cycles describe Jesus as a man with extraordinary powers who is not above using magical techniques; he employs magical words, uses magical manipulations, and holds a long discourse with a demon. All of these features are absent from the stories of the Semeia Source. Here Jesus documents his power in a different way, not as a magician but as a god...The miracles of Jesus are more than miracles, they are epiphanies." *Ancient Christian Gospels*, 204-205.

15   *Jesus Outside the New Testament*, 176.

Few scholars would deny the existence of "strata" of sources for the gospels, documents and oral traditions that appeared at particular points in the evolution of the Jesus myth and that reflect that evolution. Crossan attempts to arrange sources "by chronological stratification." *The Historical Jesus*, 427-450.

16   *Pagans and Christians*, 340.

Of the many gospels rejected by the early church, Eusebius remarked, "they obviously turn out to be inventions of heretical men." *Ecclesiastical History*, III, 25, 7.

17   The assumption that the original text of each portion of each New Testament document is to be found in at least one surviving manuscript is accepted as a mostly unspoken article of faith by nearly all textual critics. If this assumption is not correct, then recovery of the original text can never be absolutely assured and the project of textual criticism –establishing the exact text of the original documents– ultimately fails.

18   There is good evidence that this did, in fact, occur with some frequency.

19   Bart Ehrman in a lecture, "The Neglect of the Firstborn in New Testament Studies," 2. Elsewhere Ehrman notes, "…the earliest copyists appear to have been untrained and relatively unsuited to the tasks; they made lots of mistakes, and these mistakes were themselves then copied by subsequent copyists (who had only the mistake-ridden copies to reproduce) down into the Middle Ages." *Lost Christianities*, 49.

20   Ehrman's *The Orthodox Corruption of Scripture*, which concentrates on the effects of the emerging christological controversies on the New Testament text, is the most comprehensive examination of the evidence for doctrinally motivated textual tampering. The corrupted form of the text is essentially that of the *King James Version*, the so-called "majority text." For a thorough discussion of the majority text and its ever thinning ranks of defenders, Daniel Wallace's essay in *The Text of the New Testament in Contemporary Research*, 297-320, is recommended.

21   Holmes, *Text of the New Testament*, 348-350. A *critical text* is a master text thought to preserve the most accurate wording of the New Testament based on close comparison of all existing manuscripts. The critical text used for this work is the 27th edition of the Nestle-Aland *Novum Testamentum Graece*.

Chapter Two:
The Infancy Narratives

To the modern reader, a *history* is by definition a dispassionate examination of the facts, and many Christians past and present have read the gospels as if they were histories in this sense: simple, unbiased accounts of facts. From the presentation of the New Testament writers themselves, the reader might easily assume that a history in the modern sense is being proposed:

> Inasmuch as many have set their hand to organize a coherent narrative concerning the events which have been fulfilled in our midst, even as those who from the beginning became eyewitnesses and attendants of the word handed down to us, I too resolved to carefully trace the course of events from the beginning and to write them down in a logical sequence for you, most excellent Theophilus,[1] so that you might know with certainty the matters about which you have been instructed.
>
> Luke 1:1-4

A close reading of the introduction reveals that the writer was not himself an eyewitness to the events he describes, but is compiling accounts of events which were "handed down to us," the "us" in question being Christians of Luke's generation who had not personally witnessed the events of Jesus' life. Moreover, Luke has written his account with a stated goal in mind which is *correct religious instruction*, not mere acquaintance with the facts of Jesus' life. The gospels are not simple reportage. The purpose of the gospels is to generate belief.

It is estimated that at least 30 years passed between the events of Jesus' life and the writing of the gospels. To appreciate the implications of the estimated time lapse between the events of Jesus' life and the writing of the gospels, try to imagine the eyewitness accounts of the assassination of John F. Kennedy, which occurred in 1963, being passed from person to person in oral form until the year 2000, at which point someone finally commits *some* of the oral versions to written form. Our confidence in the reliability of such a report might be tentative at best.

Two points must be clearly understood before a person can undertake an intelligent reading of the New Testament. The gospels are religious propaganda, missionary literature with a double agenda: the conversion of unbelievers and the defense of Christianity before a skeptical pagan audience, and as such the gospels make and support absolute religious claims:

> "I am the way and the truth and the life. No one comes to the Father except through me." *Hidden meaning*
>
> John 14:6

> "And there is no salvation in anyone else, for there is no other

31

name under heaven given among men by which we must be saved."

Acts 4:12

Whether or not Jesus himself ever taught the things here attributed to him, they nevertheless express a clear Christian claim which categorically excludes believers in other religions from approach to God. Every invitation to belief should be an occasion for scrutiny, and a claim as sweeping as this invites the most rigorous form of examination.

The second issue which must be addressed is the nature of our approach to the gospels as documents. It is clear that the gospels were constructed of bits and pieces of oral and written precursors —the primitive written sources are sometimes called *proto-gospels*, but the form these sources may have taken is necessarily a matter of conjecture since they no longer exist. These pre-existing scraps of data are known as *pericopes*, a term which literally means "cut around." A pericope is similar to a modern *blurb*, a short, memorable line excerpted from a longer text. Present scholarship holds that lists of sayings, miracles, and lines from debates with opponents were the likely sources of the pericopes.[2]

> The earliest Christians did not write a narrative of Jesus' life, but rather made use of, and thus preserved, individual units — short passages about his words and deeds. These units were later moved and arranged by editors and authors. This means that we can never be sure of the immediate context of Jesus' sayings and actions.[3]

After noting that authorship is an implicit guarantee of the unity of a work, a noted analyst of narrative goes on to observe of the biblical texts:

> The anonymity of the biblical writer and the absence of context for him are enormously complicated by the intricate process of editing through which his work has come down to us. As with any ancient text, local puzzlements abound —scribal glosses, other kinds of brief interpolations, errors in transcription, and at times wholesale scrambling of passages. But what is far graver for the literary critic is that the stories as a rule appear to have been patched together from disparate and perhaps even conflicting literary sources.[4]

To the modern mind, the gospels contain a host of glaring omissions. There is no physical description whatever of Jesus or of any of his disciples.[5] Jesus' mother, brothers, and sisters are referred to in Mark, but none of the gospels has much to say about Jesus' father once Jesus' career begins. [6] Of Jesus' own marital status, nothing is said and it is difficult to know just what to make of the gospels' silence on this subject.

Even more to the point, apart from the mention that he was a disciple of John the Baptist, *the gospels provide no information on the source of Jesus' ideas.* According to the most primitive tradition, Jesus does not become a person of interest until after he receives the spirit. In other words, John the Baptist and Jesus simply *appear.*[7]

Despite all attempts by historians to determine them, the exact dates of Jesus' birth and death remain a matter of conjecture. The length of Jesus' career is also uncertain; the chronology of the gospel of John suggests a career of about three years, but the earlier account of

33

Mark is consistent with a much shorter period, perhaps less than a year in length. The later synoptic gospels, Matthew and Luke, both polish Mark's prose and ease into Jesus' story by including infancy narratives which are clearly fictitious. Matthew and Luke also omit many of the more radical details and sayings found in Mark, features with which they were obviously uncomfortable.

The gospel of Mark contains this revealing bit of dialogue:

> Peter began to say to him, "Look, we have given up everything and followed you."
> Jesus replied, "Truly I say to you, there is no one who has left house or brothers or sisters or mother or father or children or fields on my account and on account of the good news who will not receive a hundred times as much now in this present time, houses and brothers and sisters and mothers and children and fields —with persecutions— and in the age to come, eternal life"

> Mark 10:28-30

It appears that Jesus' closest disciples abandoned their homes, families, and means of living to follow him. This naturally raises the question of what happened to those families his disciples left behind —*wives and children* are nowhere mentioned as a part of Jesus' entourage. How Jesus and his band of followers managed to support themselves is also unclear, but the accounts imply that while on the road they lived from the charity of those receptive to Jesus' message. [8]

At least one passage implies that Jesus was alienated from his own family:

> And his mother and brothers came, and standing outside, they

sent for him, calling him. A crowd sat around him, and they said to him, "Look, your mother and brothers and sisters are outside asking for you."

He answered, "Who are my mother and brothers?" And looking at those who were sitting around him, he said, "Behold my mother and my brothers! For whoever does the will of God, this is my brother and sister and mother."

Mark 3:31-35

This episode is also reported by Matthew and Luke. [9] At the wedding in Cana, Jesus' mother tells him that the host has run out of wine and is basically told to mind her own business. [10] As we will see in a different context, those looking for support for "family values" may take cold comfort from the words of Jesus of Nazareth.

The Infancy Narratives

Of the city of Bethlehem the prophet Micah wrote:

But you, O Bethlehem Ephrathah, who are little to be among the clans of Judah, from you shall come forth for me one who is to be ruler in Israel, whose origin is from of old, from ancient days.

Micah 5:2, *Revised Standard Version*

The first Christians were eager to apply this prediction to Jesus, but to do so they had to get Jesus born in Bethlehem. There was, unfortunately, a problem: Jesus and his family were from Nazareth, a village so insignificant that it is never even mentioned in the Old Testament. Mark, the writer of the earliest gospel,[11] simply ignored the issue, but Matthew and Luke elected to take it up.

It is well known that people of Jesus' time often concocted fabulous stories about the birth and childhood of famous figures. In the centuries after Jesus' death, apocryphal tales about him and his mother were collected in the form of books, two of which, the *Infancy Gospel of Thomas*[12] and the *Gospel of James*, still survive. Matthew and Luke needed to get Jesus born in Bethlehem, in David's city,[13] so that David, the past king of Israel, could function as a prophetic prototype of Jesus, the future King of Kings. Toward this goal they created our earliest recorded fables about Jesus' childhood, but their fictional solutions created many more difficulties than they resolved.

Matthew places Jesus in the family line of Abraham and David, two pivotal characters in Jewish salvation history, and even enumerates a span of 42 generations between Abraham, David, and Jesus. Matthew completes Jesus' connection to David by having him born in Bethlehem, [14] after which time magi from the east[15] appear at the court of the Judean king, Herod the Great:

> In the days of Herod the king, after Jesus was born in Bethlehem of Judea, magi came from the east to Jerusalem, saying, "Where is he who has been born King of the Jews? For we saw his star ascend, [16] and we came to render homage to him." But after hearing this, King Herod became troubled and all Jerusalem with him, and he assembled all the chief priests and scribes of the people and inquired of them where the Christ was to be born.
>
> Matthew 2:1-4

Herod then sends the magi on to Bethlehem with orders to report back. The star goes ahead of them and stops over the house —*not*, it should be noted, a manger— where the infant Jesus lives with his parents. The magi are warned in a dream not to return to Herod, and an angel appears to Joseph in a dream and warns him to flee with his family to Egypt. Herod, seeing that the magi have not returned as promised, then kills all the children in Bethlehem who are under two years of age. When Herod dies, an angel again appears in a dream to Joseph and orders him to return from Egypt to Judea, but on returning, Joseph discovers that Archelaus, Herod's son, is ruler of Judea (and Bethlehem) and, warned yet again in a dream, resettles his family in Nazareth of Galilee. All of these events —the flight to Egypt, the slaughter of the children, and the move to Nazareth— supposedly fulfill Old Testament prophecies.[17]

There are many problems with this story, beginning with the magi, who, if represented to be Persian officials, could be presumed to have some slight knowledge of royal courts and how they worked. They appeared before Herod the Great —who no doubt regarded *himself* as King of the Jews— inquiring about "he who has been born King of the Jews." Although his reputation for rapacious cruelty was not out of keeping with the standards of his times, this is the same Herod widely known to have murdered two of his ten wives, three sons, a brother-in-law, and a wife's grandfather.[18] How, one cannot help but wonder, did the magi think that Herod would react to the news of the birth of a rival king?

Herod dispatches the magi to Bethlehem on the promise that they will return and report the child's location to him, but according to the story, the magi evade Herod, returning to their country by a different route. But if Herod was so disturbed by the news of the kingly birth, "and all Jerusalem with him," why didn't he simply have the magi followed? Why, for that matter, didn't Herod just kill all the children in Bethlehem at once and have done with it, having learned about Bethlehem *from the prophecy of Micah*, not the magi?

When the magi set out from Herod's palace on their mission to find Jesus, the star again appears and stops over the house where Jesus and his parents live. But if the star led them to Jesus, why didn't it just take them there in the first place? Why did it lead them first to Herod and why would they need to inquire of Herod's scribes and priests where the Christ would be born if the star stopped over the very house where Jesus lived? Obviously the story as we have it traces a ridiculously convoluted path to Bethlehem.[19]

Joseph Hoffman has suggested a strong secondary motive for Matthew's elaborations:

> Some passages in the gospels…show the clear imprint of Christian counter-polemic…the story of the flight to Egypt (Matt. 2:13-15), which the author of the first Gospel strains to relate to an Old Testament prophecy…is perhaps a response to the Talmudic charge that Jesus had learned magic and sorcery in Egypt.[20]

According to this reading, Matthew's infancy story reflects past or current accusations of magical practice leveled against Jesus and seeks to disarm them by explaining Jesus' association with Egypt —and its powerful magic— as strictly circumstantial and not as the true source of his amazing powers. Nevertheless, Christian apologists found themselves defending Jesus against charges of practicing sorcery for years after his death, including allegations that he had returned from Egypt with spells tattooed on his body.[21]

If Matthew's story is to be judged improbable, Luke's is, if anything, even worse. The birth narrative of Luke starts, not with Jesus, but with his predecessor, John the Baptist. There was, according to this version of events, a priest named Zechariah who was married to a barren woman named Elizabeth. While Zechariah fulfilled his priestly duties in the temple, the angel Gabriel appeared to him and announced that Elizabeth would bear a son who would be called John. When Zechariah objected that both he and his wife were too old to have children, Gabriel struck him mute.[22]

In the sixth month of Elizabeth's pregnancy, Gabriel appeared to Mary, a virgin girl[23] living in Nazareth of Galilee.

> And the angel said to her, "Do not fear, Mary, for you found favor before God, and behold, you will conceive in your womb and give birth to a son and you will call his name Jesus. This one will be great and will be called Son of the Most High, and the Lord God will give him the throne of David his father, and he will rule over the house of Jacob for [all] ages and of his kingdom there will be no end.
>
> Luke 1:30-33

Having established the connection between Jesus and his forefather David through Gabriel's announcement, Luke must now somehow get Mary to David's home town of Bethlehem where she will deliver the promised child. It is here that Luke makes an egregious misstep, for according to him,[24] the Roman Caesar Octavian (titled *Augustus*) issued a decree that "all the world" must go to the town of their forefathers to be registered. Luke says this occurred while Quirinius was governor of Syria, an event which, according to Luke 1:5, was contemporaneous with the rule of Herod the Great.

There are two fatal problems with this part of Luke's story: Quirinius was, in fact, a governor in Syria, but not until ten years *after* Herod's death. And of the world-wide census supposedly ordered by Augustus, there is no record, nor indeed could there have been. How could people all over the empire have possibly known where their ancestors had lived *a thousand years previously* and gone there to be registered as Luke claims Joseph did? Ancient sources are understandably silent about this fictitious registration as noted by Ehrman who asks, "…are we to imagine that this massive migration of millions of people, all over the empire, took place without any other author from the period so much as *mentioning* it?" [25]

There are other problems in harmonizing the infancy narratives of Matthew and Luke. In Luke, we are informed that following Mary's ritual purification according to Jewish law, she and her husband "returned to Galilee, *to their town Nazareth*," where the child grew up and that *every year thereafter* his parents went down to Jerusalem for the Passover festival.[26] Where, then, does the family's flight to Egypt and their return to Palestine fit in? In Luke's account of Jesus' childhood, there is never any sense that Jesus is in danger. To the contrary, following the saccharine tale of Jesus being left behind in the temple, Luke assures us that the young Jesus increased in favor with both God and men.[27]

Luke's reconstruction of events forges yet another, less obvious, link between Jesus and his forefather David: even as the prophet Samuel, conceived by a barren woman, anointed David, John, also conceived by a barren woman, baptizes Jesus. The correspondence between the two stories is far too extensive to be coincidental. Indeed, it appears that Luke has taken what he regarded as the essential elements of one story and used them as a framework for the construction of his own account. Luke was particularly adept at raiding the text of the Old Testament for material with which to construct Luke-Acts. For ease of comparison, I have listed the similarities between the two stories below:

Elizabeth is barren.	Hannah is barren.
Elizabeth miraculously conceives John.	Hannah miraculously conceives Samuel.
Zechariah sings a psalm of praise:	Hannah sings a psalm of praise:
Israel saved from enemies.	Enemies will be shattered.
Jesus grows in favor with God and the people.	Samuel grows in favor with God and the people.
John baptizes Jesus.	Samuel anoints David.
(Luke, chapters 1-3)	(1 Samuel, chapters 1-16)

The parallelism between the stories of Samuel the Anointer and John the Baptizer suggests that Luke deliberately used the Old Testament as a model for his story, seeking to show another, deeper, correspondence between David, the king of Judah, and Jesus, to whom God will give "the throne of David his father." [28] Despite the piling up of historical references at Luke 2:1-2, the author of the gospel was not writing history as we know it, but rather locating Jesus and his predecessor John in the stream of salvation history. Thus Samuel becomes a prototype of John even as David becomes a prototype of Jesus —what the first of each pair did, the second will do in an even larger way.

The foregoing discussion illustrates some of the ways in which the text of the gospels has been composed to score theological points. It is probable that we catch a brief glimmer of the real Jesus and the controversy surrounding him in the references to magi and Egypt, but it is clear that these stories do not approximate any modern definition of history.

Notes

1 Κρατιστε Θεοφιλε: "most excellent Theophilus." Most excellent –κρατιστος (kratistos)– is used elsewhere in the New Testament only by Luke and only in addressing the Roman officials Felix (Acts 23:26, 24:3) and Festus (Acts 26:25). Lane Fox concludes that Theophilus ("beloved of God") "is the cover name for a highly placed figure in Roman circles…Acts and the third Gospel are the first, and greatest, of Christian apologies to be addressed to highly placed pagans." *Pagans and Christians*, 430.

2 "The prepassion Gospel narratives were constructed from units of tradition whose divergent forms and contents, locations and interpretations underlined the artificiality of the narrative frames that now encompass them." *The Historical Jesus*, 367.

3 Sanders, *The Historical Figure of Jesus*, 57.

 "It is impossible to avoid the suspicion that historical Jesus research is a very safe place to do theology and call it history, to do autobiography and call it biography." *The Historical Jesus*, xxviii.

4 Alter, *The World of Biblical Literature*, 2-3. Although his observations are made about the Old Testament text, they fit the New Testament situation equally well.

5 "Nobody remembered what Jesus looked like…by c. 200, he was being shown on early Christian sarcophagi in a stereotyped pagan image, as a philosopher teaching among his pupils or as a shepherd bearing sheep from his flock." *Pagans and Christians*, 392.

 The very earliest representation of Jesus appears to be the Roman *Alexamenos grafitto*, which depicts Jesus as a crucified man with a donkey's head. The familiar Jesus of the rather elongated, bearded face comes to us from the 6th century when such a likeness is said to have been miraculously imprinted on a facecloth or *mandylion*, becoming the ancestor of the Greek (and later Russian) Orthodox icon. Such a miraculous image is known as an *acheiropoietos*, "made without hands."

6   Mark 3:31. Mark describes Jesus as "the son of Mary" (6:3), which, given the custom of patrilineal genealogy (as at Matthew 1:1-17, for example), implies that the identity of Jesus' father was a question of dispute. On the subject of fatherhood, his opponents chide him, "we were not born from fornication" (John 8:41). The taunt clearly implies that Jesus' legitimacy is in question. Luke says only ων υιος **ως ενομιζετο** Ιωσηφ: "being a son –**so it was thought**– of Joseph" (Luke 3:23). It is interesting to compare this remark with the explanation of Jesus' parentage at Matthew 1:18-20.

Jesus' brothers are also mentioned at John 7:3, 1 Corinthians 9:5, and Galatians 1:19. According to Paul, Jesus' brothers and the other apostles were married.

7   As at Mark 1:4: **εγενετο** Ιωαννης ο βαπτιζων εν τη ερημω: "John the Baptizer **appeared** in the wilderness." Similarly, Jesus simply "comes" from Nazareth of Galilee (Mark 1:9). Compare this with the more elaborate account of John 1:19-34. This is a remarkable contrast with the documenttation of a later religious career: "[Mother] Teresa's supporters have worked endlessly to compile a complete volume of records documenting her case. More than 100 witnesses answered a 263-question survey, and a 35,000-page, 80-volume report was assembled, according to the promoter of her cause, the Rev. Brian Kolodiejchuk." *Austin American-Statesman*, October 17, 2003.

8   Women are mentioned who provided for Jesus (Luke 8:1-4), and John notes that the disciples kept a purse (John 12:6, 13:29).

9   Matthew 12:46-50, Luke 8:19-21. Jesus' saying that his disciples must hate their families as well as their own lives (Luke 14:26) may reflect an element of his own psychology as suggested by

Smith. *Jesus the Magic*ian, 24-28.

10   John 2:3-4.

11   That Mark was written before the other gospels is agreed upon
     by the majority of New Testament scholars. A excellent summary
     of the evidence for Markan priority has been written by Daniel
     Wallace: "The Synoptic Problem," *www.bible.org.*

12   Not to be confused with the Coptic *Gospel of Thomas.*

13   David's father, Jesse, was a native of Bethlehem (1 Samuel 16:1).

14   Matthew 1:1, 17, 2:1.

15   A μαγος (magos) is usually understood to have been a Persian
     court official, an expert in astrology, dream interpretation, and
     the occult arts generally. However, in the Greek speaking world
     the practice of magic was often attributed to foreigners,
     particularly Persians and Egyptians, simply as a matter of custom.
     An intriguing parallel in the Greek translation of the Old
     Testament recounts how Nebuchadnezzar, disturbed by a
     prophetic dream, summons the "enchanters," επαοιδος
     (epaoidos), the "magi" μαγος (magos), and the "sorcerers,"
     φαρμακος (pharmakos), to interpret his dream (Daniel 2:2).

     Georg Luck: "The history of the terms *magos, mageia,* suggests
     and old misunderstanding. What, for the Persians, was their
     national religion, was, in the eyes of the Greeks, ritual magic."
     Witchcraft and Magic in Europe: Ancient Greece and Rome, 95 Morton
     Smith believed that the story was meant to mark Jesus out as
     "the supreme magus and master of the art," worthy of the
     submission of other magi. *Jesus the Magician,* 96.

16   If the star was a comet or some other spectacular celestial event,
     why had Herod and his court not seen it? Matthew probably had
     in mind Isaiah 60:3 (*RSV*): "And nations shall come to your light
     and kings to the brightness of your rising."

17   Matthew 2:8-23.

18   Metzger, *The New Testament: Its Background, Growth and Content,*
     24.

19   A possible motive for the story of the slaughter of the children

by Herod was to create a parallel between Jesus and Moses by recalling Pharaoh's murder of the Israelite children (Exodus 2:15-16).

20　*Jesus Outside the Gospels*, 40. The Jews, like many ancients, regarded Egypt as the cradle of magic. Clement of Alexandria famously referred to Egypt as "the mother of magicians."

21　*Magic in Ancient Egypt*, 47.

22　Luke 1:5-20. The impregnation of barren women is practically a cottage industry in the Old Testament. Sarah, the wife of Abraham and mother of Isaac, was barren (Genesis 17:17-19) as was Hannah, the mother of Samuel.

23　The Greek word παρθενος (parthenos), virgin, translates the Hebrew word for young woman in Isaiah 7:14 in the *Septuagint*, the Greek translation of the Old Testament favored by early Christians. Mark does not mention Jesus' childhood, and John appears not to have heard of the virgin birth; the disciple Philip identifies Jesus as "Jesus the son of Joseph from Nazareth" (John 1:45) and the Jews also identify Jesus simply as "the son of Joseph" (6:42). The story of the virgin birth is an attempt to make Jesus fulfill the prophecy of Isaiah 7:14, where the Hebrew word *almah*, "young woman," is (mis)translated *parthenos*, "virgin," in the *Septuagint*.

24　Luke 2:1-4.

25　*Jesus: Apocalyptic Prophet of the New Millennium*, 38-39.

26　Luke 2:39-41. The ritual period of purification, in the case of a male child, lasted 33 days according to Leviticus 12:4.

27　Luke 2:42-52.

28　In Acts 3:24 Luke even has Peter say that the prophet *Samuel* predicted the coming of Jesus!

you continuing to fit your facts to parts of the gospel to make your point just as those who wrote the gospels.

45

Chapter Three: Confrontation

The gospels pass over the life of Jesus quite rapidly, concentrating most of their attention on his trial and execution. Indeed, it is the death and resurrection of Jesus that become essential to early Christian theology, and an enormous amount of firepower is expended on this subject, particularly by Jesus' chief advocate, the apostle Paul. The first letter to the Thessalonians, widely believed to be the oldest surviving Christian document, defines the centrality of Jesus' death and resurrection, a theme which is sounded again in the letter to the Corinthians:

> Concerning us, they report what sort of welcome we had from you, and how you turned away from idols to serve a living and true God, and to wait for his Son to come from the heavens, who he raised from the dead, Jesus, who delivers us from the coming wrath.
>
> 1 Thessalonians 1:9-10

> Because in the wisdom of God the world did not know God through its wisdom, God resolved through the foolishness of what is proclaimed to save those believing. Because Jews ask for

signs and Greeks demand wisdom, but we proclaim Christ crucified, for the Jews a cause of revulsion, to the Gentiles foolishness, but to those who are called, both Jews and Greeks, Christ the power of God and the wisdom of God. So that the foolish thing of God is wiser than the wisdom of men, and the feebleness of God is stronger than the strength of men.

And coming to you, brothers, I did not come with superior speech or wisdom proclaiming the mystery of God to you. No, for I decided not to know anything among you except Jesus Christ, and him crucified.

1 Corinthians 1:21-25, 2:1-2.

These passages are the verbal equivalent of a crucifix Paul thrusts forth before his readers. Given that the death and resurrection of Jesus is the bedrock on which Paul's theology rests —he rarely specifically quotes Jesus' teachings and shows almost no interest in his biography— it is important to examine the accounts of those key events.

The final confrontation

Six days before the feast of Passover, Jesus and his disciples arrived at Bethany, a small town within walking distance of Jerusalem. [1] Jesus sent two of the disciples into the village where they found a donkey. The disciples threw their cloaks over the animal, Jesus mounted it, and rode into Jerusalem much as described in the prophecy of Zechariah:

Rejoice greatly, O daughter of Zion! Shout aloud, O daughter of Jerusalem! Lo, your king comes to you; triumphant and

47

victorious is he, humble and riding on an ass, on a colt, the foal of an ass.

Zechariah 9:9, *RSV*.

The gospel of Matthew reconstructs this prophetic scene as follows:

This happened to fulfill what was spoken through the prophet, saying, "Tell the daughter of Zion, Behold, your king is coming to you, humble, and mounted on a donkey and on a colt, the foal of a donkey."

And the disciples went and did just as Jesus directed them. They brought the donkey and the colt, and laid their outer garments over them, and he sat upon them. And a very large crowd spread their outer garments in the road, and others cut branches from the trees and were spreading them in the road. And the crowds that preceded him and those following him shouted, saying, "Hosanna to the son of David. Blessed is the one coming in the name of the Lord! Hosanna in the highest heavens!"

And coming into Jerusalem, the whole city was in commotion, saying, "Who is this?" And the crowd said, "This is the prophet Jesus from Nazareth in Galilee."

Matthew 12:4-11

The writer of the gospel was obviously not an eyewitness of the events he describes. He misunderstands the parallelism of the Old Testament passage, mistakenly reading the text of Zechariah to refer to *two* animals —Mark, Luke, and John[2] all have one donkey— and presents the reader with the absurd image of Jesus astraddle two animals, and adult *and* its colt. The gospel of John nearly concedes that the connection between Jesus' trip into Jerusalem on a donkey and the prophecy of Zechariah is a later invention:

His disciples did not realize these things about him at first, but after he had been glorified, then they recalled that these things had been written about him and they had done these things to him.

John 12:16

On the day of his arrival, possibly the first day of the six days mentioned in John, Jesus went to Jerusalem, entered the temple for a look around, and then left, "as it was already late," and went back to Bethany to spend the night.[3] On the following day —day two according to Mark[4]— he returned from Bethany with a group of disciples and created a disturbance in the temple, overturning the tables of the moneychangers and generally obstructing business, but was not arrested by the temple police at that point.

Jesus and his followers left the city that evening and returned the following day, the third day of Jesus' temple activities according to Mark's account. At this point the temple authorities confronted him, but were unable to arrest him publicly because they feared the crowds that Jesus attracted.[5]

The confrontations the gospels describe between Jesus and the temple authorities were an ugly business. Jesus denounced them in offensive terms, quoting from the prophet Jeremiah:

And he was teaching them, saying, "Has it not been written, my house will be called a house of prayer for all the nations? But you have made it a hideout of robbers!" And the chief priests and the scribes heard about this and they began to seek how they might kill him, for they feared him because the whole crowd was overwhelmed by his teaching.

Mark 11:17-18

"Woe to you, scribes and Pharisees! Hypocrites! You build the tombs of the prophets and you adorn the graves of the righteous, and you say, 'If we lived in the days of our forefathers, we would not have been their partners in shedding the blood of the prophets.' So you testify against yourselves that you are sons of those who killed the prophets!"

"Fill up the measure of your fathers, you! Snakes! Offspring of vipers! How are you to flee from the judgment of Gehenna?"

"Why for this reason I am sending forth prophets and wise men and scribes to you. You will kill and crucify some of them and some of them you will whip in your synagogues and pursue from city to city, so that there may come upon you all the righteous blood spilled on earth from the blood of innocent Abel down to the blood of Zechariah the son of Barachiah who you murdered between the sanctuary and the altar."

"Yes, indeed, I say to you, all this will come upon this generation!"

"Jerusalem, Jerusalem, she who kills the prophets and stones those sent forth to her! How many times I wanted to gather your children to me the way a hen gathers her chicks under her wings, but you did not want it. Now look! Your house is left desolate! For I say to you, from now on you will by no means see me until you say, 'Blessed is he who comes in the name of the Lord!'"

Matthew 23:29-39

As extreme as these words are, the modern reader can scarcely appreciate the offense they must have caused the temple authorities. The Gehenna to which Jesus refers is the same valley of Hinnom[6] mentioned in Jeremiah, which in Jesus' day was a steep, narrow ravine outside the southern wall of the city into which the city's sewage drained and rubbish was thrown to be burned. Gehenna was a combination of cesspool and garbage dump.

The valley's unsavory associations dated from the remote past; the area is the likely site where the apostate king Solomon built an altar to Moloch, a Canaanite deity associated with child sacrifice by burning. [7] Long after the reign of Solomon, the Judean king Josiah led a violent religious reformation movement during which the altars and furnishings of the pagan gods were destroyed, their priests killed, and the grounds of their holy sites desecrated by the burning of human bones. [8]

In this scathing denunciation, Matthew even has Jesus include converts to Judaism, calling them "sons of Gehenna." [9] In short, the context of this bitter denunciation repeatedly associates the temple officials not only with filth, but with apostasy. Do these exchanges reflect the words of the historical Jesus? [10]

It is nearly certain that they do. The woes pronounced against the temple leadership culminate in the prediction that the temple itself will be destroyed.

> As he left the temple, one of his disciples said to him, "Teacher, look what large stones and amazing buildings!" And Jesus said to him, "Do you see these great buildings? By no means will a stone be left upon a stone here and not be demolished!"
>
> Mark 13:1-2

Jesus' curse upon the temple is reported by all four gospels, repeated by his accusers at his hearing before the temple authorities, and is thrown back in his face as a taunt during his crucifixion. It appears in the Coptic *Gospel of Thomas*, and in Acts the witnesses against Stephen accuse him of repeating Jesus' prediction that the temple will be destroyed.[11] There is certainly no reason to doubt Jesus' animosity toward the temple authorities and their fear of him is well documented. They believed the crowd would riot if they arrested him publicly.[12] It is likely that from this moment forward, Jesus' fate was sealed. The leaders determined to arrest him and turn him over to Pontius Pilate to avert the possibility of greater disturbance.

The apocalyptic content of Jesus' preaching is the subject of a subsequent chapter, but suffice to say at this point that Jesus came proclaiming the imminent arrival of the kingdom of God and the overthrow of the old order, including, as we have seen, the destruction of Herod's temple. It is difficult to imagine how any prophet foretelling the overthrow of kings and kingdoms in the midst of the vast Passover throngs —caught up during the festival on the high tide of nationalistic religious fervor— would be tolerated.

Preventing disturbances during Passover was the job of the Jewish temple police operating under the authority of the High Priest, Joseph Caiaphas. For the sake of all involved, it was acknowledged that the administration of Jewish affairs was best left in the hands of the Jewish authorities whenever possible. The provocation of pagan soldiers entering the sacred temple grounds during this most holy of festivals would be a recipe for disaster,[13] so Roman intervention within the temple precinct would have been used only as a last resort.

Given the potential for rioting among the Passover crowds, the Roman prefect —Pontius Pilate[14] at the time of Jesus' arrest— traveled to Jerusalem from his usual residence in the sea coast city of Caesarea accompanied by a contingent of 3000 troops. A permanent Roman garrison in the fortress of Antonia, adjacent to the temple precinct, warily surveyed the Jewish pilgrims from the ramparts of the heavily fortified walls and towers, alert for any signs of disturbance. In the event of problems during Passover, the entire political leadership, Jewish and Roman, would present a united front, quickly and efficiently dealing with troublemakers.

Joseph Caiaphas' responsibilities to his people during the festival were particularly extreme: if a mob should slip from the control of the Jewish temple police, the Roman prefect would be forced to intervene, a provocation that would impel the restive population to open rebellion. Should that occur, Pilate would next petition for legions of troops from the neighboring Syrian legate. All of Judea could erupt into war with incalculable loss of life, a disaster for Caiaphas and an even greater tragedy for the Jewish nation.

> Therefore the chief priests and the Pharisees assembled the High Council and they said, "What will we do? This man is performing many signs! If we tolerate him like this, everyone will believe in him and the Romans will come and take over both our place and people!"
>
> But one of them, Caiaphas, being the High Priest that year, said to them, "You don't understand anything! You don't even take into account that it is more advantageous for you that one man die for the people than to have the whole nation destroyed." He did not say that of his own accord, but being High Priest that year he prophesied that Jesus was about to die for the nation, and not only for the nation, but to gather together God's

dispersed children into one.

So from that day forward they planned how they might kill him.

John 11:47-53

The betrayal, arrest, and trial of Jesus are deeply overlaid with Christian iconography and facts are hard to separate from fable. Luke reports that the temple police used spies to follow Jesus[15] in preparation for his delivery to the authorities, so it makes little sense to suppose that they would pay Judas to betray Jesus' location. It has been suggested that Judas betrayed the content of Jesus' secret teaching, an idea supported by the charge that Jesus considered himself the future "King of the Jews." [16]

The accounts of Jesus' arrest are contradictory. Mark has Judas indicate which man is Jesus by approaching him and kissing him. In John's gospel, on the other hand, Jesus steps forward, asks the temple police who they are seeking, and identifies himself not once but three times while Judas simply stands by. At the time of his arrest, the disciples initially offer armed resistance, and then flee.[17]

If the disciples abandoned Jesus in disarray and followed the subsequent progresssion of events from a safe distance,[18] then it was, of course, impossible for them to overhear Jesus' exchanges with his accusers. It is already established by the gospels themselves that the authorities arrested Jesus by night, hastily interviewed him, pronounced his guilt, and hustled him away to Pilate for speedy execution *because they were in fear of the reaction of the crowd of Jesus' supporters.* It is therefore absurd to have Pilate stand Jesus before the crowd and argue repeatedly for his acquittal.

The gospels, especially Matthew and John, want Jesus to have been condemned by the Jewish mob, against Pilate's better judgement. Pilate worried, he was advised by his wife to do nothing, he consulted the crowd, he pleaded on Jesus' behalf; finally, weakling that he was, he could not withstand the clamour of the crowd, and so he had Jesus executed (Matt. 27.11-26; John 18.28-19.16). These elements of the story of Jesus' last hours derive from the desire of the Christians to get along with Rome and to depict the Jews as their real opponents. In all probability Pilate received Caiaphas' charge, had Jesus flogged and briefly interrogated, and, when the answers were not completely satisfactory, sent him to the cross with not a second thought. Philo, who was Pilate's contemporary, wrote an appeal to the emperor Gaius (Caligula), which included a description of Pilate. Philo wrote of "the briberies, the insults, the robberies, the outrages and wanton injuries, the executions without trial constantly repeated, the ceaseless and supremely grievous cruelty" that marked Pilate's rule (*Embassy to Gaius*, 302). Moreover, Pilate was eventually dismissed from office because of large-scale and ill-judged executions (*Antiq.* 18.88f). This evidence agrees precisely with the sequence of events that the gospels narrate: Jesus appeared before Pilate and was executed almost immediately, with no further witnesses and no trial procedure. The stories of Pilate's reluctance and weakness of will are best explained as Christian propaganda; they are a kind of excuse for Pilate's action which reduces the conflict between the Christian movement and Roman authority.[19]

In summary, the trail of events seems to have run roughly like this: Jesus and his disciples left the temple area and crossed the Kidron valley to a garden where Jesus was arrested by the temple police.[20] He was taken before Annas, the father-in-law of Caiaphas, and other members of the High Council, where he was questioned by some number of Jewish rulers, including the High Priest.[21] The Jewish authorities, satisfied that Jesus was recalcitrant, then sent Jesus posthaste to Pilate with the recommendation that he be executed. Pilate briefly interrogated him and sent him away to die.[22]

Even the accounts of the crucifixion present difficulties. Mark informs us that certain women among Jesus' followers watched his crucifixion from a distance, an observation probably in keeping with historical possibility.[23] *Women* viewing the execution *from a distance* would not likely have aroused the suspicions of the Romans. John, on the other hand, has female members of Jesus' family, along with at least one male disciple, standing at the foot of the cross engaging the dying Jesus in conversation.[24] This admittedly adds a nice dramatic touch, but is historically improbable.

The accusation of sorcery

One further detail, perhaps the most relevant to our investigation, must be addressed. It would appear that the Jewish leaders accused Jesus of sorcery. The evidence for such an accusation, *considered apart from other information*, is inconclusive, but given the editing to which the gospel accounts have been subjected, one could hardly expect the situation to be otherwise.

The imputations of practicing sorcery are based on two passages, one of which is found in John. Asked by Pilate what charges they are bringing against Jesus, the Jewish leaders reply:

> "If this man were not an evildoer, we would not have handed him over to you." [25]

> John 18:30

It is apparent from the context that whatever evil Jesus was accused of doing, it was a capital offense. It is also clear from the gospels that the Jewish authorities considered Jesus to be in control of evil spirits. In addition to *evildoer*, the term κακοποιος (kakopoios) could also mean *sorcerer*, and under Roman law some forms of sorcery, in particular the attempt to predict the death of Caesar by any form of divination, was considered *lèse majesté* and was punishable by death.

Early Christians were also accused of being "evildoers" and the charge of evildoing was serious enough to warrant execution:

> Nor may any of you suffer death as a murderer, or an evildoer, or a thief, or as a receiver of stolen goods.[26]

1 Peter 4:15

The second passage cited in support of a charge of sorcery comes from Matthew, and is again voiced by the Jewish authorities to Pilate:

> "My Lord, we remember that that impostor said while still alive, 'After three days I will raise myself.'" [27]

Matthew 27:63

The term πλανος (planos), translated *imposter*, can also mean *deceiver* or *sorcerer* and as an adjective is used elsewhere in the New Testament in relation to spiritism.[28] After a lengthy analysis of the passage in question, Samain concluded:

> ...by the epithet πλανος, Matthew refers to a man who has won over the crowd not only by his doctrines and his words, but also by his activities and his wonders, that is to say, a magician.[29]

Some conclusions

The gospels are simultaneously missionary literature, apologies, and polemics, written to defend an obscure Jewish sect before the greater Greco-Roman world while at the same time squashing unwanted theological speculation within Christian ranks by defending correct teaching. The gospels, as we are beginning to see, are back formations, responses to unexpected historical developments which put the most primitive theological tradition in serious doubt.

As to whether Jesus practiced sorcery, we have thus far the allusions to Egypt in Matthew's infancy narrative and the oblique accusations made by the Jewish leaders when they turned him over to Pilate. Taken alone, this evidence is inconclusive, but the aim of the gospel writers was to exonerate Jesus before the world, not convict him of charges of practicing magic. Christian belief is on trial in the gospels and at no point would we expect full disclosure.

The first and most serious jolt to the disciples' hopes came at the crucifixion, and it is to a consideration of how that shock was repaired that we turn next.

Notes

1   Mark 11:1, John 12.1.

2   Mark 11:2, Luke 19:30, John 12:14. In John's account, Jesus finds the donkey on his own.

3   John 12:1, Mark 11:11.

4   Mark 11:12. The confrontation recorded in Mark 11:15-19 is, as astutely noted by Crossan, "not at all a purification of the Temple but rather a symbolic destruction." *The Historical Jesus*, 357.

5   The gospels are unanimous that the temple authorities were afraid

of the crowds: Matthew 21:26, Mark 11:32, Luke 20:19, John 12.19.

6   Greek γεεννα (Gehenna), a transliteration of the Aramaic for "valley of Hinnom."

7   1 Kings 11:4-8, 2 Kings 16:2-4, 2 Chronicles 28:1-4.

8   2 Kings 22:1 – 23:25.

9   Matthew 23:15.

10   Some of the details of these diatribes are certainly anachronistic: none of Jesus' followers were being pursued or flogged in synagogues at this stage, and the Pharisees were never in charge of the temple cult. As the only religious sect to survive the Roman invasion following the Jewish revolt, they became the source of modern rabbinic Judaism.

11   Matthew 24:1-2, Luke 21:5-6, John 2:19-21, Mark 14:58, 15:29-30, *Gospel of Thomas*, 71 ("I shall destroy this house and no one will be able to build it."), Acts 6:13-14.

12   Mark 14.2.

13   Violent clashes between Jews and Palestinian Arabs at the site of the Western Wall in the present day are an example of the same phenomenon, the intrusion of "the other" into sacred space. An inscription putting Gentiles on notice not to enter the sacred precinct read as follows: "Let no foreigner enter within the screen and enclosure surrounding the sanctuary. Whosoever is taken so doing will be the cause that death overtaketh him." *Light from the Ancient East*, 80.

      Regarding Jesus' provocative behavior during Passover, Crossan observes, "Such an act, if performed in the volatile atmosphere of Passover, a feast that celebrated Jewish liberation from inaugural imperial oppression, would have been quite enough to entail crucifixion by religiopolitical agreement. And it is now impossible for us to imagine the offhand brutality, anonymity, and indifference with which a peasant nobody like Jesus would have been disposed of." *The Historical Jesus*, xii.

14   Pontius Pilate, *praefectus* of Judea from CE 26-36, possessed

imperium, supreme administrative power, which entitled him to deal with virtually any situation as he saw fit, the customary practice when the indigenous people of a province presented special problems of governance. Palestine was part of the imperial province of Syria which, unlike senatorial provinces, was ruled by a military governor. The districts of the province were controlled by *prefects* or *procurators*. Pilate was such a prefect.

15 Luke 20:20.

16 *Jesus, Apocalyptic Prophet*, 216-219. During his ministry, Jesus never calls himself "King of the Jews" (Mark 15:12).

17 Mark 14:43-45, John 18:3-10, Matthew 26:56, Mark 14:50. Significantly, Jesus asks if the temple police have come to arrest him as if he were a λῃστής (lêstês). The word is multivalent: it can mean *highwayman*, *robber*, or *insurrectionist*, *guerrilla*, i.e., a person who incited rebellion against Roman authority (Mark 14:48). Is is, of course, quite likely that insurrection was funded by theft, so the two categories no doubt overlapped. Given that the gospel was written during the last years of the Jewish revolt, certainly after the destruction of Herod's temple, it raises the possibility that Jesus advocated subversion. The term is also used of the two men crucified along with Jesus (Luke 23:40).

Crossan: "Social banditry and millennial prophecy may, indeed, go hand in hand...Messianic claimants invoke human violence but with divine violence undergirding it." *The Historical Jesus*, 163, 168. A modern parallel is the preaching in the church or mosque provoking terrorism in the street.

18 Matthew 26:56, Mark 14:50.

19 *The Historical Figure of Jesus*, 273-274. Luke exonerates the Romans by shifting the blame for Jesus' death to the chief priests and the scribes (Luke 22:2), omits the presence of Romans at the moment of Jesus' arrest (22:52) —contrast John 18:12— and deletes the reference to Gentile "sinners" found in Matthew 26:45 and Mark 14:41. He has Herod Antipas' officers abuse Jesus (Luke 23:11), not the Romans (Matthew 27:27-31, Mark 15:16-20). Nevertheless, that Pilate murdered Jews is conceded, perhaps

inadvertently, by Luke (13:1).

20 John 18:1-3.

21 John 18:12-14, 19-24. This proceeding was a close to a formal trial as Jesus was to get.

22 John 18:28, 19:1-16. Even the interrogation of Jesus is problematic. If Pilate spoke Latin and Greek, and Jesus spoke Aramaic, then the prolonged philosophical discussions reported in the gospels could only have transpired through an interpreter and it is doubtful that Jesus received that much of a hearing from Pilate.

23 Mark 15:40.

24 John 19:25-27.

25 ει μη ην ουτος **κακον ποιων** ουκ αν σοι παρεδοκαμεν αυτον: "If this man were not an **evildoer**, we would not have handed him over to you." Although not typically cited as evidence favoring an accusation of magic, Luke specifies that the charge made against Jesus was "**perverting** our people" –**διαστρεφοντα** το εθνος ημων– which is perhaps *not* coincidentally the very same term he has Paul use against the *magician* Bar-Jesus: ου παυση **διαστρεφων** τας οδους του κυριου: "will you not stop **making crooked** the paths of the Lord?" (Luke 23:2, Acts 13:10).

26 ως φονευς η **κακοποιος** η κλεπτης: "as a murderer, or an **evildoer**, or a thief…" Compare 1 Peter 2:12: καταλαλουσιν υμων ως **κακοποιων**: "they slander you as **evildoers**." As noted by Selwyn, Tertullian translated κακοποιος with the Latin *maleficus*, meaning *magician*. *The First Epistle of St. Peter: The Greek Text with Introduction, Notes and Essays*, 225.

27 εκεινος ο **πλανος** ειπεν ετι ζων μετα τρεις ημερας εγειρομαι: "that **imposter** said while still alive, 'After three days I will raise myself.'" If construed as the middle voice, εγειρομαι would mean *I will raise myself*. Most translators, accepting the claim that God raised Jesus from the dead, translate the passage as *I will be raised*, reading the verb as passive.

The Jewish historian Josephus, in a passage which is almost certainly authentic, refers to Jesus as a **παραδοξων εργων ποιητης**: "a performer **of amazing works**," which Van Voort notes "can be read to mean simply that Jesus had a reputation as a wonder-worker," an observation that would be consistent with a charge of practicing magical feats such as raising oneself from the dead. *Jesus Outside the New Testament*, 89.

28 As at 1 Timothy 4:1: προσεχοντες πνευμασιν **πλανοις** και διδασκαλιαις δαιμονιων: "turning to **deceptive** spirits and teachings of demons…" That Paul and his companions were regarded ως **πλανοι**: "as **impostors**" (2 Corinthians 6:8) in certain circles may indirectly acknowledge that they were charged with practicing magic –Paul's relation to magicians is the subject of a subsequent chapter. Significantly, the same authorities who accuse Jesus of controlling demons also say "he **deceives** the crowd" –**πλανα** τον οχλον (John 7:12, 20).

"To begin with the terminology used in speaking of itinerant magicians: in Greek they continue to be classified as *agyrtai* or begging holy men, although sometimes they are also called *ageirontes*, a participle from the same root as *agyrtes* that means 'those taking up a collection,' and sometimes yet again as *planetai*, 'wanderers or vagabonds,' or *planoi* [plural of πλανος, *my note*], the deeply ambiguous term that means primarily 'one who creates delusions in the minds of other men,' then 'sorcerer,' but that may also have connotations of vagabond or wandering beggar; the term *laoplanos*, 'one who deludes the masses,' is also found." *Magic and Magicians in the Greco-Roman World*, 224-225.

29 My translation of: "pour…l'épithète de πλανος Matthieu désigne un homme qui a séduit la foule, non seulement par sa doctrine et ses paroles, mais aussi par ses gestes prodiges: c'est à dire un magicien." *Ephemerides Theologicae Lovanienses* 15:458-459.

more than magic it is spiritual science

Chapter Four:
The Resurrection as
Ghost Story

If what happened when the Jewish leaders turned Jesus over to the Roman authority was predictable, what happened when the Roman authority turned Jesus over to history was simply amazing.

Jesus' post mortem appearances fall generally into three categories: visions, epiphanies, and apparitions, but the distinctions are not always maintained, nor are the details wholly consistent. For example, the account of Jesus' appearance to Saul on the road to Damascus, reported in three places in the book of Acts,[1] differs in detail with each retelling. According to the first report, the men with Paul hear a voice but see no one,[2] but in the second the men see a light but do not hear a voice.[3] In the first account, Paul alone falls to the ground,[4] but in the third retelling, all the men fall to the ground.[5]

Soon after his conversion, Saul (aka Paul) again sees Jesus, but under different circumstances:

> It happened that after returning to Jerusalem, while I was praying in the temple, I came to be in a state of ecstasy, and I saw him saying to me, "Hurry and leave Jerusalem at once because they will not accept your testimony about me."
>
> Acts 22:17-18

Jesus' appearance to Paul in the temple is an ecstatic vision,[6] whereas his manifestation on the road to Damascus has characteristics of post-resurrection epiphanies: light, voices, glowing raiment,[7] supernatural entities, and natural upheavals.[8]

A text often cited as the first report of Jesus' post-resurrection appearances comes to us from a letter written by Paul:

> For I passed on to you as of first importance what I also received, that Christ died for our sins according to the scriptures, and that he was buried, and that he was raised on the third day according to the scriptures, and that he appeared to Cephas, [9] then to the twelve, then he appeared to more than five hundred brothers at one time, the greater number of whom remain until now, but some have fallen asleep [in death].
> Then he appeared to James, then to all the apostles. Last of all, he appeared even to me, as to one born before his time.
>
> 1 Corinthians 15:3-8.

However, the claim that Jesus appeared to 500 witnesses at one time is the sort of exaggeration one would expect from a later apocryphal account, and the fact that none of the gospels report this remarkable confirmation of the resurrection almost certainly marks the passage as having been inserted into the text long after Paul's death. Robert Price has proposed that the chain of connectives —"*that* Christ died...*that* he was buried...*that* he was raised...*that* he appeared..."—

How can the author prove otherwise
Every TWP is recorded on the other
So we will eventually know the truth.

64

is the relic of an interpolated liturgical confession, i.e., *not* written by Paul,[10] which if true, would make the gospel of Mark the oldest report of the resurrection:

> When the Sabbath had passed, Mary the Magdalene and Mary the mother of James and Salome bought spices so that they might go and anoint him, and very early in the morning on the first day of the week, the sun having risen, they went to the tomb. They were saying to one another, "Who will roll the stone away from the door of the tomb for us?"
>
> Looking up, they saw that the stone —which was extremely large— had been rolled away. And entering the tomb, they saw a young man clothed in a white robe, sitting off to the right, and they were alarmed. But he said to them, "Do not be alarmed. You are seeking Jesus of Nazareth who was crucified. He is not here. He has been raised. Look at the place where they laid him! But go tell his disciples and Peter that he goes ahead of you into Galilee. You will see him there just as he told you."
>
> And after they left, they fled from the tomb, for trembling and panic[11] seized them. And they said nothing to anyone because they were afraid.

> Mark 16:1-8

The account contradicts our expectations for several reasons, most obviously because the women do not actually see Jesus, but a young man who we assume to be an angel. [12] There is no sense of reassurance here —the women flee the tomb in panic, too frightened to speak of their experience.

The writers of Matthew and Luke were dissatisfied with this ending and set about repairing it, introducing a number of new difficulties in the process.[13] Matthew's expansion has the eleven faithful apostles go to Galilee where they receive the commission to make disciples of all nations, but, we are told, *some doubted.*[14]

The doubt of some to the eleven faithful apostles clearly troubled the early church —the resurrection and glorification of Jesus was already the keystone in the arch of Christian belief as Paul explains to the Corinthians:

> If Christ has not been raised, your faith is useless. You are still in your sins and those who have fallen asleep in Christ are truly dead. If in this life only we have hoped in Christ, we alone among all men are the most pathetic.
>
> But now Christ has been raised from the dead, the beginning of the harvest of those who have fallen asleep in death.
>
> 1 Corinthians 15:17-20

But when Luke set about removing the last element of doubt about the reality of Jesus' resurrection, he created a startling narrative shift: the appearances of the risen Christ begin to take on the characteristics of classic ghost stories.

The longest of these stories concerns the stranger that two disciples meet on the road to Emmaus. As they walk with him, they repeat the details of the story of the women at the tomb and the vision of angels. Jesus, who they have been prevented from recognizing, then explains all the prophecies relating to himself in the Old Testament. Finally, as they eat the evening meal together, Jesus blesses the bread, breaks it, and hands it to them. The account of the appearance comes to this jarring conclusion, a conclusion which is particularly unsettling because of the association between invisibility and magic:

Their eyes were opened and they recognized him and he

became invisible to them.[15]

Luke 24:31

Surely Luke was not unaware of the ghostly nature of this story. Indeed, the next account he relates appears designed to prove that the stranger on the road to Emmaus was *not* a ghost:

> But while they were talking about these things, he stood in their midst and said to them, "Peace be with you!" But they were alarmed and became afraid, thinking they were seeing a spirit. And he said to them, "Why are you terrified, and why do doubts arise in your hearts? Touch me and see,[16] because a spirit does not have flesh and bones as you see I have."[17] And saying this, he showed them his hands and feet.
>
> But even in their joy they did not believe him, and while they were wondering, he said to them, "Do you have anything here to eat?" And they gave him a piece of fish. And he took it and ate it in front of them. *The salamander.*

alexander

the monks

has fathersürite

Luke 24:36-43

In this passage Jesus proves his corporeal nature to his disciples by having them touch him and by eating food in their presence. But the disciples wonder —as well they might— how a body of flesh and bones has suddenly materialized in their midst. *The same way as when we are born from spirit.*

Jesus' appearances in the gospel of John retain this spectral quality. Twice Jesus appears in the disciples' midst even though the doors are locked:

> So being the evening of that day,[18] the first of the week, and the doors having been locked[19] where the disciples were for fear of the Jews, Jesus came and stood in their midst and said to them, "Peace to you!" and having said this, showed his hands *the asters*

and side to them. Consequently the disciples rejoiced at seeing the Lord.

…

And after eight days his disciples were again indoors and Thomas was with them. Jesus came, the doors having been locked, and stood in their midst and said, "Peace to you!"

Then he said to Thomas, "Put your finger here, and look at my hands, and reach out your hand and stick it into my side, and be not unbelieving, but believing."

Thomas exclaimed, "My Lord and my God!"

Jesus said to him, "You have seen me and believed. Happy are those who not having seen yet believe."

John 20:19-20, 26-29

In these various manifestations Jesus exhibits traits of a *revenant*, an embodied ghost that appears once or for a brief period of time following the death of the subject[20] and performs bodily functions such as speaking and eating, displays premortem wounds, is associated with an empty tomb, and vanishes suddenly without leaving any physical trace, all of which are characteristics noted by Debbie Felton, a scholar who has produced a particularly productive analysis of the ancient Greco-Roman ghost story.[21] As noted by Finucane, "…late classical tradition attributed various activities to ghosts, such as informing, consoling, admonishing, and pursuing, the living." [22]

It is well known that people of antiquity thought certain classes of the dead particularly likely to become ghosts: the αωρος (aôros), the *prematurely dead*, the αγαμος (agamos), the *unmarried*, the αταφος (ataphos), the *unburied*, and the βιαιοθανατος (biaiothanatos), the *dead by violence*. It is clear that Jesus could be numbered among at least three of these groups, all of whom share a commonality identified by Sarah

those who choose to come back e show themselves

Johnston: "Those who died before completing life were understood to linger between categories, unable to pass into death because they were not really finished with life." [23]

It is possibly significant that the Greek of Luke's gospel reveals a higher social register than that of Matthew or Mark —the historiographic preface to Luke's gospel, in keeping with official histories of the era, "indicates that the author has done extensive research."[24] If that is the case, it is not unlikely that the writer was also familiar with accounts of ghosts included in secular histories and the popular *paradoxa*, collections of uncanny and bizarre events which quite naturally included ghost stories.[25]

If Luke sought, consciously or not, to imitate the genre of the classical ghost story in framing his accounts of Jesus' post-resurrection appearances, his technique would at the very least have set a precedent for the author of the gospel of John. Alternatively, of course, it is possible that the accounts of Luke and John were not influenced by Greco-Roman literary conventions, in which case we are confronted with a primitive New Testament tradition that contains examples of ghost stories.

Notes

1   Acts 9:1-19, 22:6-16, 26:12-18.

2   Acts 9:7.

3   Acts 22:9.

4   Acts 9:4.

5   Acts 26:14.

6   The term εκστασις (ekstasis), which literally means "to be outside oneself," is the obvious source of *ecstasy*. An altered state of

consciousness is clearly in view, and the word is often translated *trance*. Peter also sees a vision while in a state of ecstasy (Acts 10:10-11).

7 As at Matthew 28:3, Luke 24:8.

8 Matthew 28:2, 5.

9 The usual words meaning to "see" are βλεπω (blepô) and θεωρεω theôreô), but here Paul repeatedly uses forms of οραω (horaô), a verb often employed in the New Testament for preternatural visions and similar experiences. The related noun, οραμα (horama), usually denotes *vision* in the sense of "supernatural experience."

10 *Journal of Higher Criticism* 2/2: 69-99.

11 Another occurrence of εκστασις, which I have rendered *panic*. The Greeks believed the sight of the nature divinity Pan induced irrational fear, hence our word.

12 In a subsequent chapter I will make the case the *young man* is derived from a different strand of the tradition.

13 Peter Kirby's summary is recommended: "The Case Against the Empty Tomb," www.depts.drew.edu. Later manuscripts of the gospel of Mark append several spurious endings designed to improve on the original. Matthew appropriates the youth's words from Mark (Matthew 28:5-7), but in his retelling the women are not struck silent from fear but run joyfully to inform the apostles that Jesus has risen, being met by Jesus on the way (Matthew 28:9-10).

14 Matthew 28:17.

15 και αυτος **αφαντος εγενετο** απ' αυτων: "and he **became invisible** to them." This is the only occurrance of αφαντος (aphantos) in the New Testament. The preposition απο (apo) in the construction απ' αυτων is often used with verbs of concealment and separation, and could be taken to imply that Jesus' manifestation became invisible to them *as he left*, i.e., dematerialized in some way.

Three days in the tomb reflects the Jewish belief that the soul remained in the vicinity of the tomb for three days following burial. *Ancient Christian Gospels*, 235.

The Greek magical papyri preserve this spell: "Arise, demon from the realm below…whatever I may command of you, I, *X*, in that way obey me…if you wish to become invisible, just smear your forehead with the mixture and you will be invisible for however long you want." *Papyri Graecae Magicae*, I, 14 (I, 254-257). The wording of the spell, **αφαντος γενεσθαι**: "**to become invisible**," duplicates the phraseology of Luke's story. *Jesus raised the level of his thought & achieved this.*

The Greek ο δεινα (ho deina), which I translate *X*, means *a certain one*, indicating that the name of the magician or the subject of the incantation is to be supplied as the occasion requires. The term is very common in the spell books.

16 **ψηλαφησατε με και ιδετε**: "**touch me and see..**"

17 The 4th century church historian Eusebius quotes an ancient variant of this story: εφη αυτοις λαβετε **ψηλαφησατε με και ιδετε** οτι ουκ ειμι **δαιμονιον ασωματον**: "Take, **touch me and see** that I am not **a disembodied demon**…" *Ecclesiastical History*, III, 36.11. "Demon" in this context might reflect a Christian belief that ghosts were evil spirits pretending to be dead people.

During the 3rd century some Jews explained Jesus' post-resurrection appearances as works of sorcery, claiming that Christians "could conjure [his spirit] up and had already brought it back to earth by making their magical sign of the cross." Lane Fox, *Pagans and Christians*, 479-480.

18 Interestingly, Jesus' appearances tend to occur at night or in the intervals between day and night, i.e., "between times" typically associated with works of sorcery (Matthew 28:1, Mark 16:2, Luke 24:29, John 21.4).

19 The verb κλειω (kleiô) means *to lock, to shut with a key* –κλεις (kleis), *key*. Translations that render the verb as simply *to shut* fail to fully convey the idea that the doors were locked, not merely

[*] closed, and that *in spite of that fact*, Jesus "came and stood in their midst." *Read the teachings of the masters of the Far East.*

20 Evans, *Field Guide to Ghosts*, 19.

21 *Haunted Greece and Rome*, 7, 14, 17, 23-26, 28.

22 *Ghosts*, 25

23 *Restless Dead*, 149. Such a person was ατελεστος (atelestos), *unfulfilled*.

24 Ehrman, *The New Testament*, 115.

25 Such as Phlegon of Tralles' story of the newly dead Philinnion who returns to have sex with her family's guest, to cite a particularly famous example.

That an element of the fantastic is already present in the canonical gospels is clear from Matthew's claim that following Jesus' resurrection many of the "holy ones" who had died rose bodily from their tombs and went into "the holy city" where they were seen by many (Matthew 27:52-53). Defeating expectations, this alleged resurrection *en masse* is mentioned by none of the other evangelists.

[*] *The masters of the Far East are able to do this because it is written in a much spiritual context.*

Chapter Five: The Apocalyptic Prophet

All four gospels agree that Jesus came from Nazareth to John the Baptist and was baptized by him in the Jordan River. [1] The descent of the spirit following his baptism constitutes Jesus' anointing and it is from this point onward that we first hear of his teachings and miracles.

About John himself the gospels have little to report. Herod Antipas, one of the sons of Herod the Great, had John executed after he rashly criticized Antipas' marriage to Herodias, the wife of his brother Philip.[2] Aside from John's critique of Herod's irregular family life, the gospels have this to say about his message:

> So he said to the crowds that were coming out to be baptized by him, "Brood of vipers! Who showed you how to flee from the coming wrath?"
> "Therefore produce fruits worthy of repentance and do not start to say among yourselves, 'We have Abraham for a father,' for I tell you that God can raise up children for Abraham from

the stones. The ax is already laid at the root of the tree! Every tree not producing good fruit will be cut down and thrown into the fire!"

"The winnowing fork is in his hand, ready to clean out the threshing floor and gather the wheat into his barn, but the husks he will burn with fire that cannot be put out!"

Luke 3:7-9, 17

John's is a message of rapidly impending judgment that no Jew can escape by pleading special status as a son of Abraham. The separation of the righteous from the unrighteous is imminent: the ax is already laid at the root of the tree.

We are never informed about what circumstances prompted John's denunciations, but the fact that Jesus came to him to be baptized indicates that he agreed with John's message and became his disciple.[3]

According to Mark, Jesus' career began even as John's was about to end, and —it is important to note— Jesus adopted John's apocalyptic message:

It happened in those days that Jesus came from Nazareth of Galilee and was baptized in the Jordan by John. And at once, while he was coming up out of the water, he saw the heavens being ripped open[4] and the spirit descending on him like a dove.[5]

And a voice came out of the heavens, "You are my son, the beloved In you was I pleased."

At once the spirit drove him out into the wilderness, and he was in the wilderness for forty days being tempted by Satan and he was with the wild animals and the angels served him.

But after John had been arrested, Jesus came into Galilee proclaiming the good news of God, and saying, "The time allotted has run out and the kingdom of God has almost arrived!

Repent and believe in the good news!"

Mark 1:9-15

Like John the Baptist, Jesus proclaimed a message of impending judgment and called for repentance. The kingdom of God was coming quickly. But just how quickly? What sort of judgment did Jesus visualize? And what sort of kingdom? Fortunately, the gospels provide fairly coherent answers to these questions.

That Jesus imagined the kingdom to be coming soon —*very soon*— is made abundantly clear by Mark:

> He said to them, "Truly I say to you, there are some standing here who will by no means taste death until they see the kingdom of God already arrived in power."[6]

Mark 9:1

> "Truly I tell you, by no means will this generation disappear until all these things happen."

Mark 13:30

> The High Priest was standing in their midst, and he asked Jesus, "Have you nothing to say in response? What are these men testifying against you?"
>
> But he kept silent and did not reply to anything. Again the High Priest asked him, "Are you the Christ, the son of the Blessed One?"
>
> Jesus said, "I am. And you will see the Son of Man seated at the right hand of power and coming with the clouds of heaven!"

Mark 14:60-62

According to Jesus, the High Priest himself will witness the coming of the heavenly Son of Man. Jesus own generation —"*this*

75

generation"— will not disappear before "*all* these things" happen, nor will most of his followers die before personally seeing the kingdom of God arrive "in power."

When Jesus sends his disciples out on a round of healing and kingdom preaching, he tells them,

> "But whenever they run you out of one town, flee to another, for truly I tell you, by no means will you finish going through all the towns of Israel before the Son of Man arrives."
>
> Matthew 10:23

Jesus is quite explicit about what the coming of the Son of Man will mean for both the righteous and the wicked:

> "But in those days, after that affliction, the sun will be darkened and the moon will not give its light and the stars will fall out of the sky and the powers in the heavens will be shaken. And they will see the Son of Man coming in the clouds with great power and glory. Next he will send forth his angels and gather his chosen ones from the four winds, from the ends of the earth to the ends of the sky."
>
> "Learn this comparison from the fig tree: whenever you see its branch sprout and put forth leaves, you know that summer is almost here. In the same way, whenever you see these things happening, you know that he is at your door. Truly I tell you, under no circumstances will this generation disappear until all these things happen."
>
> Mark 13:24-30

> "Just the way it happened in the days of Noah, that is the way it will be in the days of the Son of Man. They were eating and drinking, marrying and giving brides away right up to the day

Noah went into the ark, and the Deluge came and destroyed everyone."

"It happened the very same way in the days of Lot. They were eating, drinking, buying and selling, planting and building, but the day Lot left Sodom, fire and sulfur rained from heaven and destroyed everyone. It will be like that the day the Son of Man is revealed."

Luke 17:26-30

The verb translated "to reveal" in Luke 17:30 is αποκαλυπτω (apokaluptô), and the corresponding noun, αποκαλυψις (apokalupsis), is the source of our word *apocalypse*. Apocalypticism is the ideological substrate of the most primitive Christian theology, the sudden revelation of God's judgment with all that that implies. In this particular passage Jesus describes how in the remote past the mundane façade of everyday life was suddenly ripped away by revelations of divine judgment. In the case of Sodom [7] and the near extinction of the human race during the Deluge,[8] the overthrow of the wicked was sudden, violent, and complete. The reversal of fortune for people then living was also total: the complacent wicked were utterly annihilated, the watchful righteous exalted. Apocalypse seized the imagination of Jesus as it has seized the imagination of many men before and since. Indeed, what could possibly motivate men to action more than the idea that the world as we know it is about to end?

Did Jesus mean to identify himself with the apocalyptic Son of Man whose coming he foretold? The evidence is ambiguous, and like many other issues dealing with the correct interpretation of Jesus' words, the controversy has raged back and forth only to end in stalemate. In the passages concerning world judgment such as the ones quoted

77

above, Jesus speaks of the Son of Man in the third person. A reader unacquainted with Christian belief might easily assume that Jesus was speaking of someone else and not himself.

What is clear is that Jesus' earliest followers came to identify him as the Son of Man, probably due to the influence of an apocalyptic passage from Daniel.[9] Mark has Jesus refer to himself as the Son of Man in connection with his betrayal, death, and resurrection,[10] and Matthew relates the term to Jesus' authority to forgive sins, heal on the Sabbath, and with his identification as the Messiah.[11] It has been argued that in these passages the church was simply reading its subsequent under standing of Jesus' mission back into the institutional memory of his life.

> As far as we can determine, this was not a message about himself, but a message about the coming day of judgment on which the Son of Man...would be licensed by God to take direct control of a new kingdom (c.f. Mark 14:62). *The failure of these signs to materialize led to the curious result that Jesus was retroactively declared 'Son of Man'...by his followers after his death...*" [12]

It is notable that apart from the gospels, the disciple Stephen is the only other person to identify Jesus as the Son of Man,[13] and oddly enough, Paul, for whom the resurrection *cum* glorification of Jesus is the theological event of all time, never speaks of Jesus as the Son of Man, nor do the early church fathers seem at all interested in the term.

Desperate times, it has been said, call for desperate measures. If Jesus really believed in the impending end of the political and religious order, we would logically expect to hear it reflected in his ethical advice, and we do. The disciples are not to imagine that Jesus came to bring peace on earth. Indeed, family members will turn on one another, becoming bitter enemies[14] and those who expect to follow Jesus into the coming kingdom should do so now, not even stopping to say goodbye to those left behind.[15] A man on his roof must not linger to gather his possessions, and a man in the field must not stop even to pick up his cloak.[16] The urgency of the times abrogates even the most basic filial responsibilities:

> Another of his disciples said to him, "Lord, first permit me to go and bury my father." But Jesus said to him, "Follow me and let the dead bury their dead."
>
> Matthew 8:21-22

For those who expect to inherit the coming kingdom, the costs will be steep. No one can become a disciple without hating his own father, mother, brothers and sisters, and even wife and children, as well as relinquishing all possessions. The would be disciple must therefore count the cost. Little wonder that the rich heard Jesus' words with regret.[17]

Even Jesus' exorcisms are evidence of the coming kingdom:

> "For if I cast out the demons by means of Beezeboul, by whom do your sons cast them out? That is why they will become your judges. But if I cast them out the demons by the finger of God, [18] then the kingdom of God has already overtaken you."
>
> Luke 11:19-20

Seen from this point of view, Jesus' exorcisms are harbingers of the coming kingdom. The raising of the dead foreshadows the raising of all the dead at the final judgment, the healing of the sick foretells the elimination of all disease, and casting out demons anticipates the final expulsion of the Prince of Demons. So sure is Jesus of this that he describes it proleptically, as if already done:

> And the seventy-two returned with rejoicing, saying, "Lord, even the demons are subject to us in your name!" And he said to them, "I saw Satan thrown down from heaven like lightening!"[19]
>
> Luke 10:17-18

It is, in fact, quite possible to see most of the events of Jesus' career in this way. The confrontation with the temple authorities is understood as a parable-in-action, a preview of God's impending judgment of the temple and his rejection of its leadership. Jeremiah is understood —probably by Jesus himself— as a prototype or forerunner. Jesus takes up both the Old Testament prophet's mantle of office and his words. All the judgments of the past, the Deluge, the end of Sodom, and the destruction of Solomon's temple, foretell the judgment Jesus speaks against his own generation, "this generation" that will not pass away until all Jesus' words are fulfilled upon it.

It is probable that Jesus thought his confrontation with the Jewish leaders would in fact inaugurate the New Age, an interpretation demanded by the phraseology of the so-called "eucharistic words":

> "Truly I tell you that I will never by any means drink of the fruit of the vine until that day when I drink it anew in the kingdom of God."
>
> Mark 14:25

> "Truly I tell you that I will by no means eat [the Passover]

until it is consummated in the kingdom of God…I tell you that from now on I will by no means drink from the fruit of the vine until the kingdom of God arrives."[20]

Luke 22:16, 18.

As noted by David Martinez, these passages are examples of *issar*, a self-binding vow of abstinence employed "to activate the realm in which divine power operates." By vowing abstinence from the Passover meal, the supreme cultic celebration of Judaism,

> Jesus consecrates himself to the necessary action, making himself the instrument through which God will establish the new order…He seals his absolute commitment to the apocalyptic age with the vow that he will not partake of the sacred bread and wine until that age is ushered in.[21]

Similar binding vows of abstinence are well known elements of the erotic spells of the Greek magical papyri, formulae which find very close parallels in Jesus' repeated demands for exclusive devotion.[22]

Jesus' disciples envisioned a physical kingdom that would replace the kingdoms soon to be swept away. And how could they have thought otherwise? Jesus had promised them that he would drink wine with them in the kingdom, where they would enjoy families, houses, and fields, and sit on thrones, judging the twelve tribes of Israel. Even the mother of two of the disciples asks Jesus to seat her sons at his right and left hand in his coming kingdom.[23] Paul himself preached that the Christian saints would sit in judgment of the world and the angels.[24]

According to Luke, as Jesus approached Jerusalem for his final Passover celebration, the disciples supposed that the kingdom was about to appear, and after Jesus' resurrection they again asked if he was about to restore the kingdom to Israel.[25] For a period of time, expectations of Jesus' triumphant return ran so high that those with property sold off what they had and Jesus' followers lived communally.[26] Paul, writing to the newly converted, advised slaves to remain slaves, and virgins and the unmarried to remain in their present state. Married men were to behave as if they had no wife, which probably meant that married couples acted as if celibate, for "the time allotted has become short." [27] So pervasive was the sense of impending doom that the early Christians resorted to the most extreme behavior: Origen, a church father of the 2nd century went so far as to castrate himself, using Matthew 19:12 as justification, and Justin Martyr, another early church father, praised a young Alexandrian convert who petitioned the Roman governor to give a surgeon permission to castrate him. Like many apocalyptic movements since, early Christianity was characterized by sexual psychopathology and extremism.

Convinced that Jesus had risen and would soon return, the believers waited expectantly. It is to an examination of those expectations and what became of them that we turn next.

Notes

1   Matthew 3:13, Mark 1:9, Luke 3:21, John 1:32.

2   Mark 6:17-18.

3   After carefully tracing the way in which John's message was adapted to meet Christian needs, Crossan notes "that John's message was an announcement of imminent apocalyptic intervention by God and not at all about Jesus" and of John's execution says "No matter what John's intentions may have been, Antipas had more than enough materials on which to act. Desert

and Jordan, prophet and crowds, were always a volatile mix calling for immediate preventive strikes." *The Historical Jesus*, 235.

4   In Mark 15:38, the curtain which closes off the Holy of Holies where God is symbolically present is similarly ripped from top to bottom following Jesus' death.

5   το πνευμα ως περιστεραν καταβαινον **εις** αυτον: "the spirit descending **on** him like a dove." Regarding the preposition Ehrman observes, "The prepositon εις commonly means "into," so that the text as Mark originally wrote it is especially vulnerable to the Gnostic claim that at Jesus' baptism a divine being entered into him. Whether Mark himself understood the event in this way is not the question I'm concerned to address here. It is worth noting, however, that both Matthew and Luke changed the preposition to επι ("upon"). *The Orthodox Corruption of Scripture*, 141.

6   According to Matthew's version, the disciples will not die before seeing the Son of Man "coming in his kingdom" (Matthew 16:28).

7   Genesis 19:24-27.

8   Genesis 7:1-5.

9   Daniel 7:13-14.

10   Mark 8:31, 9:31, 10:33-34.

11   Matthew 9:5-6, 12:8, 16:13-17.

12   *Jesus Outside the Gospels*, 11-12.
      Neither Hebrew nor 1st century Greek employed lower case letters, so the mere convention of capitalizing "Son of Man" in English makes it into a title, implying that the ancients so regarded it. That, of course, is not necessarily the case.

13   Acts 7:56.

14   Matthew 10:34-37, Luke 12:49-53.

15   Luke 9:61-62.

16   Matthew 24:17-18.

17   Luke 14:26-28, 33, 18:23-25.

18   The "finger of God" had magical connotations (Exodus 8:19), so Matthew changed it to "spirit of God." John Hull: "Matthew's reticence about technique is seen in 12:28 (= Luke 11:20) where the change from 'finger' to 'spirit' is to be explained in terms of the association with magical technique which the finger of God had. The only place in the gospel where Jesus seems to be on the point of disclosing his method is thus spiritualized." *Hellenistic Magic and the Synoptic Tradition*, 129.

Schlier: "There is mention of a magical finger on an Egypt[ian] ostracon: εξορκιζω κατα του δακτυλου του θεου ("I cast you out by the finger of God," *my translation*)." *Theological Dictionary of the New Testament*, II, 22.

Deissmann also noted that "It is the finger of God!" is used by the magicians of Egypt to designate powerful magic. *Light from the Ancient East*, 306.

19   "This passage, in which Jesus remarks that he saw Satan 'fall like lightening from the sky,' depicts an unabashedly apocalyptic scene in the midst of a document not usually considered to be 'apocalyptic.'" *The Demise of the Devil*, 46.

If Satan is overthrown, then his followers must also fall. The metaphor of opposing kingdoms of light and darkness is a powerful element in the apocalyptic view. "The figure of Satan becomes, among other things, a way of characterizing one's actual enemies as the embodiment of transcenddent forces. For many readers of the gospels ever since the first century, the thematic opposition between God's spirit and Satan has vindicated Jesus' followers and demonized their enemies." *The Origin of Satan*, 13.

The arrest of Jesus therefore became a temporary triumph of "the power of darkness" (Luke 22:53). The meaning is clear: the Jewish leaders are the minions of Satan, doing his bidding.

20   The formula ου μη + the aorist subjunctive used in these passages

constitutes the most negative statement possible in Greek, denying not only the fact, but even the *possibility* that an event might take place.

21 *Ancient Magic and Ritual Power*, 346, 350-351.

Regarding the connection between prophecy and magic, Crossan notes that "among colonized people there appear not only thaumaturgical or magical but also millennial or revolutionary prophets, or, more simply, magicians and prophets." *The Historical Jesus*, 137.

22 As, for example, at Matthew 10:37 and Luke 14:26.

23 Mark 10:30, 14:25, Matthew 19:28, 20:20-21.

24 1 Corinthians 6:2-3. Paul almost certainly had in mind the fallen angels he believed were the real rulers of the world (2 Corinthians 4:3-4).

25 Luke 19:11, Acts 1:6.

26 Acts 4:34-35.

27 1 Corinthians 7:21-31.

Chapter Six:
The Apocalypse Postponed

Generations of people come and go, and as one year passed into the next, the people of Jesus' generation began to die. There was no Apocalypse, no host of angels, no Judgment Day for the wicked, no glorious return of the Son of Man, and no Kingdom of Heaven to replace the kingdoms of this world. In 70 C.E., only a few years after the finishing touches were put on it, Herod's temple was destroyed, not by the wrath of God, but by wrathful Roman soldiers who burned the magnificent structure to the ground. Some stones were left standing upon stones; the massive blocks of the Western Wall —the Wailing Wall— which in Jesus' day towered as much as 100 feet above the surrounding terrain, survived the Roman siege engines.

Paul and his parousia

The letter of Paul to the church in Thessalonika is thought to be the oldest surviving Christian document. Its principle subject is the dead, specifically those of the first generation of Christians who died awaiting Jesus' return. What, the faithful wondered, would become of those who had already died? What hope could Paul hold out for them?

Here are the parts of Paul's letter that specifically touch on those concerns:

> ...And to wait for his Son from the heavens, who he raised from the dead, Jesus, the one who delivers us from the coming wrath...For what is our hope, or joy, or crown of exaltation? Is it not you in the presence [1] of our Lord Jesus Christ at his coming?
>
> ...In order to strengthen your hearts, blameless in holiness, before our God and Father at the coming of our Lord Jesus with all his holy ones...For we do not wish you to be ignorant, brothers, concerning those who are sleeping, so that you do not grieve like the others, those who have no hope. For if we believe that Jesus died and rose again, in the same way, through Jesus, God will bring those who have fallen asleep with him. For this we tell you by the word of the Lord, that we the living who are left remaining until the coming of the Lord will by no means get ahead of those who sleep [in death]. Because the Lord himself will descend from heaven with the commanding voice of an archangel and with the sound of God's trumpet, and the dead in Christ will be raised first. Then we the living who are left remaining will be snatched away in the clouds together with them to meet the Lord in the air, and so we will always be with the Lord...But concerning the times and the seasons, brothers, you have no need to have anything written to you. For you yourselves know exactly that the day of the Lord is coming like a thief in the night. Whenever they are saying, "Peace and security," then suddenly destruction will overtake them like the labor pains that come upon a pregnant woman, and they will by no means escape.
>
> But you, brothers, are not in darkness so that the day might

catch you like a thief, for you are all sons of light and sons of day. We are not of the night or of the darkness. Therefore let us not sleep like the others do, but let us keep watch and stay sober. For those who sleep, sleep at night, and those who get drunk, drink at night. But we, belonging to the day, should be sober, having on the breastplate of faith and love, and as a helmet, the hope of salvation.

For God has not consigned us to wrath, but to the gaining of salvation through our Lord Jesus Christ who died for us so that whether we stay awake or fall asleep, we might live together with him. Therefore comfort one another and edify one another just as you are doing.

…May the God of peace sanctify you completely and my your spirit, soul, and body be preserved blameless at the coming of our Lord Jesus Christ. He who calls you is faithful and he will do this.

1 Thessalonians 1:10, 2:19, 3:13, 4:13-17, 5:1-11, 23-24

Paul escapes the dilemma of the delayed parousia —for the moment, at least— by making the resurrection of dead believers a part of the coming of the Lord. The dead will be raised and swept up, as if snatched away by the wind, to meet those still alive in the clouds. But the astute reader will have already detected the slippage: gone are the houses, relatives, and fields to be replaced a hundredfold in the age to come as described by the gospels. The coming of the Lord has already shifted from a glorious promise made to a generation still living to words of comfort and edification made to a generation already dying.

The letter to the Thessalonians reveals the intensely apocalyptic orientation of the early church. That focus on their expectations for the near future —"we the living who are left remaining until the coming of the Lord"— very naturally shifted their attention away from the historical Jesus and onto the exalted Lord Jesus Christ who might at any moment arrive in glory to collect his saints. Schweitzer described the result in *The Quest of the Historical Jesus*:

> Paul shows us with what complete indifference the earthly life of Jesus was regarded by primitive Christianity. The discourses in Acts show an equal indifference, since in them also Jesus first becomes the Messiah by virtue of his exaltation ...The fact is, if one reads through the early literature one becomes aware that so long as theology had an eschatological orientation and was dominated by the expectation of the parousia, the question of how Jesus of Nazareth 'had been' the Messiah not only did not exist, but was impossible. Primitive theology is simply a theology of the future, with no interest in history. [2]

Paul himself informs his converts that in the (unlikely) event that they had known Jesus "according to the flesh" they know him so no more. [3] By Paul's time, the Galilean laborer-turned-prophet has completely disappeared behind the dazzling glory of the exalted Christ. We strain to catch some glimpse of him in Paul's writings, but are blinded by the light. But as Jesus' contemporaries continued to die off and hope in the parousia began inevitably to wane, the attention of the church shifted backward, to the historical figure of Jesus, and finally, even further back, to the Word who coexisted with God from deep time, before the beginning of the world. That shift in theological focus is not the subject of this book, but the point to be made is this: by the time the attention of the church moved back to the historical figure of Jesus, most of the eyewitnesses to his life were likely dead. The writers of the gospels were forced to fall back on oral and fragmentary written traditions to construct an official biography, traditions which had already been in circulation for decades. It is at this point that the early church began in earnest to ransack the texts of the Old Testament in search of "prophecy" that Jesus might "fulfill."

As time passed and the doubts about its reality increased, Christian teaching about the Second Coming became more complex and the language used to describe it ever more shrill.

> First know this, that in the last days will come ridiculers with their derision, living in accord with their own lusts, and saying, "Whatever happened to the promise of his coming? Ever since our fathers fell asleep [in death], everything goes on just like it has from the beginning of creation!"
> By maintaining this opinion it escapes their notice that there were heavens long ago and an earth that emerged from the water and through water by the word of God, and that afterward the world was destroyed by being flooded with water. By the same word, the heavens and earth that are now have been stored up for fire. They are being reserved until the day of judgment and the destruction of the ungodly men.
> But do not let this one thing escape your notice, beloved ones, that for the Lord a day is like a thousand years and a thousand years like a day. But the Lord of the promise does not delay as some define slowness, for he is patient with you, not desiring that anyone be destroyed, but that everyone attain repentance.
> But the day of the Lord will come like a thief in which the heavens will come to an end with a roar and the elements will be destroyed by fire and the earth and all that is done on it will be uncovered. If all these things are to be destroyed in this way, what kind of people should you be in holy conduct and godliness, awaiting and hastening the coming of the day of God by which the heavens will be destroyed by fire and the elements will melt? For we await a new heavens and a new earth according to his promise in which righteousness will dwell. *? in the hearts of people. It is happening.*
>
> 2 Peter 3:3-15

It is clear from the language of this passage that the tone has changed from one of questioning to one of frank skepticism. All the previous generation has apparently died by now —"our fathers fell asleep in death"— and the promise made to the fathers has yet to be fulfilled. [4] A minor adjustment —"the dead in Christ will be raised first"— will no longer suffice. Instead, the writer conjures up vast vistas of time: lest we forget, a day to the Lord is like a thousand years!

By the time the last books of the New Testament were composed, Christianity had already followed the apocalyptic road to a dead end, and the explanations for its non-occurrence had become as pre- posterous as the language used to describe it. The parousia is first delayed, then indefinitely postponed, then finally —and *thankfully* most would agree— forgotten by all but a fringe element. Concerning the theological demise of the parousia in one of its final expressions, the book of Revelation, Lane Fox says,

> ...Dionysus [the bishop of Alexandria, Egypt, *my note*] explained away the plain words of Revelation as an allegory, and when Irenaeus' tract against heresy was translated into Latin in the early fifth century, the translator omitted the millennium from its text. To many thinking Christians it had become an embarrassment.[5]

Coming to terms

As we move away from the relative simplicity of the gospels' vision of the coming of the heavenly Son of Man, we find ourselves ever more entangled in the thickets of theological jargon. It seems to be a recurring fantasy among fundamentalist Christians that the Greek of the New Testament is a species of *über*-language, a divine speech of infinite precision, logic, and clarity. No human language fits such a description, of course, and the conviction that the New Testament was written in such a tongue could only be voiced from the depths of the most abysmal ignorance.

In point of fact, nearly all words are polysemous; they carry multiple meanings and shades of meaning, and words used to describe spiritual experience are among the most slippery of all —even the early Christians acknowledged that Paul's letters contained language that was hard to understand.[6]

The New Testament is without a doubt the world's most intensively scrutinized set of documents, and its interpreters have spotted some highly significant meaning lurking in the tense of every verb and in every preposition. Indeed, so much emphasis has been placed on the supposed subtlety of the Greek text that the modern reader could be forgiven for thinking that the authors of the New Testament were the world's most polished grammarians instead of moderately literate members of society. Yet oddly enough, despite centuries of relentless study and an outpouring of commentary that continues unabated, there appears to be doubt and disagreement about the meaning of nearly everything the New Testament says. As one scholar wryly notes, "The Bible may, in fact, be the only feature of the Christian religion that all Christians have in common." [7]

That Jesus preached an apocalyptic message of imminent judgment is as sure as any feature of his teaching. Indeed, the preaching of Jesus forms a seamless continuum of apocalyptic thought that begins with his predecessor, John the Baptist, and extends to the early churches founded in his name. This observation, which is crucial for locating

Jesus and his first followers in the stream of religious ideas, has been emphasized recently by Bart Ehrman:

> This means that Jesus' ministry began with his association with John the Baptist, an apocalyptic prophet, and ended with the establishment of the Christian church, a community of apocalyptic Jews who believed in him. The only connection between the apocalyptic John and the apocalyptic Christian church was Jesus himself. How could both the beginning and the end be apocalyptic, if the middle was not as well? My conclusion is that Jesus himself must have been a Jewish apocalypticist. [8]

Both the historian who has spent his life studying Jesus and the theologian who believes that Jesus is the Christ, the Son of God, purely as a matter of faith, work from the assumption that Jesus is relevant in some way to the modern world. Both understandably want Jesus to speak to each and every generation, including ours. They want a Jesus who *matters*. But a Jesus who foretells an end of the world that never happens, a Son of Man whose kingdom never arrives, is an embarrassment, or worse, a complete failure. Albert Schweitzer, the author of one of the first and finest modern analyses of the historical Jesus, came to this rather grim conclusion: "The historical Jesus will be to our time a stranger and an enigma." [9]

The early church found itself stuck with a terrible problem: its theology had been built on the coming of the glorified Lord, and initially the message of his coming must have been a most effective inducement to discipleship. Yet with every year that passed and every believer that died, the parousia became a more hollow promise. What was the church to do?

To the pagan world, *deification* would have recommended itself as an obvious first step. Why not simply declare Jesus to be a god and have done with it? And as Christianity gradually changed from a Jewish splinter sect to become an increasingly cosmopolitan cult, that is, in effect, what happened.[10] I do not mean to leave the impression that the Christians cleanly extricated themselves from the impasse of the deferred parousia, deifying Jesus in a series of neat, logical steps. Their progress was tentative and centuries in the making, and there were divergent solutions along the way, most of which the church subsequently declared to be heretical.[11] But as the church moved ever closer to its deified Lord, it pushed his Second Coming ever farther away. As reported by Eusebius, by at least the 3rd century the doctors of the church had begun to characterize belief in the earthly rule of Christ as "trivial and befitting mortals and too like the present,"[12] and by the time of Augustine, *chiliasm*,[13] the belief in a 1000-year reign on earth entertained by many early churches, had been relegated to the uttermost fringes of Christian belief though never formally declared heretical.

Notes

1   The παρουσια (parousia), or *presence*. It is the opposite of απουσια (apousia), *absence*. In Paul's time the word appears to have had two main uses: it was used in the pagan cultus for the revelation of divine beings, and for the arrival of persons of exalted rank who had come to visit a province. The phrase seems to have already become a Christian cultic formula which Paul uses repeatedly: εμπροσθεν του κυριου ημων Ιησου εν τη αυτου παρουσια: "before our Lord Jesus in his presence."

2   *The Quest of the Historical Jesus*, 344-345

3   2 Corinthians 5:16.

That they would not know him so from Paul is clear: regarding the "transformation of the historical Jesus into the cultic Christ," Hoffmann notes the "comparative disinterest in the facts of his life and the substance of his teaching. Paul's preaching clearly reflects this lack of interest," and adds that the writing of the gospels took place *"under the influence of specific doctrines about Jesus as the Christ*, and not out of any purely historical interest in preserving the facts of his existence." *Jesus Outside the Gospels*, 34.

4   There is a near consensus among New Testament scholars that neither 1 or 2 Peter was written by the apostle, and that 2 Peter was written by a different author than 1 Peter. In fact, the epistle of Jude is so similar to 2 Peter that one is almost certainly a copy of the other. Peter the apostle was martyred in Rome about the year 64, but both epistles that bear his name appear to have been written near or after the end of the 1st century. Some put the terminus a quo for 2 Peter as late as 110.

5   *Pagans and Christians*, 266.

6   2 Peter 3:16.

Wenham, in his classic introductory grammar, observes, "It needs to be stressed that words in one language seldom have a precise equivalent in another language. Any word has a range of meanings and the nearest equivalent word in another language will have a range of meanings which overlaps but does not exactly coincide with it." *The Elements of New Testament Greek*, 192.

7   Burton Mack, *Who Wrote the New Testament*, 276.

8   *Jesus: Apocalyptic Prophet of the New Millennium*, 139.

9   *The Quest*, 400.

10 That some measure of deification has already occurred in the later documents of the New Testament is beyond question (John 1:1, 18, 20:28, Hebrews 1:8, for example), but the exact doctrinal

significance of these passages has been debated ad nauseam up to the present day.

11   Richard Rubenstein's is an accessible, well written account (*When Jesus Became God: The Epic Fight Over Christ's Divinity in the Last Days of Rome*).

Joseph Hoffman, who appears to be more agnostic than I am about rescuing much of historical value from the gospels, gives a lucid presentation of the problem of the delayed parousia in *Jesus Outside the Gospels*, 9-34.

12   *Ecclesiastical History*, VII, 24.4-5. The receiving of houses and land as well as the restoration of the kingdom of Israel presupposes and earthly kingdom (Mark 10:29-30, Acts 1:6) and many of the first Christians so believed.

13   From χιλια (chilia), *one thousand* (Revelation 20:4-5). Most of the early Christians who accepted the book of Revelation apparently believed the number to be literal.

[handwritten note:] you are barking up the wrong tree. Those who came to our group knew the truth that you academics & agnostics have failed to grasp :: your eyes & ears are closed to that truth. Yes you are right to say the bible is a manipulated record but from what? Even with your quotes from magic papyri you haven't realized that the motive of the enactors was totally different to the motives of Jesus, a lot of magic was evil in intent because of the times but Jesus wasn't. his intentions he stood out from the crowd :: his intentions were pure & god like for the good of mankind.

Life is to be considered as ... giving birth to use the body to make another.

+ received ... the ... ... this ... you live life through. And it ...

+ iii you have been brought up in a faith which does give respect for the life of mankind & yet within that faith you still tolerate experimentation on the human being. Pain & suffering are not part of man's inheritance. they are only that which mankind has brought upon himself.

David Hairshow - genetics - understanding that will eliminate in the children of the future genetic - understanding that will eliminate in the children of the future eliminate the 'sins' of the fathers.

1. We are so soul/mind & body, a spirit we come to earth into a ph body to learn lessons ... need to knowledge gained in the life, & remember before this one.

vii many who refuse to accept the spiritual aspect of their life & we have to recognise the importance to the soul and spirit within our lives in order to know less friction, our lives and consequently less disease within ourselves.

Zodiac "the soul passes through infinite lives. How can you understand if you haven't been through the experience, ever?"

3rd line...only the Garden of Gethsemene 'quote
" you have come into a physical
" many are tempted at times to throw away their cross...

Chapter Seven: Magic and Mystery

A t times the obvious bears pointing out: the sources on which we rely for information about magical practices were not written for our instruction. They were written by people of antiquity for other people of antiquity, for people who regularly saw processions of pagan priests, participated in annual festivals in honor of the dead, were initiated into mystery cults, witnessed the performances of itinerant miracle workers, wore amulets and trusted in their powers, and walked in temples that were not yet ruins, but places of active worship and service of the transcendent.

Unlike people of today, most people of antiquity made no clear distinction between religion and magic, or between medicine and magic, and to impose such distinctions on records from the past is not only anachronistic, but precludes real comprehension of what rituals of healing, exorcism, cursing, and divination may have meant for the participants. With this caveat in mind, the reader should understand that *magic* might apply to any ritual behavior that involves speaking or performance, and that when a term like *sorcery* is used, it basically means something like "religion that works."[1]

The sources of our very incomplete knowledge deserve a brief comment. The oldest magical texts known to us are the pyramid and coffin texts from Egypt, but to what extent these texts still reflected popular practice in the time of Jesus is uncertain. Something of the magic of ancient Mesopotamia is also known to us, and the Old Testament contains occasional references to sorcery. Since several of them are germane, they will be cited. That leaves the Greek magical papyri which are roughly contemporaneous with Jesus' era and have the added advantage of preserving traces of the magic performed by and for common people.

Most of our historical sources, however, were critical of magical practice and may have been preserved down through the *Christian* centuries partly for that very reason. Even in pre-Christian times magicians were regarded with suspicion and their books were considered dangerous, and under the Christian regime, the persecution of magic and its practitioners intensified. As Betz observes, "the systematic destruction of the magical literature over a long period of time resulted in the disappearance of most of the original texts by the end of antiquity."[2]

Moreover, the official histories were composed by members of the upper echelon of a stratified society that regarded the magic of the lower classes much as they regarded the people themselves, with a mixture of condescension, fear, and contempt. As Frederick Cryer notes, "In hierarchically ordered societies there is vastly more magic

98

at the bottom of society than there is at the top...It is also full of the elite disdain for the welter of popular superstition that the masses below advocate." [3]

The implications of these negative attitudes toward magic for an understanding of the New Testament are potentially enormous. As has already been noted, Jesus, his disciples, and the majority of those to whom he preached, were drawn from the rural laboring class, so when the time finally came to present Jesus and his wonder-working to the greater Greco-Roman world, there would be plenty of incentive to downplay the magical elements of Jesus' performances. And that, as we shall see, is exactly what we find when examining the gospel accounts. *spiritual science.*

The sorcerer and his works

Several terms were used of magicians during the period in which the New Testament was being composed. Fritz Graf defines the αγυρτης (agurtês) as "an itinerant and beggar priest" [4] associated particularly with the worship of Cybele —in response to which I would merely point out that Christian religious orders, such as the Dominicans and Franciscans, that lived by collecting alms are typically known as *mendicants*, not as beggars. The role of gender variance and homoeroticism in connection with the priests of Cybele is well established, [5] an added incentive, no doubt, for itinerant wonder-working Christian missionaries to distance themselves from their pagan counterparts.

The term μαγος (magos), encountered in a previous chapter, is one of the most generally used and hence one of the least specific words for *magician*. It is the obvious source of our word in English. Of these men Luck notes, "It seems the *magos* had a bit of everything —the bacchantic (i.e. ecstatic) element, the initiation rites, the migratory life, the nocturnal activities."[6]

A complete description of the γοης (goês) and the nature of his type of sorcery —γοετεια (goeteia), "the invocation of the dead"— has been given by Sarah Iles Johnston. The *goês* is a man who raises the dead through wailing, a typically female role, but is also associated by ancient writers with initiation into mystery cults, protecting the living from the wrath of angry ghosts, and enchantments and incantations, both written and sung.[7] Graf defines the *goês* as "a man who combines healing, weather magic, and the calling up of dead souls…"[8]

Other terms include the ριζοτομος (rhizotomos), or "rootcutter," the forebear of the herbalist or "kitchen witch," and the more sinister φαρμακος (pharmakos), which could mean *sorcerer* or *poisoner*, or both. Lest the latter term be completely misunderstood, however, it should be pointed out that the term φαρμακον (pharmakon) means both *medicine* and *potion*.[9] That most substances used as remedies are also potent poisons comes as no great surprise —even modern over-the-counter medications are lethal if taken in sufficient quantity as many patients have learned to their dismay.

The intimate connection in the ancient mind between medicine, magic, and the art of writing is exemplified by this reference in a Greek magical papyrus:

I am Thoth, inventor and creator of spells and writings…[10]

in which the word translated "spells," φαρμακον (pharmakon), covers both magical potions and medicines. Within the New Testament itself there is no clear distinction between exorcism and healing in connection with Jesus' miracles.

None of the terms for magician necessarily excludes other functions. Graf therefore describes the γοης-αγυρτης-μαγος as "the itinerant specialist who practices divination, initiation, healing, and magic." [11] It is unlikely that these terms were used in any consistent way by the people of the era to distinguish between "specialists" in magical practice, [12] all of whom were working in what Hans Dieter Betz has most felicitously called "the energy jungle," [13] the human dependency on universal forces conceived under the rubric of divinities of varying rank.

To enter the inner circle

Of the many forms of religious experience current in the days of Jesus, the practices of at least five mystery cults are still known to us in some detail. The Eleusinian mysteries, located at Eleusis, [14] a small town about fourteen miles west of Athens, were held in high regard even by skeptics. The cult of Mithras, in which the membership was restricted to males, was popular among the Roman legions. The cult of Isis and Osiris (Serapis) enjoyed a wide popularity, particularly among women. [15] The ecstatic cults of Dionysus and Cybele, or Mater Magna, finish out our brief list.

Rather little is known with any certainty about the inner life of these cults, [16] but it is clear that they shared certain broad characteristics: initiation, reenactment, personal transformation following the revelation of secret knowledge —often called *rebirth* [17] — and particularly in the cults of Dionysus and Mater Magna, ecstatic possession by the god.[18] Mystery cults shared one other noteworthy trait: a close association with magic.[19]

The vocabulary of the mystery cults proved irresistible both to Hellenistic Judaism and to primitive Christianity —both assimilated mystery cult terminology to describe the inner workings of their respective faiths.[20]

The μυστης (mustês), the *initiate* into a mystery cult, was typically introduced to the rites by a sponsor, the μυσταγωγος (mustagôgos), or *mystagogue*. The body of secret knowledge revealed to the initiate was usually called τα μυστερια (ta musteria), *the mysteries*. In the cults of Dionysus and Cybele, *possession* by the god was a regular feature of the rites, resulting in εκστασις (ekstasis) or ενθυσιασμος (enthusiasmos) —the obvious sources of our *ecstasy* and *enthusiasm*— altered mental states associated with visions, oracular speech, and frenzied behavior. For the Greeks, the oracle at Delphi with its "pythoness" speaking in a trance exemplified oracular possession.[21] In the case of the Bacchic rites associated with the worship of Dionysus, the god of wine,[22] the participants entered a state of μανια (mania), a condition of violent frenzy in which live animals were ripped apart[23] and their raw flesh consumed. Female participants in the rites of Dionysus were called *maenads*, which roughly translated means "crazies."

The Greeks distinguished between four categories of divinely inspired madness: *mantic*, or prophetic, associated with Apollo, the god of prophecy, *poetic*, associated with the Muses, *erotic*, linked to Aphrodite, and *telestic*,[24] connected to Dionysus.

The roots of modern theater trace back to the Bacchic initiation rites, the Dionysia held in Athens in honor of Dionysus, at which performances were given by actors speaking from behind masks. Our word *tragedy*, meaning *goat song*, comes from this source, as does *thespian*.[25] Accompanied by flutes, drums, and cymbals,[26] a chorus of men dressed as satyrs, half-man and half-goat, chanted the dithyramb in unison as the dancing celebrants tossed their heads in a violent, whirling motion, entering a state of ecstatic frenzy.

Dionysus was a god of paradox, often portrayed as effeminate,[27] yet whose symbols included the φαλλος (phallos), a likeness of the erect penis, a symbol of the generative power of nature, and the θυρσος (thursos), the Bacchic wand wreathed with ivy with a pine cone at the tip. The wand, an obvious phallic symbol, doubled as a tool of magic and as a weapon.[28]

The power of music to inspire ecstatic speech is reported in the Old Testament. Elisha, asked to foretell the fate of the army of Judah, requests a musician and, as the instrument is played, is seized "by the hand of the Lord" and begins to prophesy.[29] The connection between prophecy and possession is made again when Elisha sends a young prophet to anoint Jehu as king. The prophet calls Jehu aside, gives him the message, and flees.

> When Jehu came back to his master's officers, they said to him, "Is everything all right? Why did that madman come to you?" He answered them, "You know the sort and how they babble."

> 2 Kings 9:11, *NRSV*

103

The Greek Old Testament labels the young "madman" with a revealing term: επιληπτος (epilêptos), source of *epileptic*, one *seized* —even as was Elisha— by the hand of God. The connection between song and magic, and between "seizure" and prophecy is evident in Greek culture: the term for *enchantment* (which itself means "to chant in") —επωδη (epôdê)— is literally a *song* —ωδη (ôdê)— chanted *over* —επι (epi)— the subject of a spell. From this comes the term επαοιδος (epaoidos), *enchanter*, a close associate of the *magos*. [30] Similarly, we find πυθοληπτος (putholêptos), literally "seized by the python" —the python is a symbol of Apollo, god of prophecy— to describe the ecstatic frenzy entered by the priestess of the god as she utters oracles. The transcultural nature of this method of divination can be appreciated from the following quotation regarding the Scottish Celts:

> The Dingwall Presbytery Records tell of the *derilans* who appear to have been officiating priests on the island. Dixon suggests that this title comes from the Gaelic *deireoil*, "afflicted," inferring that the priesthood was composed of people enthused by "divine madness" in the manner of shamans the world over." [31]

The mystery cults incorporated three fundamental types of observances: (1) *invocations* —the λεγομενα (legomena), or "things said," (2) *performances* — the δρωμενα (drômena) or "things enacted," and (3) the δεικνυμενα (deiknumena) or "things shown." The New Testament contains several sacred *formulas* —known in the mystery cults as συμβολα (sumbola)— confessions of faith called "Christ hymns," as well as cultic invocations to which some verbal response was probably expected:

For everything that is brought to light is light. Therefore it is said, "Awake, O sleeper, and rise from the dead and the Christ will shine upon you!" [32]

Ephesians 5:14

Pilgrims to the temples of Asklepius, the god of healing, hoped for εγκοιμησις (enkoimêsis), the manifestation of the god in a healing or prophetic dream.[33] To achieve that goal, the patient might have to sacrifice a sheep and sleep on its fleece, a practice known as *incubation* from Latin *incubare*, "to lie down on."[34] Whether through dreams, visions, or ecstatic rites, the participants sought γνωσις (gnosis), *knowledge* based not on mere facts, but on transcendent experience. Could the contents of such revelations ever have been adequately expressed in mere words?[35] Yes.

Magic and New Testament studies

That Jesus and his first disciples were centered in the Jewish tradition, at the margins of the Hellenistic mainstream, appears beyond doubt. Nevertheless, *pace* Metzger, who denies in Paul's writings "a syncretistic amalgam,"[36] the evidence for ecstatic possession in the New Testament is quite plain, as are elements of magic, initiation, mimesis or reenactment, the existence of an inner circle, and knowledge based on special revelation.

Due to its status as sacred scripture, the text of the New Testament has to a large extent been immunized to critical examination, and such examination as it has received has usually been conducted by scholars already committed to the belief that it is *at the very least* a great religious document that enshrines eternal truths. An additional barrier to critical analysis of the text is its host of defenders, practitioners of advocacy

105

scholarship who react to any observation deemed insufficiently respectful as an attack on their faith. With religion, as with magic, the way in which basic assumptions are framed tends to predetermine the course of all subsequent discussion.[37]

Unconformity on any subject that impacts upon deeply felt values and entrenched beliefs can provoke a firestorm of reaction, making scholars think twice before writing and publishers wary of printing divergent opinions, and nowhere is this more true than criticism of the New Testament. That said, the reader is invited to step boldly into the minefield of the gospels.

Notes

1   "The religious beliefs and practices of most people were identical with some form of magic, and the neat distinctions we make today between approved and disapproved forms of religion…did not exist in antiquity except among a few intellectuals." Betz, *The Greek Magical Papyri in Translation*, xli.

"In Republican Rome, as in Archaic Greece, magic was never thought as something special and radically different from religion or medicine." *Ancient Magic and Ritual Power*, 41.

Of religious wonder-workers and his decision to call them *magicians*, Crossan says, "The title *magician* is not used here as a pejorative word but describes one who can make divine power present *directly through personal miracle* rather than *indirectly through communal ritual*…magic renders transcendental power present concretely, physically, sensibly, tangibly, whereas ritual renders it present abstractly, ceremonially, liturgically, symbolically…*Magic*, like *myth*, is a word and a process that demands reclamation from the language of sneer and jeer." *The Historical Jesus*, 138.

2   *The Greek Magical Papyri*, xl.

3   *Witchcraft and Magic in Europe: Biblical and Pagan Societies*, 116-117.

4   Fritz Graf, *Magic in the Ancient World*, 22. The noun is derived from a verb meaning "to collect."

5   Conner, *Blossom of Bone*, 99-131.

6   Luck, *Witchcraft and Magic in Europe: Ancient Greece and Rome*, 104.

7   *Restless Dead*, 103, 105-123. Johnston's is an indispensable reference for the cultural background and practice of *goeteia*.

8   Graf, *Magic*, 33.

9   "In fact, references to *veneficium* throughout Roman literature, and to Φαρμακον in Greek literature, are always ambiguous. The potions were powerful; whether that power was for good or for evil depended on the outcome of each specific case." *Magic in the Roman World*, 12.

10   Εγω ειμι Θωυθ **φαρμακων** και γραμματων ευρετης και κτιστης: "I am Thoth, inventor and creator of **potions** and spells..." *Papyri Graecae Magicae*, I, 190 (V:249).

     "Thoth was said to be the inventor of both magic and writing and he was the patron deity of scribes...Thoth was linked in myth with two potent images of power used in magic, the sun eye and the moon eye...The image of the Thoth baboon beside a *wedjat* eye occurs on magic wands as early as the twentieth century BC." *Magic in Ancient Egypt*, 28-29.

     The connection between magic and writing is commemorated in the double meaning of the English word *spell*, to say nothing of the term *gospel*, literally, "good spell."

11   Graf, *Magic*, 49.

12   *Magic and Magicians in the Greco-Roman World*, 12-15.

13   Betz, *Papyri*, xlvii.

14   The sanctuary at Eleusis –ελευσις, *arrival*– was destroyed in 394

CE by the troops of Alaric, a Goth who had converted to Arian Christianity.

15 "Isis was a mistress of magic and a saviour goddess who initiated human beings into the mysteries of everlasting life." *A History of Pagan Europe*, 23.

16 μυω (muô), the Greek verbal base from which *mystery* and its cognates are formed in both Greek and English, means *to shut*, in the particular case of mystery cults, *the mouth*. The initiate's lips were sealed and the oath of secrecy was taken seriously.

Meyer: "…the mysteries emphasized an inwardness and privacy of worship within closed groups." *Ancient Mysteries*, 4.

17 Samuel Angus: "Common to the Mysteries and Gnosticism were certain ideas, such as pantheistic mysticism, magic practices, elaborate cosmogonies and theogonies, rebirth, union with God, revelation from above, dualistic views, the importance attaching to the names and attributes of the deity, and the same aim at personal salvation. As Gnosticism took possession of the field East and West, the Mysteries assumed an increasingly Gnostic character. The dividing line is sometimes difficult to determine." *The Mystery Religions*, 54.

18 A discussion of the phenomenon of induced ecstasy, written by Georg Luck, can be found in *Religion, Science, and Magic*, 185-217.

19 Luck: "*Mystes*…applies also to the sorcerer who has reached a certain level. *Mysterion* or *telete* [τελετη, *my note*] could designate a high degree of magical knowledge, while telesma [τελεσμα, *my note*] (hence 'talisman') also means 'amulet,' sometimes also *alexikakon*, [αλεξικακον, *my note*] 'averter of evil.'" *Witchcraft..*, 100.

On the connection between magic and the mystery cults, Graf notes, "It must be concluded that there existed, at the level of ritual, affinities between the mystery cults and magic…Magic in general, as a combination and linked series of different rites, is called *ta musteria* or *hai teletai*, 'mysteries'…the *musterion* also designates magical objects or tools, like a ring or ointment." Graf, *Magic*, 92, 97.

20 Betz, *Magika Hiera*, 250-251.

21 On the archeology, see the recent discussion by John Hale, *et al*, *Scientific American* 289/2: 66-73.

22 Compare John 15:1: εγω ειμι **η αμπελος** η αληθηνη: "I am **the** true **vine**." One of Dionysus' many miracles connected with wine were the εφημεροι **αμπελοι**, *one-day vines* that flowered and bore grapes in the space of a single day. Otto, *Dionysus*, 98.

Dionysus (Διονυσος) or Bacchus (Βακχος), the god of wine, known to the Romans as *Liber*, meaning *free, unrestrained*. The worship of Dionysus involved intoxication, music, trance dancing, ritual violence and frenzy, performance of miracles, orgiastic rites, and ecstatic speech. It is likely this association that leads to the accusation that the ecstatic Christians are drunk (Acts 2:15).

23 Of Sampson, "and the Spirit of the LORD came mightily upon him, and he tore the lion asunder as one tears a kid; and he had nothing in his hand." Judges 14:6, *RSV*.

24 From τελεστικος (telestikos), *initiatory*, or *mystical*, having to do with τελετη (teletê), *initiation* into the mysteries.

25 τραγωδια, *goat ode*, and θεσπις, *inspired*, having words from the gods. The male goat, along with the bull and snake, were sacred to Dionysus.

"The theatrical use of the mask presumably grew out of its magical use: Dionysus became in the sixth century the god of theatre because he had long been the god of masquerade." *The Greeks and the Irrational*, 94.

26 The flute and tympanum, associated with gender variance and homoeroticism, were used to induce an altered mental state. *Blossom of Bone*, 114-122.

"The pandemonium in which Dionysus, himself, and his divine entourage make their entry –that pandemonium which the human horde, struck by his spirit, unleashes –is a genuine symbol of religious ecstasy." *Dionysus: Myth and Cult*, 92.

Deissmann quotes from a letter written in Greek during the 3rd century BCE: "And send us also Zenobius the effeminate, with tabret, and cymbals, and rattles." *Light from the Ancient East*, 164.

27   "The priest in female clothes is typical of trance religion…in eastern shamanism the male shaman also crossdresses as a sign of his separateness from normal life." *History of Pagan Europe*, 118.

28   The *wand* or *staff* –ραβδος (rhabdos)– is a very old magical tool, well attested in both the Greek magical papyri and in the Greek translation of the Hebrew Old Testament, where, in the story of the confrontation between Aaron and Moses and the magicians of Egypt, Aaron is told: λαβε την **ραβδον** και ριψον επι την γην εναντιον Φαραω: "take your **staff** and cast it on the ground before Pharoah" (Exodus 7:9, *Septuagint*).

29   2 Kings 3:13-15. The *Septuagint*, the Greek translation of the Old Testament favored by early Christians, says: εγενετο επ' αυτον **χειρ** κυριου και ειπε: "**the hand** of the Lord came to be upon him and he spoke." Confronted with magic they cannot duplicate, Pharoah's sorcerers declare, "It is the finger of God!" (Exodus 8:19).

30   As at Daniel 2:2, 4:7, for example.

31   *History of Pagan Europe*, 107.

32   και **επιφαυσει** σοι ο Χριστος: "and the Christ **will shine upon** you," or alternative, "**will enlighten** you." The double meaning was obviously intentional.

33   In Matthew's infancy narrative, prophetic warning dreams are sent to Joseph (1:20), to the magi (2:12), again to Joseph a second (2:13), third (2:19), and fourth time (2:22), and later to Pilate's wife (27:19). As noted by Hull, "No less than five dreams surround the divine birth and Messiah goes to his death in the ominous

mystery of Pilate's wife's dream…The parousia of the Messiah is also to be accompanied by warning portents. The reference to 'the signal of your coming' and 'the sign that heralds the Son of Man' (24:3, 30) are unique to this gospel. So the birth, death and reappearance of Jesus Christ are all authenticated by signs." *Hellenistic Magic and the Synoptic Tradition*, 116-117.

Prophetic dreams are common in the Old Testament (Genesis 37:5-8, 41:7-41, Daniel 2:1-30).

34 Also the source of *incubus*.

The temple area where sleepers awaited dreams was the κοιμητηριον (koimêtêrion), the source of our *cemetery*.

"Incubation must involve, somehow, a magic procedure, for a god is conjured or summoned by some ritual, but it is performed within a religious context, under the supervision of priests who may have had some medical knowledge." Luck, *Arcana Mundi*, 141. Again we note the melding of magic, religion, and medicine.

Consulting ghosts, or necromancy —νεκυομαντεια (nekuomanteia)— was also an important function of dreams. Daniel Ogden: "It is not surprising that ghosts should have been sought in dreams, since they often visited the living spontaneously in this way," and notes that various Greek characters return to visit the living in their dreams. *Greek and Roman Necromancy*, 76.

Incubation would appear to be a crosscultural phenomenon: the calling of a "man of high degree" in the Australian aboriginal cultures "may be deliberately sought by sleeping in an isolated place, particularly near the grave of a medicine man or some other enchanted spot." *Aboriginal Men of High Degree*, 17. And of the Scandanavian people: "The *Flateyjarbók* tells of a man who was inspired with the gift of poetry by a dead *skald* on whose howe he slept." *History of Pagan Europe*, 142.

The Israelites "who sit in tombs, and spend the night in secret places" (Isaiah 65:4) were likely using graveyards to provoke necromantic visions.

35   Compare 2 Corinthians 12:4.

36   *The New Testament: Its Background, Growth, and Content*, 2nd edition, 245-246.

37   John Gager: "from the time of Sir James Frazer to the present, the ruling assumption has been spells, charms, and amulets cannot work –by definition. Once again, the initial assumption sets the agenda for the ensuing discussion and interpretation: because the beliefs are assumed to be false and because the practices are taken to be ineffective, how are we to explain the persistent irrationality of those who pursued them through so many centuries."

"What would happen, however, if we changed our initial assumption and began with the idea that these beliefs and practices must have worked *in some sense*; if we indicated that we can no longer accept the notion that those who hold to them are irrational; and if we recovered our sense of poetic language and expressive ritual as fundamental constituents of all human experience?" *Curse Tablets and Binding Spells from the Ancient World*, 22.

Naomi Janowitz makes much the same point: "In the main magic was dangerous because it *worked*. In the eyes of our ancient sources magic produced real results. It did so, however, by means of evil powers." *Magic in the Roman World*, 3.

John Dominic Crossan: "hocuspocus or mumbo jumbo may be found not only in ritual acts but also in philosophical theories, ideological claims, and theological systems. There may be, in other words, one gobbledygook, to use Betz' term, for the oral masses and another for the scribal elites, but it is still gobbledygook in each case." *The Historical Jesus*, 310.

Regarding modern Christianity's denial of the effects of magic, the comments of the late Ioan Couliano are apropos: "A religion once instituted, can endure only by the active control it exercises over the education of individuals, a control that must also be repressive in order to prevent the individual from losing his state of depersonalization or becoming capable of being re-programmed. The same criterion, of course, applies to the promotion of an individual in the religious hierarchy." *Eros and Magic in the Renaissance*, 108.

We cannot hope to understand magic as the people of the 1st century understood it unless we step outside the magisterium of concensus scholarship.

Chapter Eight:
Jesus the Magician

esus' contemporaries accused him of sorcery, of practicing magic. We know of this accusation because it is reported —*repeatedly*— by the gospels.[1] So it may be fairly asked how closely the behavior of Jesus of Nazareth matched that of the magicians who were his contemporaries.

The beginning of his powers

With a few exceptions, Jesus' miracles are exorcisms and healings, and they begin almost immediately after his return from the wilderness:

> It happened in those days that Jesus came from Nazareth of Galilee and was baptized in the Jordan by John. And at once, while he was coming up out of the water, he saw the heavens being ripped open and the spirit descending on him like a dove. And a voice came out of the heavens: "You are my son, the beloved. In you was I pleased."
>
> At once the spirit drove him out into the wilderness,[2] and he was in the wilderness for forty days, being tempted by Satan

and he was with the wild animals and the angels began serving him.[3]

After John had been arrested, Jesus came into Galilee proclaiming the good news of God, saying, "The allotted time has run out and the kingdom of God has almost arrived! Repent and believe in the good news!"

...

They came to Capernaum and as soon as the Sabbath came, he entered the synagogue and taught. They were astounded by his teaching, for he was teaching them as one having authority and not like the scribes.

Now in their synagogue there was a man with an unclean spirit and he shouted out, "What have we to do with you, Jesus of Nazareth? Did you come to destroy us? I know who you are! The Holy One of God!"

Jesus rebuked it,[4] saying, "Shut up and come out of him!" The unclean spirit convulsed him and screamed with a loud voice and came out of him.[5]

They were all amazed and they were asking one another, "What is this? A new teaching with authority! He commands the unclean spirits and they obey him!" Immediately the report about him spread through all the surrounding region of Galilee.

Mark 1:9-15, 21-28

Some have interpreted Jesus' extended time in the wilderness as having shamanistic overtones consistent with a vision quest, but due caution should be exercised in this regard; there is no evidence for an exact equivalent of shamans in the Middle East.[6]

The extent to which Jesus might have been influenced by magical practices outside the Jewish milieu is impossible to assess completely. There was a strong Hellenistic[7] presence in Galilee in Jesus' day —the Decapolis, a league of ten Greco-Roman cultural enclaves, is

115

mentioned in the gospels[8] — but the antecedents of Jesus' own wonder-working powers cannot be determined. However, the gospel of Mark repeatedly mentions how quickly his fame as an exorcist spread through Galilee and beyond.[9] Herod Antipas had heard of his exploits[10] and other exorcists were quick to use his name.[11] It seems incredible to think that this osmotic transfer of fame and knowledge flowed only in one direction.

Regarding the magical texts recovered from the Cairo *geniza*, Gager notes that they "reveal how widespread such beliefs and practices were in the Jewish communities of the ancient world and how broadly this material circulated, crossing linguistic, chronological, cultural, and religious boundaries."[12] The archeological evidence suggests that extensive cross-pollination of belief and practice was the rule in the Mediterranean world of Jesus' day and it is certain that he knew of and used common magical techniques because the gospels of Mark and John record them in some detail.

In Jesus' case, the spirit which has descended on —or perhaps more correctly speaking *into* him— immediately drives him out into the wilderness. The verb translated "drove him out" —εκβαλλω (ekballô)— is used of driving out unclean spirits in it very next occurrence.[13] The language used of Jesus' initiatory experience is the same as that used for spirit manipulation, and it is probably for that reason that both Matthew and Luke not only changed the verb, but even recast it in the passive voice when using Mark's account.[14]

The angelic assistant

Modern people, conditioned by countless depictions of angels, have entirely lost touch with the understanding of spirit entities that existed in antiquity. Even as Christianity corrupted the term *demon* —originally δαιμων (daimôn) referred to a being greater than a human, but of lesser rank than a god— giving it a permanent connotation of evil, so *angel* —αγγελος (angelos)— has been similarly distorted from its original sense. In classical Greek, the word meant *messenger*, and the related αγγελια (angelia), *report* or *message*. A being of intermediate rank that communicates between the gods and men is an extension of that basic meaning.

The word *angel* still has a fairly wide application even in the New Testament. Paul, for example, refers to a physical malady as "an angel of Satan,"[15] and some early Christians advocated the worship of angels, in all probability in the role of intercessors, a function now fulfilled in some Christian sects by saints.[16] Of the angels that appeared to Jesus in the wilderness we are told:

> Then the Devil left him and, Look! angels came and began to serve him.[17]
>
> Matthew 4:11

The angels in question first appear after Jesus has been challenged by Satan to perform magic —read *miracles*— transforming stones into bread and flying into the air. After Jesus asserts his own authority, angels come and begin to serve him. Who were these "angels"? As Georg Luck observes, "An essential part of the magician's training consisted in acquiring a *paredros* (παρεδρος, *my note*), i.e. an 'assistant' (daemon). This acquisition is a step toward complete initiation…"[18] Morton Smith: "Further, the report that after the temptation the angels served Jesus attributes to him the success magicians strove for —to

117

be served by supernatural beings." [19] "After the gods, the παρεδροι (plural of *paredros*, my note) are most frequently identified as αγγελοι (*angels*, my note) and δαιμονες (*demons*, my note) of an unspecified character. These two types of beings occur frequently in the Greek magical papyri."[20]

Joshua Trachtenberg:

> The peculiar rôle of the angels, heavenly counterparts of all earthly phenomena, as well as the direct servants and emissaries of God, closest to His ear, rendered powerful indeed the man who possessed the secret of bending them to his will. [21]

The one with authority

Mark tells us that Jesus taught with "authority" and "not like the scribes." In point of fact, the scribes were a highly literate class charged with both copying and interpreting the laws of Moses and they worked to be self-supporting so as to impose no financial burden on the population. They were the men to whom questions of religious observance might be referred, and they were deeply respected.[22] It is not possible that they had *no authority*. *a different kind.*

The word Mark uses for *authority* is εξουσια (exousia); it refers particularly to "the belief that some people have supernatural powers as a gift."[23] In Jesus' case the accounts make clear that the authority in question had nothing whatever to do with interpreting the laws of Moses. Jesus had the power to command demonic spirits. Hull notes that of the ten instances of *exousia* in Mark, only one is *not* connected with exorcism or healing, and concludes, "The people do not admire Jesus for his learning but for his power over the demons."[24] Mark himself clearly defines what the *authority* in question meant: "He *commands* the unclean spirits and they *obey* him."

Some of the methods by which Jesus commands obedience from unclean spirits are revealed in this account of an exorcism:

> After he got out of the boat, immediately he encountered coming out of the tombs a man controlled by an unclean spirit. He lived among the tombs since no one was able to bind him even with a chain. He had been bound with chains and shackles many times, but he snapped the chains apart and broke the shackles in pieces, and no one was strong enough to subdue him.
>
> He screamed day and night in the tombs and in the hills, lacerating himself with stones.
>
> When he saw Jesus from far away, he ran and fell at his feet and screamed out in a loud voice, "What have I to do with you, Jesus, son of the Most High God? I beg you in God's name do not torture me!"
>
> Because Jesus had said to it, "Come out of the man, unclean spirit!" and asked him, "What is your name?"
>
> He said, "Legion is my name, because we are many." He entreated him not to banish them from the region. There was a large herd of pigs grazing on the hill and the demons begged him, saying, "Send us into the pigs so that we can enter them." He gave them permission and the unclean spirits came out and entered the pigs and the herd of about two thousand pigs stampeded over the cliff and into the sea and drowned in the sea.
>
> Mark 5:2-13

Mark's account has a number of points in common with the manipulation of demons described in ancient sources: (1) the imagery of binding demons,[25] (2) the reference to the man as "demon-possessed,"[26] (3) the threat of torture,[27] (4) the demand that the demon tell its name,[28] and (5) the casting of the demons into the swine.[29]

We are given some further insight into the nature of Jesus' authority by the story of the centurion's boy.

> As he entered Capernaum, a centurion came to him, entreating him, "Lord, my boy[30] is lying at home paralyzed, suffering terribly."
> Jesus said to him, "I will come and heal him."
> The centurion replied, "Lord, I am not worthy for you to step under my roof, but say a word and my boy will be healed. For I, too, am a man with authority, having soldiers under my command, and I say to this one, "Go!" and he goes, and to another, "Come!" and he comes, and to my slave, "Do this!" and he does it."
>
> Matthew 8:5-9

The point of the story is that the centurion intuitively understands Jesus' command of the spirits to be the same as his command of his soldiers,[31] and for this insight is rewarded with the healing of his boy.

The pericope about the centurion finds a remarkable parallel in the language of the magical papyri and its description of the *paredros*, the magical assistant: *Today you would ask someone of that level.*

> No spirit of the air that is joined to a powerful assistant will draw back into Hades, for all things are subordinate to him, and if you wish to do something, merely speak his name into the air and say, "Come!" and you will see him standing near you. Say to him "Do this task," and he does it immediately, and having done it, he will ask, "What else do you wish, for I am hurrying into the sky." If you have no orders at that moment, tell him, "Go,

Lord," and he will leave. In this way the god will be seen by you alone, nor will anyone except you alone hear his voice when he speaks. [32]

The notion that superior authority may encompass the idea of superior strength agrees entirely with Jesus' own characterization of exorcism: the strong are overcome and bound by the stronger:

> "How can Satan cast out Satan? If a kingdom divides against itself, that kingdom cannot stand, and if a house divides against itself, that house will not be able to stand. So if Satan rises up against himself and becomes divided, he cannot stand. To the contrary, his end has come."
>
> "No one can enter the strong man's house[33] to plunder his possessions unless he first binds the strong man, and then he plunders his house."

Mark 3:23-27

The claim being made is that Jesus is stronger than "the strong man," able to bind him and take away his possessions.[34] On this passage Grundmann notes:

> The mission of Christ means that the ισχυτερος ["stronger," *my note*] comes, that he binds the ισχυρος ["strong"] when he has entered his house, and that He robs him of his spoil. This is how the exorcisms are to be understood.[35]

As Susan Garrett notes in connection with the metaphor of plunder, "whenever Jesus exorcises or heals, he takes spoil from Satan's kingdom and adds it to God's own…he as 'the stronger one' is entering and plundering the domain of the conquered Satan."[36] The gospels consistently represent Jesus as operating from a position of superior strength in regard to demons.

In keeping with his authority, the gospels speak of Jesus *rebuking* demons. The verb in question, επιτιμαω (epitimaô), is variously translated *rebuke, warn, reprimand*, or *reprove*, and it is used not only for exorcism, but for healing and for the performance of weather magic. In addition to demons,[37] Jesus "rebukes" the wind,[38] a fever,[39] and the apostle Peter —where the wording, "Get away from me, Satan,"[40] has the character of an exorcism.

Working magic: the technical details

A brief account in the gospel of Mark reveals some of the magical elements of Jesus' healing technique:

> They brought a deaf mute[41] to him and they entreated him to lay his hand upon him. Taking him away from the crowd to a private place, he put his fingers in his ears,[42] spit,[43] and touched his tongue, and looking up into the sky, he groaned[44] and said, "Ephphatha!" that is, "Be opened!"
>
> Instantly his ears were opened, and the bond that held his tongue was loosed[45] and he spoke normally.
>
> Mark 7:32-35

The several steps in this healing ritual —"he put his fingers in his ears, spit, and touched his tongue, and looking up into the sky, he groaned"— find very close parallels with similar rituals in the magical papyri: "Facing the sun, speak seven times into your hand, and spit once, and stroke your face..." [46]

Regarding such similarities between Jesus' actions and the spells described in the papyri, John Dominic Crossan's words are particularly relevant:

Finally, Jesus as a popular first-century Jewish magician in the tradition, say, of Elijah and Elisha, may well be different from the professional magicians who owned those magical papyri, but that should be established by comparing their actions, not presuming their motives.[47]

As far back as 1927, Campbell Bonner noted that groaning had "mystical and magical associations, and that...loud cries, roarings, and bellowings were a part of the mystical-magic technique."[48] Such details of magical technique are typically omitted by Matthew and Luke, who also chose to delete any mention of healings that take place *in stages* such as the healing of the blind man recorded in Mark 8:22-26.

The stories of healing and exorcism recounted in the gospels of Mark and John reveal well-known elements of magical practice including the use of spittle, a word of power or *vox magica*, as well as sighing and gestures:

> From other stories in the New Testament, Greco-Roman and rabbinic texts we can reconstruct a fairly standard repertoire of exorcistic techniques. These included looking upwards, sighing or groaning, making hand gestures (such as making the sign of the cross), spitting, invoking the deity and speaking "nonsense" words or letter strings. Sometimes the demon was commanded to speak as a way of demonstrating both his presence in the human body and the practitioner's control over him.[49]

The invocations Jesus uses as a part of his exorcistic technique have close parallels in the magical papyri as the comparison below illustrates:

> Seeing the crowd bearing down on him, Jesus rebuked the unclean spirit, saying to it, "I order you, speechless and deaf

spirit, get out of him,[50] and may you never come back into him!"[51]

Shrieking and convulsing him horribly, it came out and left him like a corpse so that most of them said, "He's dead!" But Jesus, taking him by the hand, raised him and stood him upright.

Mark 9:25-27

Excellent ritual for casting out demons.
Spell to be recited over his head:

[*Coptic gloss inserted into Greek text.*]

I order you, demon, whoever you are, by this god...Get out, demon, [52] whoever you are, and stay away from X! Now, now! Quickly, quickly! Get out, demon...! [53]

It is worth noting that in the accounts of both Matthew and Luke, the procedural details of the exorcism of the deaf and dumb spirit, as well as the description of the dramatic physical effects of the exorcism, have been stripped away, leaving us with these insipid versions:

So Jesus rebuked the unclean spirit and the demon came out of him and the boy was healed in that very hour.

Matthew 17:18

As the boy approached, the demon threw him down in convulsions, so Jesus rebuked the unclean spirit and healed the boy and returned him to his father.

Luke 9:42

These are particularly clear examples of the way in which the exorcisms have been "edited" —*cleaned up* would be more accurate— to make them more "miraculous" and less "magical," thereby rendering Jesus more palatable to a sophisticated audience. Although the healings and

exorcisms are held up as evidence of Jesus' divine status, the details
of their performance were an embarrassment to the church —they
portray a Jesus who might be regarded merely as one among many
itinerant wonder-working holy men. By this point theology was already
moving steadily away from the historical Jesus whose flaws, particularly
his reputation as a magician, were being papered over even as his official
résumé was being prepared.[54]

The author of Matthew anxiously eliminated all references to magical
technique, including the *voces magicae*: "and he cast out the spirits *with a
word*,"[55] but the *word* is never specified. In fact, as Hull noted, Matthew
reports only one word spoken to a demon, and twenty-three words
spoken by demons, whereas Luke records nine words spoken directly
to demons, and three more indirectly, as well as thirty-four words
spoken directly by demons to Jesus.[56]

It will come as no surprise that modern Christian apologists draw the
very conclusions that Matthew, the chief editor of the exorcism stories,
intended:

> Mark reports Jesus' prayer consisting of a single word,
> "Ephphatha (be opened)" (7:34) — which stands in the sharpest
> possible contrast with the extended invocations and formulas
> of the magical texts...As in the first story, there is no hint of
> elaborate invocation of angelic powers or of therapeutic
> procedure.[57]

This line of argument, which seeks to exonerate Jesus of charges of
magical practice, begins by assuming that Jesus' word was a "prayer,"
not an "invocation" or a "formula" —the text of the gospel specifies
not only that Jesus *groaned* and *looked up* to the sky, i.e., behavior

consistent with magical technique, it tells us that Jesus took the man aside, put his fingers into his ears, spit, and touched the man's tongue *all of which* conform to "therapeutic procedure." [58]

The first assumption is then followed by another: that in the few verses Mark allots to the story, he provides a complete description of *all that happened and all that Jesus said*, something that can never be taken for granted given the obvious manipulation of the texts. This selective apologetic reading of the evidence follows on the heels of the selective apologetic reporting of the evidence in the gospels themselves, and the foregone conclusion is that what Jesus did was in some way different in *substance*, if not in form, from what other miracle workers did. This sort of pig-headed misreading of the text is completely typical of believer scholarship that simply refuses to see that which is inconvenient in the documents of the New Testament. *Quite true.*

Working magic: binding and loosing

The story of the deaf mute introduces the metaphor of binding and loosing —"the bond that held his tongue was loosed." [59] The concept of binding was basic to 1st century magical practice: the verb and noun set is δεω (deô), *bind*, and δεσμος (desmos), *bond*. A closely related set, καταδεω (katadeô), *tie down*, and καταδεσμος (katadesmos), *binding spell*, were used of magical spells designed to restrain the actions or choices of others.[60] Because sickness and possession are not clearly differentiated in the gospels, identical language is often used in connection with both healing and exorcism:

"And this woman, a daughter of Abraham, who Satan bound[61] for —just imagine! Eighteen years! Was it not fitting that she be

126

loosed from this bond [62] on the Sabbath day?"

Luke 13:16

Working magic: who controls who?

In the 1ˢᵗ century it was well known that people with supernatural gifts often exhibited unnatural behavior, an observation reflected in this account from Mark:

> He came home and a crowd gathered again, so much so that they were not even able to eat a meal. His family went out to restrain him when they heard about it, because they were saying, "He's out of his mind!" [63]
>
> The scribes who came down from Jerusalem were saying, "He has Beelzeboul!"[64] "He casts out the demons by the ruler of the demons."
>
> Calling them together, he made an analogy: "How can Satan cast out Satan? If a kingdom divides against itself, that kingdom cannot stand, and if a house divides against itself, that house will not be able to stand. So if Satan rises up against himself and becomes divided, he cannot stand. To the contrary, his end has come."
>
> "No one can enter the strong man's house to plunder his possessions unless he first binds the strong man, and then he plunders his house."
>
> "Truly I say to you, every error and blasphemy will be forgiven the sons of men, but whoever blasphemes against the holy spirit will have no forgiveness for all ages, but is guilty of everlasting sin" —because they were saying, "He has an unclean spirit." [65]

Mark 3:20-30

The verb εξιστημι (existêmi) can refer to states of confusion or amazement or to insanity, but there is certainly nothing in the context to suggest that Jesus was either so confused or so amazed that his family felt they needed to restrain him. The related noun, εκστασις (ekstasis), which has already been mentioned, refers to a state of trance or frenzy.

To Jesus' family it may have appeared that he had taken leave of his senses, but the religious authorities saw it differently. They believed Jesus to be in control of a demon, basing their belief on his erratic behavior. The claim that Jesus controlled demons led to his rejoinder concerning blasphemy against the holy spirit and his question, "If I cast out demons by means of Beelzeboul by what means do your sons cast them out?"[66] Significantly, Jesus nowhere denies being able to manipulate a spirit —which is after all the *sine qua non* of the miracle-working holy man— but replies that the spirit in question is the spirit of God, not an unclean spirit.

Mark's reference to Jesus as being "out of his mind" was too extreme for both Matthew and Luke —there is no trace of this part of the story in either of their gospels.

That the expression "He has Beelzeboul" should be taken in the *active*, rather than passive sense, was pointed out by Kraeling:

> In the relations of men and demons there are two basic possibilities, either the demon has a man in his possession, or a man has a demon under his control...in the second the demon is the servant and the man a magician. [67]

Kraeling's observation is confirmed by the nearly identical wording of Revelation 3:1 where the glorified Christ is called "the One who has the seven spirits of God and the seven stars" —"stars" which are identified in the context as angels.[68] On the meaning of *having* the seven spirits, Hanse says,

> ...These seven spirits are thought of as autonomous beings, and they are to be equated with the seven angels which stand before God...What does it mean that Christ "has" them? It obviously means that He has authority over them, that He can command them...[69]   *He works with them.*

The accusation by the Jewish leaders is not that Jesus is possessed *by* a demon, but rather that he is the magician par excellence because he has bound Beelzeboul himself, the prince of demons, to his service and works his miracles as a result of exercising that control. It is nonsense to acknowledge that Jesus has authority over demons and in the next breath claim that he is *possessed* by one. Demonic possession means that the man is controlled by the demon, not that the demon is controlled by the man.[70]

Jesus himself virtually says as much when he asks, "How can one enter a strong man's house and seize his belongings *unless one first binds the strong man?*" [71] Jesus is not only claiming to loose those bound by Satan, but to bind demons to his will, an authority he can transmit to others.[72] After a thorough review of the evidence intrinsic to the gospel accounts, Samain construed "to have a demon" in the active sense, i.e., *to have control of the demon:*

> ...Christ is the master of Beelzeboul and he controls him to the point of using him to perform his exorcisms...Christ is alleged to be a magician: joined with the ruler of the demons, he compels him, by using his name, to perform the miracles he wants, particularly exorcisms; no spirit, no demonic power can resist him ...Δαιμονιον εχει ["He has a demon," *my note*] therefore

129

means that Jesus is a false prophet, a magician." [73]

That having a demon under one's control is very different from being possessed by a demon is reflected both in the language of the New Testament and in the terminology of the magical papyri. A particular verb —δαιμονιζομαι (daimonizomai)— "to be possessed by a hostile spirit" [74] is consistently reserved for those tormented by demons and it is *never* applied to Jesus in the New Testament even by his opponents. [75] In response to the accusations that Jesus is employing an evil spirit to accomplish his miracles, the crowd correctly notes, "These are not the words of a possessed man!" [76] The verb is used of those under the control of a demon, not of a man in control of one.

Jesus is never represented as being among the demon-possessed, among the *afflicted*, those who have *lost control* of themselves —"demon-possessed and epileptic and paralysed." [77] Of such tragic figures Joshua Trachtenberg notes, "Demons who have taken possession of a human body exercise such complete control over it that the personality and the will of the victim are extinguished." [78] Such persons have most emphatically not been placed in command of spirits, whereas Jesus is everywhere presented in the gospels as operating from a position of superior strength vis-à-vis the demons. Jesus' authority —his εξουσια— "means a mysterious superhuman force whereby demons were controlled and afflictions miraculously healed." [79]

We should be perfectly clear on this point: *pace* Howard Clark Kee the scribes *nowhere* "charge that [Jesus] can control the demons because he is himself controlled by their prince, Beelzebub," a situation that would for all intent make Jesus into a puppet of Satan. [80] To the contrary,

130

their charge is that *Jesus is in control of Beelzeboul*: "He casts out demons *by the ruler of the demons*." The charge of the scribes is that Jesus is a magician so powerful that he can bind even the prince of demons to his service. But he is a *magician* nonetheless.

As noted previously, erratic or strange behavior was long associated with exorcistic ritual, prophecy, and wonder-working generally. In a hostile encounter with Jewish holy men, this very power was turned against Saul as described in the account of his hunt for his rival, David.

> Saul was told, "David is at Naioth in Ramah." Then Saul sent messengers to take David. When they saw the company of prophets in a frenzy, with Samuel standing in charge of them, the spirit of God came on the messengers of Saul and they also fell into a prophetic frenzy.
> When Saul was told, he sent other messengers, and they also fell into a frenzy. Saul sent messengers again the third time, and they also fell into a frenzy.
> Then he himself went to Ramah. He came to the great well that is in Secu; he asked, "Where are Samuel and David?" And someone said, "They are at Naioth in Ramah." He went there, toward Naioth in Ramah; and the spirit of God came upon him. As he was going, he fell into a prophetic frenzy, until he came to Naioth in Ramah. He too stripped off his clothes, and he too fell into a frenzy before Samuel. He lay naked all that day and all that night. Therefore it is said, "Is Saul also among the prophets?"
>
> 1 Samuel 19:20-24, *NRSV*

The bizarre behavior that accompanied Jesus' own miracle working is the subject of this telling passage in the gospel of John:

> Again a division of opinion occurred among the Jews because

of these words. Many of them were saying, "He has a demon and he's raving! [81] Why listen to him?"

Others said, "These are not the words of a possessed man! Is a demon able to open the eyes of the blind?"

John 10:19-21

In this text "raving" translates the verb μαινομαι (mainomai), and given the context, it is clear that Jesus' opponents are not simply accusing him of talking nonsense, but are pointing to Jesus' raving as evidence of magical ritual. The nominal form, μανια (mania), which occurs as a description of the frenzy of the Bacchic rites, refers specifically to violent behavior that accompanied possession.[82] In either case, it is important to note that the word simply designates behavior, and not its cause or motive.

At no point do Jesus' opponents deny that he casts out demons. It is only Jesus' method that is open to question, but whether accomplished by the spirit of God or by Beelzeboul, the prince of demons, the results are formally identical: the demons leave when commanded. It must also be emphasized, however, that *for the exorcist* —unlike the prophet— *raving is a magical technique, not a symptom of demonic possession.* Whereas the prophet raves as a sign of possession, the magician raves to *establish control.* For the magician, raving is an enactment, a form of mimesis. Unlike the prophet, who courts possession through music, dance, and dream, the role of the magician is active —magic is about taking control of and manipulating power. Magic is cosmic theater and the magician is the director.

Jesus and the dark side of sorcery

Given the quintessentially Christian view that connects sorcery with all that is evil, it is quite surprising to find Jesus performing acts that incorporate dark magical elements. It is even more surprising to find some of these accounts clustered in the gospel of John, widely held to be the most heavily "spiritualized" gospel.

> As he passed by, he saw a man blind from birth. His disciples asked him, "Rabbi, who sinned, this man or his parents, so that he was born blind?[83]
>
> Jesus answered, "Neither this man nor his parents sinned, but it happened so that the works of God might be manifest in him. We must perform the works of the one who sent me while it is day. A night approaches when no one can act. While I am in the world, I am the light of the world."
>
> When he had said this, he spit on the ground, made a paste from the spittle, and smeared the paste on the man's eyes and said to him, "Go wash in the pool of Siloam," which interpreted means Sent. Then he went and washed and came back seeing.
>
> Consequently the neighbors and those who had previously seen that he was a beggar said, "Isn't this the man who sat and begged?" Others said, "That's him!" But others were saying, "No, it's someone like him." The man was saying, "It's me!" So they said to him, "So how were your eyes opened?"
>
> The man answered, "The man called Jesus made a paste and smeared it on my eyes and said to me, 'Go to Siloam and wash,' and then I went and washed and received my sight."
>
> John 9:1-11

This episode, like the version in Mark which differs from it in that it requires *two* applications of spit to be effective,[84] *is not conventionally miraculous.* Indeed, it fairly reeks of magic: one must do *this*, then *this*, and next *this* to accomplish *that*. The common perception is that Jesus simply speaks and his miracles occur, but as this account shows, that is not the case. These accounts describe exactly the sort of ritualistic step-by-step behavior associated with the performance of magic.[85]

So powerful is Jesus' magic that even his clothing takes on talismanic power:

> There was a woman who had suffered from a flow of blood for twelve years, and she had endured many treatments by many doctors and had spent everything she had and had received no benefit, but had become even worse off.
>
> Having heard about Jesus, she came up from behind him in the crowd and touched his clothing, for she kept saying, "If I just touch his clothes, I will be healed." And immediately her flow of blood dried up and she perceived in her body that she was healed of the affliction.
>
> Suddenly realizing in himself that power had gone out of him, Jesus turned around in the crowd and said, "Who touched my clothes?" His disciples said to him, "You see the crowd pressing in on you and yet you say 'Who touched me?'" [86]
>
> He looked around to see who had done it, but the woman, knowing what had happened to her, came trembling with fear and fell down before him and told him the whole truth. But he said to her, "Daughter, your confidence has healed you. Go in peace and be healed of your affliction."
>
> Mark 5:25-34

This story has provoked some very interesting observations which are summarized by John Hull:

1. the woman exhibits no particular interest in or knowledge of Jesus' mission or his person,

2. she knows the healing power is available independent of Jesus' will,

3. the impersonal nature of Jesus' power is known to himself, the woman, and the evangelist,

4. the power, like electricity, flows automatically to another if their touch is deliberate and they have confidence in its efficacy,

5. the power in Jesus is also in the garment,

6. Jesus notices the flow of power, not the touch, and

7. Jesus does not find the woman's action blameworthy.[87]

Jesus' power is such that other exorcists, unknown to him or his disciples, cast out demons using his name, [88] a practice which continues after his death,[89] and his disciples also possess such power that not only can contact with articles of their clothing heal, *even their shadow falling across the sick effects a cure.*[90] All of the above examples indicate that the power in question is *impersonal*, i.e., *magical*.

These accounts reveal an attitude toward working a miracle that shares the same basic assumption as working magic: power is *value-free* and hence available to those who master the techniques required to access it. Techniques can be taught, and power transferred from one practitioner to another. In fact, the gospel of Mark specifies that Jesus taught his disciples the techniques of exorcism,[91] and it is this understanding of the impersonal nature of the energy involved that motivated Simon to offer to pay Peter for his miraculous powers.[92]

Any magical operation presupposes that some sort of energy is available in the universe which can be used by the operator. The modern anthropologists call it *mana*, the Greeks called it *dynamis* [δυναμις, *my note*], "power," or *charis*, "grace," or *arete*, "effectiveness." In a polytheistic society, it was only natural that the one Power took on the forms and names of many powers —gods, daemons, heroes, disembodied souls, etc— who were willing, even eager, to work for the *magos*. [93]

All power has a dark side, and that was equally true of the power of Jesus:

> And Herod heard of it, for [Jesus'] name became known and they were saying, "John the Baptist has been raised from the dead and because of this the powers are at work in him.[94]
> But others said, "He is Elijah," but others, "A prophet, like one of the former prophets." But when Herod heard, he said, "John, the one who I beheaded, has been raised."
>
> Mark 6:14-16

From a superficial reading of this text, a person might assume that people were speculating that John the Baptist had been resurrected from the dead in much the same way that Lazarus or Jesus himself was subsequently raised. However, a much different reading, one not only in accord with the circumstances of the times, but with the vocabulary of the passage, was proposed by Carl Kraeling:

> Between demons as the servants of magicians, and spirits of the dead used in a similar way there is no basic distinction. Both are beings of the spiritual order, not limited by time or space, and endowed with supernatural powers...What the people and Herod originally said about Jesus' relation to John was that Jesus was using the spirit of John brought back from the dead to perform his miracles for him.[95]

136

The broader context of the story establishes that Herod Antipas not only knew and feared John the Baptist as a holy man, but that he had previously protected him. Furthermore, Herod obviously knew John was dead —Herod himself had ordered John's execution and had seen his head delivered on a platter.[96]

Whoever the "they" were that claimed John the Baptist had been raised from the dead, it is clear that they had known John. Why else would they mention him unless they had been in the crowds that went out to be baptized by him and considered him a prophet?[97] And they must certainly have known Jesus and seen him in action. What else would explain their animated speculation about the source of his powers? Why, therefore, should we suppose that the crowds who first flocked to hear John the Baptist and later witnessed the wonders performed by Jesus could not tell that John the Baptist and Jesus of Nazareth were two different people?

Note carefully how the common people explained Jesus' powers: "John the Baptist has been raised from the dead *and because of this* the powers are at work in him." The people did not mean that John had been resurrected, but that his ghost had been raised up for magical purposes. In Jesus' day it was widely believed that the ghosts of the unquiet dead, those who had died before their time, particularly by meeting up with a violent end —and John certainly qualified on that count— were earthbound sources of enormous power. Jacob Rabinowitz vividly describes such restless dead: "Needy and dangerous figures waiting in the shadows of existence...particularly those who died young or violently, the unhappy and unsatisfied dead with their restless energy and free-floating rage."[98]

Regarding a possible motive for why Jesus might have selected the ghost of John the Baptist above all others as a source of power, this observation by Daniel Ogden bears careful note:

> How significant were these categories of dead for necromancy in particular? Often the prime criterion in selecting a ghost for necromancy was the relevance of the individual ghost to the matter at hand. Hence, the ghost exploited was often a dear one…A further category that may have been particularly valued for necromancy was that of the exalted ghost.[99]

Who could have been more relevant to Jesus' career than John the Baptist? He is Jesus' forerunner, "the voice of one crying in the wilderness," even a relative according to Luke, and of those born of women, who was greater than John?[100]

Because the people believe that Jesus has raised the ghost of John, they conclude that "the powers are at work in him" —the powers of darkness.[101] In several New Testament passages "powers" make a clear reference to spirit entities,[102] and of the verb translated "be at work in" —ενεργεω (energeô)— Bertram notes that in the New Testament "theological or demonological use is predominant." [103] Both the verb and corresponding noun, ενεργεια (energeia), from whence *energy*, are used in the magical papyri for working sorcery.[104]

In the process of redacting his version of the story, Matthew has Herod say, "This man is John the Baptist. He was raised from the dead and that is why the powers are working in him."[105] The text makes an identification between Jesus and John, interpreting Jesus as John *redivivus*, thus setting the stage for most exegesis that will follow, but this gloss does not fully address the question of *why* the powers

138

would be working in someone because they had been raised from the dead, nor does it contemplate *what sort of powers* were thought to be involved.

Luke, on the other hand, produces a Herod who is "completely perplexed," at a seeming loss how to even begin to explain Jesus' famous powers. Although apologist scholars such as Susan Garrett admit that Luke rephrases "the most damaging part of the account," to avoid the charge of necromancy, she next claims that the evangelists "did not share modern readers' frequent assumption that identity of appearance implies actual identity."[106] But how else would one establish an identity *based on performance?* Are not trees known by their fruit?[107] Indeed, the frequent alterations and omissions of incriminating details by Matthew and Luke indicate that the writers of those gospels shared *exactly* the assumption that appearance implies identity and knew that their readers would also assume that appearances implied identity. Why report Jesus' healings and exorcisms at all if their performance was not thought to establish something about his identity? And why change or delete Mark's reports of Jesus' performance unless the identity being established by Mark was not to the exact liking of Matthew and Luke?

Garrett's argument also ignores the evidence for Jesus' reputation among non-Christians —Gentiles regarded Jews as accomplished exorcists and Jesus the Jew as a magician. Evidently his early critics also shared our "modern" assumption that appearances tell us something about identity:

> The charge that Jesus was a magician has been preserved outside the New Testament in both Jewish and pagan traditions...The church fathers, among them Irenaeus, Arnobius,

Justin Martyr, Lactantius, and Origen, were keenly aware of the charge —made by Jew and Gentile alike— that Jesus was a magician. In reply to this assertion, these early Christian writers made no effort to distinguish Jesus' actions from those of a wonder-worker…It was a question not of the form of the wonders, but of the relationship of the purported doer to the person speaking or writing.[108]

Those pondering the source of Jesus' power, then as now, are torn between two possibilities: he is a prophet like one of the prophets of old and his powers come from the spirit of God, or he is a necromancer and the powers at work in him include the ghost of John the Baptist. Herod Antipas appears to lean toward the latter conclusion: "John, the one who I beheaded, has been raised." Little wonder that the origin of Jesus' authority remains an issue up to the end of his life.[109]

That Jesus controlled demons is everywhere acknowledged, even by his enemies, but the fact that he could send unclean spirits into animals and men has received far less attention.

> After saying this, Jesus became disturbed in spirit and declared, "Most certainly I tell you, one from among you will betray me!"
> The disciples looked around at one another, uncertain about whom he was speaking. One of the disciples —the one that Jesus loved— was lying up against Jesus. Simon Peter motioned him to ask him about whom he was speaking, so the disciple leaning against Jesus' chest said to him, "Lord, who is it?" [110]
> Jesus answered, "It is the one I give the morsel of bread that I dip. Then he took the morsel and dipped it and gave it to Judas, the son of Simon Iscariot. And after the morsel, then Satan entered into him.
> Jesus said to him, "Do what you are doing more quickly." [111]

140

But none of those reclining with Jesus knew why he said that to him.

John 13:21-28

As soon as John tells us that Jesus "became disturbed in spirit" we are put on notice of an impending supernatural event. Such "disturbances" —the verb is ταρασσω (tarassô)— in the gospel of John always precede miraculous occurrences. When the water of the pool of Bethzatha is "stirred" by an angel, the first sick person in is healed —a sort of divinely-sponsored 'race for the cure'— and when Jesus' soul is "troubled" a heavenly voice is heard. Jesus becomes similarly "disturbed" on first encountering the mourners at Lazarus' tomb and again as he stands before the tomb itself —the raising of the beloved Lazarus quickly follows.[112]

In the case of the final meal with his disciples, Jesus' disturbance of spirit again signals a preternatural event, two of them to be exact. First, Jesus foresees Judas' betrayal,[113] and next he hands Judas over to Satan so that Satan can destroy him. There is a clear precedent for this action: he has previously handed a herd of swine over to the horde of demons that drove the pigs over a cliff to their death —as previously noted, "transference of the disease or demon from the man to the animal" is a well-attested magical technique in the ancient Middle East.[114] The piece of bread that Jesus dips in the bowl and hands to Judas is the equivalent of Judas' kiss of betrayal: it is the sign to the Adversary to approach and take control. Morton Smith: "The notion that a demon can be sent into food so as to enter anyone who eats the food is common."[115] Jesus betrays Judas to Satan before Judas betrays Jesus to the temple police. In so doing, Jesus is merely following the example set in the Old Testament where God regularly sends evil spirits into those of whom he disapproves. [116]

Specific references to Jesus cursing people, if such events occurred, have been removed from the gospels, but the fact that Jesus could directly curse someone to death is supported by the story of the withered fig tree.[117] After his death, Jesus' followers exercise the power both to strike people dead on the spot and to deliver them over to Satan, issues that will be explored in the following chapter.

Conclusions

It is primarily through the holes in the narrative seams of the gospels that we catch a fleeting glimpse of Jesus the man, the man condemned to stand forever in the shadow of the Christ. To the office of apocalyptic prophet we may now add a second, that of ecstatic wonder worker. Jesus would likely have been regarded by the pagan population of his day as a γοης (goês), or "wailer," a sorcerer, a necromancer, or merely as a charlatan, a fraud.[118] The ancient world was a full of wonder-workers —θαυματουργος (thaumatourgos), *thaumaturge*, is only one of many terms we moderns have inherited from it— as ours is of faith healers and smarmy televangelists, and like their modern counterparts, the religious actors of Jesus' day were received with responses that spanned the spectrum from bugeyed credulity to smirking derision.

It is initially surprising how easily exorcism, magic, and apocalyptic speech flow together in the person of Jesus, breaking through the artificially imposed categories laid down by centuries of theology. In point of fact, we see little distinction in our texts between religion and

142

magic, or between healing and magic. In both Mark and John, the magical details of Jesus' workings are reported quite ingenuously, with little awareness of a difference between magic and miracle, whereas Matthew and Luke carefully filter the same details out of their accounts, attempting at every turn to distinguish Jesus from other prophets, exorcists, and healers. But as Mark and John reveal, at the level of the earliest, most primitive tradition, it is a distinction without a difference.

Notes

1   Mark 3:22, 6:16, John 8:48, 52, 10:20.

2   ευθυς το πνευμα αυτον **εκβαλλει** εις την ερημον: "at once the spirit **drove** him **out** into the wilderness..."

3   οι αγγελοι **διηκουν** αυτον: "the angels **began serving** him."

4   επετιμησεν αυτω ο Ιησους: "Jesus rebuked it..."

5   "In Mark 1:24 the demon cries out to Christ, 'I know who you are' continuing with the holy name as proof of recognition. This is a magical formula well attested in the [magical] papyri...This is rather similar to the girl with the oracular spirit in Acts 16.17 who greets Paul and his friends with the warning exclamation, 'These men are servants of the most high God' just before the spirit is exorcized." Hull, *Hellenistic Magic and the Synoptic Tradition*, 67-68.

Naomi Janowitz: "In the first centuries in order to unmask a daimon and drive it from somebody's body the officiant himself had to have more-than-human status...Divine names...function similarly to signatures and signature guarantees in our culture, which are understood to be legally binding representations." *Magic in the Roman World*, 36, 40.

A Greek term for a person of such power was ανθρωποδαιμων (anthrôpodaimón), *man-demon*.

6   "There is little secure evidence for the existence of shamans in Northern Asia in antiquity and no evidence for the transfer of shamanistic practices from Asia to Greece." *Magic and Magicians in the Greco-Roman World*, 13.

7   Hellenization "means only to express indigenous concepts and traditions in Greek, not to transform traditions and concepts according to a Greek mold…" Graf, *Magic in the Ancient World*, 5.

8   At Mark 5:20, for example, where the mention is made in the context of a report of an exorcism.

9   Mark 1:28, 45, 3:7-8, 5:20.

10 Mark 6:14.

11 Mark 9:38. Exorcism was a quintessentially Jewish technique that rapidly spread throughout the Roman world.

12 *Curse Tablets and Binding Spells from the Ancient World*, 107. Jewish practice forbids the destruction of any text in which the divine name has been written. Worn out scrolls were therefore retired to a storage area called a *geniza* which was located in or next to the synagogue.

13 Mark 1:34.

14 ο Ιησους **ανηχθη** εις την ερημον υπο του πνευματος: "Jesus **was led up** into the desert by the spirit" (Matthew 4:1); και **ηγετο** εν τω πνεματι εν τω ερημω: "and he **was led** by the spirit into the desert" (Luke 4:1).

15 **αγγελος** σατανα: "an **angel** of Satan" (2 Corinthians 12:7).

As "an intermediary between the worlds of gods and men" the chthonic goddess Hecate is repeatedly called an "angel." *The Rotting Goddess*, 22.

Gerhard Kittel, noting the frequent use of angel in Greek magical curse tablets, says, "There are chthonic as well as heavenly αγγελοι ["angels"]." *Theological Dictionary of the New Testament*, I, 75.

16 Colossians 2:18.

17 ιδου αγγελοι πσοσηλθον και **διηκονουν** αυτω: "Look! Angels came and **began to serve** him." Following Young, I have construed the tense as an example of the inceptive imperfect. *Intermediate New Testament Greek*, 115.

18 Luck, *Witchcraft and Magic in Europe: Ancient Greece and Rome*, 108. παρεδρος (paredros) means *associate*, and is equivalent to the Latin *famulus* and the English *familiar* (spirit).

19 *Jesus the Magician*, 105.

20 Leda Jean Ciraolo, *Ancient Magic and Ritual Power*, 283. A thorough discussion of the role of magical assistants in the papyri.

21 *Jewish Magic and Superstition*, 25. For further comments on angels as assistants to initiated magicians, see Graf, *Magic in the Ancient World*, 90-91, 117.

22 The respect accorded the scribes is indirectly acknowledged in Mark 12:38.

23 Luck, *Witchcraft and Magic*, 99.

Significantly, Satan offered Jesus εξουσια, "authority," which Jesus refused (Luke 4:6). The gospels everywhere present Jesus as already in possession of authority. When Luke records Jesus' first exorcism, the demon being cast out screams "Have you come to destroy us?" (Luke 4:31-37). Given Jesus' superior authority, there can be no doubt regarding the answer.

24 Hull, *Hellenistic Magic*, 165. The exceptional use of *exousia* is found in Mark 13:34, where the reference is apocalyptic.

25 ουδεις εδυνατο αυτον **δησαι**: "no one was able **to bind** him..." (Mark 5:3).

"because I bind you with **unbreakable bonds**:" επει σε δεσμευω δεσμοις αδαμαντινοις.

26 θεωρουσιν **τον δαιμονιζομενον** καθημενον: "they saw **the demon-possessed man** sitting…" (Mark 5:15).

"If you say the name **to the demon-possessed** while putting sulfur and asphalt under his nose, instantly [the demon] will speak and go away:" εαν **δαιμονιζομενω** ειπης το ονομα. *Papyri Graecae Magicae*, II, 99 (XIII, 243-244).

27 ορκιζω σε τον θεον **μη με βασανισης**: "I beg you in God's name **do not torture me!**" (Mark 5:7).

"God of gods, King of kings, now compel a kindly demon, a giver of oracles, to come to me lest even **more severe tortures be applied:**" ινα μη εις **χειρονας βασανους ελθω**. *Papyri Graecae Magicae*, I, 24 (II, 53-55).

28 "The invocation of angelic names in Jewish magic may be regarded as in part the parallel to the pagan invocation of many deities, and in part as invocation of the infinite (personified) phases and energies of the one God. Both Jewish and pagan magic agreed in requiring the accumulation of as many names of the deity or demon as possible, for fear lest no one name exhaust the potentiality of the spiritual being conjured." *Jewish Magic and Superstition*, 86-87.

29 Marie-Louise Thomsen: "Sumerian incantations against evil demons describe how an animal, usually a goat or pig, was offered as a substitute for the sick person. The purpose of the ritual was the transference of the disease or demon from the man to the animal…the demon was conjured to leave him and take possession of the animal instead." *Witchcraft and Magic in Europe: Biblical and Pagan Societies*, 71-72.

30 "My boy," could also be translated "my servant," or even "my boyfriend." Luke completely recasts this story, inserting Jewish elders who make the plea on the centurion's behalf, and friends who speak for the centurion himself, thereby destroying the

immediacy of Jesus' interaction with the centurion and his "boy," who, as Gentiles, are ceremonially unclean. Nevertheless, one wonders, since Luke was writing *to* Gentiles, if there might have been another motivation. Luke also redescribes the boy as a "slave" (7:2) who was "precious" to the centurion (7:7), a valuation usually interpreted as merely financial.

In John's account, the centurion becomes a "royal official," and the enigmatic boy is variously described as his "son" (4:46), as "my child" (4:49), and "his boy" (4:51). None of these accounts entirely succeed in clearing up the relationship between the centurion and his "boy" which is perhaps the point.

The word παιδιον (paidion) used of the "boy" carries sexual connotations, and homosexual relations with slaves were apparently common. The story and its redaction give us a nearly perfect example both of the ambiguity of the Greek text and of the editing and rephrasing to which the New Testament material has been subjected. For addition discussion of the possible homoerotic implications of the passage, see Theodore Jennings' *The Man Jesus Loved*.

31 Compare Matthew 26:53. Jesus can say the word and summon 12 legions of angels, 72,000!

32 *Papyri Graecae Magicae*, I, 10-12 (I:179-189).

Compare Matthew 8:9: τω δουλω μου **ποιησον τουτο και ποιει**: "to my slave, **"Do this,"** and he does it..." and *PGM*, I:182: λεγε αυτω **ποιησον τουτο το εργον και ποιει** παραυτα: "say to him, **"Do this task, and he does it immediately..."**

33 την οικιαν **του ισχυρου**: "the **strong man's** house..." Regarding ισχυρος (ischuros), *mighty one*, as a description of a demon, compare εγω ειμι ο ακεφαλος δαιμων **ισχυρος** ο εχων το πυρ το αθανατον: "I am the headless demon...the

mighty one who has the unquenchable fire…" *Papyri Graecae Magicae*, I, 185 (V:14-147).

34   Compare Matthew 3:11, "The one coming after me is *stronger* than I…"

35   *Theological Dictionary of the New Testament*, III, 401.

36   *The Demise of the Devil*, 45.

37   επετιμησεν δε ο Ιησους τω πνευματιχ τω ακαθαρτω και ιασατο τον παιδια: "Jesus **rebuked** the unclean spirit and the boy was healed." Luke 9:42 (Compare Luke 4:41). Howard Kee emphasizes the notion of exorcism *as subjugation by force*, as in Mark 3:27. *New Testament Studies* 14: 232-246.

38   και διεγερθεις **επετιμησεν** τω ανεμω: "and arising, he **rebuked** the wind." Mark 4:39.

39   **επετιμησεν** τω πυρετω και αφηκεν αυτην: "he **rebuked** the fever and it left her." Luke 4:39.

40   **επετιμησεν** Πετρω και λεγει **υπαγε** οπισω μου **σατανα**: "he rebuked Peter and said, 'Get away from me, Satan!'" Mark 8:33. Compare the language of Matthew 4:10: λεγει αυτω ο Ιησους **υπαγε σατανα**: "Jesus said to him, 'Get away, Satan!'"

41   Mute because the demon possessing him is mute (Matthew 9:32, Luke 11:14).

42   Hull: "Whilst healing this man, Jesus put his fingers into the man's ears…in other biblical contexts the finger appears as the symbol of God's power. In this latter use it may have connections with magic and exorcism, and there are many parallels in the magical literature." *Hellenistic Magic*, 82.

43   Spit was a well-known magical substance: "The old woman pulled a string made from threads of different colors from her dress and tied it around my neck. Then she took some dirt, mixed it

with her spittle, and with her third finger made a mark on my forehead…" from the *Satyricon*, quoted by Luck, *Arcana Mundi*, 89. The witch uses spittle to cure Encolpius' erectile dysfunction.

"Spittle is used in three of the miracles. In John 9.6 paste is made from the spittle of Jesus and clay is smeared on a man's eyes; in Mark 8.23 and 7.33 spitting is used in cases of blindness and dumbness…All races of antiquity attached magical significance to spittle. The Pyramid Texts (late third millennium BC) speak of Atum spitting out Shu, the air, in the act of creation…The Epidaurus inscriptions describe miraculous cures wrought by the lick of sacred snakes and dogs within the temples of Asclepius…" *Hellenistic Magic*, 76-77.

44   και αναβλεψας εις τον ουρανον **εστεναξεν**: "And looking up into the sky, he **groaned**…"

45   και ελυθη ο **δεσμος** της γλωσσης αυτου: "and the **bond** that held his tongue was loosed…"

46   *Papyri Graecae Magicae*, I, 50 (III, 422-423).

47   *The Historical Jesus*, 310.

48   Bonner notes, "στεναζω ["groan," *my note*] and αναστεναζω ["cry out," *my note*] are words which have mystical and magical associations, and that the action denoted by them may be considered as a conventional part of the mystical-magic technique." *Harvard Theological Review* 20: 172.

Hull: "In general the accounts of the miracles are remarkable for the lack of interest shown in the emotions of Jesus and his patients. Oddly enough, the use of the strongly emotional εμβριμαομαι ["be deeply moved," *my note*] in connection with miracles is also illuminated by magical usage." *Hellenistic Magic*, 84.

Εμβριμαομαι (embrimaomai) is used in the context of the performance of miracles at Mark 1:43, the healing of the leper, and at John 11:33, 38, the raising of Lazarus. Matthew's version of the story of the healing of the leper (8:1-4) omits εμβριμαομαι, as does Luke's (5:12-14). Both are evidently suspicious of the verb because of its association with works of magic.

49   Janowitz, *Magic in the Roman World*, 39.

50   **εξελθε** εξ αυτου: "**get out** of him…"

51   Geller: "Jesus' specific exorcism formula, 'Go out from him and never enter him again' can also be identified in contemporary magical literature." *Journal of Jewish Studies* 28: 145.

52   **εξελθε** δαιμων οστις ποτ' ουν ει: "**get out**, demon, whoever you are…!" The procedure reflects a widely-known formula for exorcism used by Jesus among others. The exorcist is supposed to fill in the name or characteristics of the particular demon – "whoever you are"– in question.

53   *Papyri Graecae Magicae*, I, 114 (IV:1229-1246). The textual history of this spell presents many difficulties: an Old Coptic gloss has been inserted into the Greek text. The Coptic reads: "Hail, God of Abraham; hail, God of Isaac; hail, God of Jacob; Jesus Chrestos, the Holy Spirit, *etc…*" *The Greek Magical Papyri in Translation*, 62. The Greek χρηστος (chrêstos), –*not* χριστος (christos), *Christ*– means "auspicious" or "true," "trustworthy." *Auspicious* for the working of magic.

Morton Smith: "These uses of Jesus' name in pagan spells are flanked by a vast body of material testifying to the use of his name in Christian spells and exorcisms…The attestations are confirmed by a multitude of Christian amulets, curse tablets, and magical papyri in which Jesus is the god most often invoked…" *Jesus the Magician*, 63.

Several possibilities exist: the formula represented a widely-known Jewish exorcistic invocation which finds an echo in Mark and the Coptic gloss was interpolated to make it more "Christian," or the formula was derived from Mark or a source like that of Mark and adopted to pagan use after which the Coptic interpolation was added.

54   Hull notes, "Matthew has a suspicion of exorcism. We have seen how though the messianic authority over the evil spirits is maintained, almost all details of techniques are omitted. This is because exorcism was one the main functions of the magician. The magic consisted in the method; Matthew retains the fact without the method, trying in this way to purify the subject." *Hellenistic Magic*, 139.

55   Matthew 8:16.

56   Hull, *Hellenistic Magic*, 130.

Even scholars who tend toward the apologetic concede that the gospel accounts have been severely edited. Susan Garrett: "Matthew excised not only the more blatant thaumaturgical traits but even whole incidents, such as the stories of the healing of the deaf mute (Mark 7:31-37) and of the blind man near Bethsaida (Mark 8:22-26), both of which might lend themselves to magical interpretation...Luke seems to have made an intentional effort to distance Jesus and church leaders from magical notions." *Religion, Science, and Magic*, 143.

57   Howard Clark Kee, *Religion, Science, and Magic*, 136.

58   "To the Greeks, a magician not only uttered spells, he also prayed to the gods: Plato, for one connects the ἐπωιδαι (spells) and the ευχαι (prayers) of the magician...I count five instances where ευχη ["prayer", *my note*] occurs as an actual title of a spell..." *Magika Hiera*, 188, 189.

As there is no clear distinction between religion and magic in the 1st century, there is correspondingly no clear difference between prayers and spells. The imposition of such a difference is a *modern* one which does violence to the evidence.

59   Mark 7:35.

60   "Illness and death: it is these two elements of the magico-religious complex of "binding" which have had the widest currency almost all over the world…" Eliade, *Images and Symbols*, 92-124.

Hull: "Details of some of the healing stories in Mark indicate a magical context just as details of the exorcisms seem to. The healing of the deaf mute in Mark 7:32ff. is perhaps the clearest case." *Hellenistic Magic*, 73.

"…running throughout all antiquity we find the idea that a man can be 'bound' or 'fettered by demonic influences. It occurs in Greek, Syrian, Hebrew, Mandaean, and Indian magic spells." *Light from the Ancient East*, 304.

"In the book of Daniel (5:12, 16) the ability 'to loose knots' is listed as one of the magician's accomplishments." *Jewish Magic and Superstition*, 127.

Gager reports a curse tablet that refers to "this impious, accursed, and miserable Kardelos… bound, fully bound, and altogether bound…" *Curse Tablets and Binding Spells from the Ancient World*, 71.

For a discussion of knots and magical binding in the ancient Middle East, see *Witchcraft and Magic in Europe: Biblical and Pagan Societies*, 37-38.

61   ην **εδησεν** ο σατανας: "who Satan **bound**…" The verb is the past tense of δεω. Satan himself will be bound (Revelation 20:2): και **εδησεν** αυτον χιλια ετη: "and **bound** him for a thousand years."

The metaphor of binding is also used in Jesus' argument with the Pharisees regarding the source of his powers over the demons (Matthew 12:22-32). Büchsel: "[δεω] is used of supernatural binding in L[uke] 13:16 and also in A[cts] 20:23." *Theological Dictionary of the New Testament*, II, 60.

62   ουκ εδει λυθηναι απο του **δεσμου** τουτου: "Was it not fitting that she be loosed from this **bond**…?

63 ελεγον γαρ οτι **εξεστη**: "because they were saying, '**He's out of his mind!**'"

64 Βεελζεβουλ **εχει**: "**He has** Beelzeboul."

65 πνευμα ακαθαρτον **εχει**: "**He has** an unclean spirit."

66 Matthew 12:27.

67 Kraeling, *Journal of Biblical Literature* 59: 153.

68 Revelation 1:20. **ο εχων** τα επτα πνευματα του θεου: "**the One who has** the seven spirits of God..."

69 "εχω" in *The Theological Dictionary of the New Testament*, II, 821. Hanse interprets the identical expression in Mark 3:22 in a passive sense, that of possession *by* a demon, an inconsistency that seeks to avoid the implication that Jesus worked magic through the control of demons.

   The *Exegetical Dictionary of the New Testament* says of εχω in Revelation 3:1, "It probably means that [Christ] has sovereignty over these powers..." (II, 95).

70 Crossan's observation underscores the tension that must have existed between Jesus and the temple authorities: "In all of this the point is not really Galilee against Jerusalem but the far more fundamental dichotomy of magician as personal and individual power against priest or rabbi as communal and ritual power. Before the Second Temple's destruction, it was magician against Temple, thereafter magician against rabbi...If a magician's power can bring rain, for what do you need the power of temple priesthood or rabbinical academy?" *The Historical Jesus*, 157-158.

71 εαν μη πρωτον **δηση** τον ισχυρον: "unless one first **binds** the strong man..." (Matthew 12:29).

72 As at Luke 13:16. Compare Matthew 10:1, 16:19 (what is bound on earth is bound in heaven).

73 My translation of: "le Christ est maître de Béelzéboul et le domine au point de l'employer pour opérer ses exorcismes…uni au chef des demons, il le forcerait, possédant son nom, à opérer les prodiges qu'il veut et spécialement les exorcismes; nul esprit, nulle puissance démoniaque ne lui résiste…Δαιμονιον εχει signifie donc encore que Jésus est un faux prophète magician." *Ephemerides Theologicae Lovanienses* 15: 468, 470, 482.

74 Danker's *Greek-English Lexicon*, 209.

75 δαιμονζομαι occurs 13 times in the gospels and nowhere else in the New Testament.

76 ταυτα τα ρηματα ουκ εστιν **δαιμονιζομενου**: "These are not the words **of a possessed man**!" Samain also noted: "Il est vrai que δαιμονιζομενος ne se rencontre jamais pour designer un magician." My translation: "It is true that δαιμονιζομενος ["possessed by a demon," *my note*] is never used to describe a magician." *Ephemerides* 15: 482.

77 **δαιμονιζομενους** και σεληνιαζομενους και παραλυτικους: "**demon-possessed** and epileptics [literally, "moonstruck"] and paralyzed" (Matthew 4:24).

78 *Jewish Magic and Superstition*, 51.

79 Joshua Starr, *Harvard Theological Review* 23: 303. Jesus even gives others authority over demons (Luke 9:1). How would that happen if Satan were using Jesus?

80 *Religion, Science, and Magic*, 138.

81 δαιμονιον εχει και **μαινεται**: "He has a demon and he's **raving**!"

82 Burkert: "The words which the Greeks used to describe such phenomena are varied and inconsistent…These various expressions can neither be reconciled systematically nor distinguished in terms of an evolution in the history of ideas;

they mirror the confusion in the face of the unknown. The most common term is therefore *mania*, frenzy, madness." *Greek Religion*, 109-110.

83   One must wonder exactly when the man sinned, if his punishment was to be *born* blind.

84   Mark 8:22-26.

85   Regarding the healing of the blind man, Crossan notes: "The magic features of that process are also emphasized by the private nature of the cure 'out of the village.' The concluding injunction not to reenter the village may well be Markan redaction, another of those injuctions to silence that indicate the danger of misunderstanding Jesus' miracles. But the opening separation is part of the traditional story, and it underlines the dangerously deviant nature of magical healing." *The Historical Jesus*, 325.

86   Predictably, Matthew's reworking of the story shortens it by excising details, with the net result that the healing is no longer impersonal, i.e., *magical*, in nature: in Matthew's version Jesus knows he has been touched and turns and heals the woman (9:20-22).

Interestingly, both Matthew and Luke specify that the bleeding woman, who was ritually unclean (Leviticus 15:25-27), touched only the *fringe* or *tassel* of Jesus' garment (Matthew 9:20, Luke 8:44). The fringe or tassel on the four corners of the garment marked the wearer as an observant Jew (Numbers 15:37-39), and the fact that longer tassels signified greater holiness (Matthew 23:5) and that whoever touched the tassels of Jesus' robe were healed (Mark 6:56), apparently regardless of faith, attests to the impersonal nature of the healing.

87   *Hellenistic Magic*, 109-110.

88   Mark 9:38-39. "The story in Mark 9:38f. of the alien exorcist who 'followed not with us' and yet cast out demons in the name

of Christ is clearly an example of a professional magical use." *Hellenistic Magic*, 72.

89 Acts 19:13.

90 Acts 5:12-16, 19:11-12.

That miracle-working power adheres to inanimate things associated with the miracle worker provides an obvious motive for the preservation of relics associated with saints, including even body parts. Regarding the habit of collecting relics, Lane Fox reports: "The new Christian attitude to the dead and their relics marked a break in previous religious life. Before long, church leaders were digging up corpses and breaking them into fragments, a type of grave robbery which pagans had never countenanced." *Pagans and Christians*, 448.

This observation, while true of *official* pagan religions, does not hold for necromantic sorcery. Ancient literature is replete with references to the theft of bodies and body parts. *Magic, Witchcraft, and Ghosts in the Greek and Roman Worlds*, 140f.

91 Mark 9:28-29.

92 Acts 8:18-19. The details of this failed transaction are examined in a subsequent chapter.

93 Luck, *Witchcraft and Magic in Europe*, 105.

It has been observed of the early Christian saints that people came seeking "a transfer of supernatural power...as if he were a talisman...the only thing believed in was some supernatural power to bestow benefits." *Christianizing the Roman Empire*, 3-4.

94 Ιωαννης ο βαπτιζων εγηγερται εκ νεκρων και δια τουτο **ενεργουσιν** αι δυναμεις εν αυτω: "John the Baptist has been raised from the dead and because of this the powers **are at work** in him."

95 Kraeling, "Was Jesus Accused of Necromancy?" *Journal of Biblical*

Literature 59: 154-155.

96   Mark 6:20, 26-28.

97   Mark 1:5. Compare Matthew 3:5, Luke 3:7-15, John 1:20-26. The gospels agree that John attracted large crowds and that he became very well known. John's fame was such that Jesus used it to trap the temple authorities (Matthew 21:24-26), and John had even sent out disciples to question Jesus (Matthew 11:2-6). It strains credibility to suppose that people thought Jesus could literally have been John raised from the dead.

98   *The Rotting Goddess: The Origin of the Witch in Classical Antiquity,* 104

The unquiet ghost –the νεκυδαιμων (nekudaimôn)– fell into several categories: the αωρος (aôros), the *untimely dead,* the βιαιοθανατος (biaiothanatos), the *dead by violence,* the αγαμος (agamos), the *unmarried,* and the αταφος (ataphos), the *unburied. Arcana Mundi,* 165-168, *Magic, Witchcraft, and Ghosts in the Greek and Roman Worlds,* 146-152. The νεκυια (nekuia), the rite by which ghosts are raised, is pre-Homeric.

Regarding the unburied, "The atelestoi [ατελεστοι, "not completed," *my note*] are the dead that have not received the due rites. Such spirits, like the ones of those that have died by violence or before their time, cannot achieve rest..." *Witchcraft and Magic in Europe: Ancient Greece and Rome,* 22.

Richard Gordon on the use of ghosts of those dead by violence: "a biaiothanatos, those who have been killed by violence, part of the wider class of the restless dead, who came to be thought of as the typical instruments of malign magic." *Witchcraft and Magic in Europe: Ancient Greece and Rome,* 176.

For similar concerns about the unquiet dead in Mesopotamia, see *Witchcraft and Magic in Europe: Biblical and Pagan Societies,* 79-82.

Modern ghost hunter Hans Holzer: "Ghosts by their very nature are not unlike psychotics in the flesh...there are poltergeist phenomena, which are nothing more than products of the phase of a haunting when the entity is capable of producing physical effects, such as the movement of objects." *Ghosts*, 24-25.

99 *Greek and Roman Necromancy*, 226-227.

Kraeling cites the fact that John was a *biaiothanatos* in his article and observes that the verb used of raising John is also used in the Greek magical papyri for conjuring spirits of the dead. *lower adas*

100 John 1:23, Luke 1:36, Matthew 11:11.

101 Compare Colossians 1:13.

102 As at Romans 8:38, 1 Peter 3:22.

103 *Theological Dictionary of the New Testament*, II, 653.

104 *Léxico de magia y religión en los papiros mágicos griegos*, 39.

105 ουτος εστιν Ιωαννης ο βαπτιστης αυτος ηγερθη απο των νεκρων και δια τουτο αι δυναμεις **ενεργουσιν** εν αυτω: "This man is John the Baptist. He was raised from the dead and that is why the powers **are working** in him."

106 *The Demise of the Devil*, 3.

107 Matthew 7:20.

108 Steven Ricks, *Ancient Magic and Ritual Power*, 141.

109 Matthew 21:23, Mark 11:28, Luke 20:2.

110 The disciple Jesus loves is εν τω κολπω του Ιησου: "lying up against Jesus." The term κολπος (kolpos), which is often translated "bosom," can mean "lap" when applied to humans (Luke 6:38), or can refer to the fold of a garment, or to a bay where it "folds" into the land. It is the hollow formed where the trunk of the body bends at the waist. The picture John presents is that to two men lying close enough to "make spoons."

John also uses the imagery of the preexistent Word who is "in the bosom of the Father" (John 1:18), an expression meant to pointedly emphasize intimate association and the knowledge that flows from it.

Paintings of the "Last Supper" that have the disciples seated around a table are falsifications. In Jesus' time people reclined to eat. I cannot resist an observation on supercatholic Mel Gibson's depiction of Jesus making a chair in *The Passion of the Christ*. One can only pray it will enable Jesus and his disciples to sit up sufficiently straight.

111 As noted by Morton Smith, this comparative use of ταχυς (tachus), *quickly*, appears to echo a frequently attested conclusion to magical spells, ηδη ηδη ταχυ ταχυ: *now, now, quick, quick. Jesus the Magician*, 111.

112 John 5:7. The longer text found in the *King James Version*, which explains the agitation of the water as the result of an angel, likely originated as a marginal gloss which was later copied into the body of the text.

John 12:27-29, 11:33, 38.

113 That Jesus has the power to read thoughts is everywhere stated in John (John 1:47-48, 2:24-25, 4:16-18, 5:42, 6:61, etc.). John even says that Jesus foreknew which of his disciples did not believe and which would betray him (6:64). Compare Mark 2:8.

114 *Witchcraft and Magic in Europe: Biblical and Pagan Societies*, 71-75.

115 *Jesus the Magician*, 110

116 Judges 9:23, 1 Samuel 16:15, 16, 23, 18:10, 19:9.

117 Mark 11:13, 21-24.

118 The term γοης occurs only once in the New Testament at 2 Timothy 3:13: "Evil men and *frauds* will give ever worse offense, misleading and being misled."

When Marcus Aurelius speaks of τερατευμενοι, *miracle-mongers*, and γοητες, *charlatans*, in *Meditations* I, 6, it is thought likely that he had Christian exorcists in mind. *not factual*

Chapter Nine:
Spirit Versus Spirit.

The book of Acts records several encounters between Christian missionaries and pagan miracle workers, and it comes as no surprise that the accounts demonstrate the superiority of the power *spiritual on a higher level.* of the apostles over the powers of their pagan contemporaries — pagan accounts of Christian miracle working were equally dismissive. The stories preserve much interesting information about the role of magic in primitive Christianity, and it is to an examination of them that we will turn next.

The attitude of early Christians toward their opponents, particularly toward the nonconformists arising from within their midst, was from the very first one of intense opposition. Even as Jesus handed Judas over to the Adversary, Jesus' followers exercise the power both to strike people dead on the spot, as well as hand them over to Satan.[1] The verb used in the New Testament which is translated "hand over," παραδιδωμι (paradidômi), is commonly used in magical curse tablets —known as a καταδεσμος (katadesmos) or "tie down" in Greek and as a *defixio* or "nail down" in Latin— to send a person's soul to the gods of the underworld.[2]

> Next, take [the curse written on papyrus] off to the tomb of one dead before his time,[3] dig down four fingers deep and put it in [the hole] and say:
>
> "Spirit of the dead, whoever you may be, I hand X over to you[4] so that he may not accomplish X action." Then, after burying it, go away. Better you do it when the moon is waning…[5]

Of this procedure Deissmann remarks,

> "A person who wished to injure an enemy or to punish an evildoer consecrated him by incantation and tablet to the powers of darkness below…The only difference between Jewish and pagan execrations probably lay in the fact that Satan took the place of the gods of the lower world." [6]

Meyer notes "the express authorization for the disciples to curse cities and individuals," and the practice of using magic against opponents continued until well after the death of the apostles. [7] The posture of Christianity was one of active aggression directed toward opponents, an attitude that crystallized into summary executions during the rule of Constantine, the first emperor to embrace the new religion.

after Jesus' time

his ministry in total contrast

Simon Peter versus Simon Magus

Now those who had been scattered went through the region spreading the word. Phillip went down to the city of Samaria and preached Christ to them. Everyone in the crowd was paying close attention to the things Phillip said; while listening to him they also saw the signs he performed. Unclean spirits, screaming with a loud voice, were cast out of many of the possessed, and many who were paralyzed and crippled were being healed. There was great joy in that city.

A certain man by the name of Simon, claiming to be someone great, had formerly practiced magic [8] in the city and had amazed the people of Samaria. Everyone followed him eagerly, from the least to the greatest, saying, "This man is the Power of God, the Power called Great!" They followed him for quite some time because he had amazed them with his magical feats. [9] But when they believed Phillip, who was preaching about the kingdom of God and the name of Jesus Christ, baptizing men and women, Simon himself believed and was baptized. He followed Phillip around constantly, astonished as he watched the signs and great miracles that occurred.

When the apostles in Jerusalem heard that Samaria had embraced the word of God, they sent Peter and John to them. They went down and prayed for them so that they might receive the holy spirit because up to that point it had not fallen upon any of them. They had only been baptized in the name of the Lord Jesus.

Then they laid their hands on them and they received the holy spirit. [10] When Simon saw that the spirit was given by the application of the apostles' hands, he offered them money, saying, "Give me this power too so that anyone on whom I lay my hands may receive the holy spirit."

But Peter said to him, "To hell with you and your silver! You intended to buy the gift of God with money! There is no part or share for you in this proclamation, for your heart is not upright before God. So repent of this wickedness of yours and pray to the Lord that you may be forgiven the intention of your heart, for I see in you the gall of bitterness and the shackle of unrighteousness!"

Simon answered, "You must pray for me to the Lord so that nothing you have said may befall me!"

Acts 8:4-24

The story of Simon —who will be known henceforth to history as Simon Magus— is the origin of *simony*, the purchase of church offices.

Although Acts does not tell us what became of Simon, the church fathers lost no time creating a substantial legend around him and his heresies, and his memory is excoriated in the Acts of Saint Peter, as well as by Justin Martyr, Irenaeus, Epiphanius, Hippolytus, and Pseudo-Clement.

Simon's offer of money was probably customary in his circles; when one received something, payment was quite naturally expected. [11] As will be seen in the case of Paul, apostles tended to become shrill when their authority was challenged, but Peter's response to Simon's offer borders on hysteria. The apostolic diatribe contains what may be a single telling point: "There is no part or share for you in this proclamation," literally "in this word," i.e., "the word of God" the Samaritans had embraced. Simon had attached himself to Phillip, been baptized as a Christian convert, and in all likelihood had begun to preach the word himself, to spread "the word." Simon, who had formerly amazed the Samaritans with his "magical feats," now sought to perform "signs and great miracles" in the name of Jesus. [12] That was too much for Peter. A turf war promptly ensued.

The point of the story is not as much Simon's magic as it is Peter's apostolic authority. Luke-Acts, written relatively late in the first century, long after Peter's death, reveals yet another step in the evolution of the Christian movement: the filling of an administrative vacuum. Jesus, who believed he was living on the very cusp of history, passed miraculous powers to his disciples but made no provision for the continuity of administrative authority. At first this posed no problem: the early Christians expected the quick return of the Lord and set about preparing themselves for it.

164

But the Lord did not return. The Jews grew weary of Christians proselytizing in their synagogues and kicked them out, while Gentiles began to join the movement in real numbers. Who now had the authority to decide what constituted true Christian practice? Who would determine the doctrinal content of the new religion? In the stories of magicians recounted in Acts we are witnessing the emergence of a new Christian pecking order, the establishment of apostolic authority as the beginning of a continuous chain of command that culminates in the creation of a line of bishops that starts with the apostles. [13]

Paul versus Bar-Jesus

When they had gone through the whole island as far as Paphos, they encountered a certain man, a magician,[14] a false prophet,[15] the Jew named Bar-Jesus, who was with the proconsul Sergius Paulus,[16] a man of discernment, who summoned Barnabas and Saul because he wanted to hear the word of God. But Elymas the magician —for that is how his name is translated— resisted them, trying to turn the proconsul away from the faith.

But Saul, also known as Paul, filled with the holy spirit, stared at him intensely and said, "O you who are full of every treachery and every kind of fraud, son of the Devil, enemy of all righteousness, will you not stop making crooked the straight paths of the Lord? Now look! The hand of the Lord is upon you and you will be blind, not seeing the sun for a time."

Immediately mist and darkness fell on him and he wandered around searching for someone to lead him by the hand. When the proconsul saw what had happened, he believed, having been overwhelmed by the teaching of the Lord. [17]

Acts 13:6-12

A thorough analysis of this passage has been done by Rick Strelan, whose observations I will touch upon and add several observations of my own. [18] Paul addresses Bar-Jesus —which means "Son of Jesus"— as a "son of the Devil" and pronounces a classic slander spell against him, a διαβολη (diabolê), "a spell that ascribes unholy actions to an opponent," [19] causing the offended divinity to avenge itself: Bar-Jesus is struck temporarily blind even as was Paul himself for his opposition to Jesus.

As Strelan points out, Sergius Paulus "wanted to hear the word of God," and it is over the interpretation of the "word" that Paul and Bar-Jesus are fighting. Neither Simon nor Bar-Jesus can lay claim to "the word." They are outside the prophetic circle which —as Luke is eager to show us— consists only of the apostles and their immediate associates. The conflict in sight in this passage is over true versus false representations of Christianity. Bar-Jesus, as his name strongly implies, is within or at the margins of the "Jesus community," and Paul accuses him not of denying Jesus, but of "making crooked the straight paths of the Lord," i.e., of *twisting* the gospel.[20]

The purpose of the book of Acts —the Acts of the *Apostles*— is to establish the myth of apostolic authority in the face of competing gospels. The proclamation of the true gospel belongs to the inner circle and to them alone. Henceforth the conflict between Christian sects will be characterized as a front in the universal war between the Lord and his agents of light and Satan and his army of darkness:

> Each side is represented visibly on earth by a set of human lieutenants. To the prophets correspond the false prophets, to the apostles, false apostles, to the Christ, the Antichrist. And as God empowers his "saints" to accomplish miracles that authorize

their mission, Satan and his underlings enable their fiends to perform powerful works that are, or so they would seem, equivalent. These "sons of the devil" who perform such marvels are magicians.[21]

In re: Paul and Silas

It so happened that as we were going to the place of prayer a certain servant girl who had a spirit of divination met us. [22] She used to turn a tremendous profit for her masters by making predictions. She kept tagging along after Paul and the rest of them, saying, "These men who are proclaiming a way of salvation to you are servants of the Highest God!"

She went on doing this for many days. Finally at the end of his patience, Paul turned and said to the spirit, "I command you in the name of Jesus Christ to come out of her!" It came out of her that very hour. When her masters saw that their hope of profit had fled them, they seized Paul and Silas and hauled them to the marketplace to appear before the authorities.

Acts 16:16-19

The girl who follows Paul and Barnabas has "a spirit of divination" —πνευμα πυθωνα, "a spirit of the python." This curious terminology derives from the myth of Apollo, [23] the god of prophecy, who slew the dragon Python that lived in the caves of Delphi at the foot of Mount Parnassus. As a mark of his victory over the serpent, Apollo appointed a priestess, the Pythia, or "Pythoness," who spoke oracles when she was possessed by the spirit of the god, [24] the Pythonic spirit or spirit of divination.

The Delphic oracle, which spoke continuously through its priestess for nearly 2000 years, thus became synonymous with female mediums of a type known as an εγγαστριμυθος (engastrimuthos), or "belly talker." Such mediums, like the priestess of Apollo and the slave girl who tailed after Paul, were typically women "with little education or experience of the world," [25] and their presence in the ancient world is well attested.

By far the most famous biblical medium is the witch of Endor. Misidentified in the *Septuagint* as an *engastrimuthos*, she is more correctly an evocator, or "soul-drawer" —a ψυχαγωγός (psuchagôgos)— as the account shows:

> When Saul saw the army of the Philistines, he was afraid and his heart trembled greatly. When Saul inquired of the Lord, the Lord did not answer him, not by dreams, or by Urim, or by prophets. Then Saul said to his servants, "Seek out for me a woman who is a medium, so that I may go to her." His servants said to him, "Behold, there is a medium at Endor."
>
> So Saul disguised himself and put on other garments and went, he and two men with him; and they came to the woman by night. And he said, "Divine for me by a spirit, and bring up for me whomever I shall name for you." The woman said to him, "Surely you know what Saul has done, how he has cut off the mediums and wizards from the land. Why then are you laying a snare for my life to bring about my death?" But Saul swore to her by the Lord, "As the Lord lives, no punishment will come upon you for this thing." Then the woman said, "Whom shall I bring up for you?" He said, "Bring up Samuel for me." When the woman saw Samuel, she cried out with a loud voice; and the woman said to Saul, "Why have you deceived me? You are Saul!" The king said to her, "Have no fear; what do you see?" The woman said to Saul, "I see a god coming up out of the earth." He said to her, "What is his appearance?" She said, "An old man is coming up; and he is wrapped in a robe." And Saul knew that it was Samuel, and he bowed with his face to the ground, and did obeisance.

Then Samuel said to Saul, "Why have you disturbed me by bringing me up?" Saul answered, "I am in great distress, for the Philistines are warring against me, and God has turned away from me and answers me no more, either by prophets or by dreams; therefore I have summoned you to tell me what I shall do."

1 Samuel 28:5-15

Although we know of the evocation of ghosts by female mediums, it is not possible to tell what possessed the girl who followed Paul.[26] In any case Paul makes it clear that the 'proclamation of a way of salvation' will not be shared with disembodied entities, whatever their nature. The spirits of the prophets are subject to the prophets, as are also demonic spirits —not even an angel from heaven can contradict the apostolic gospel.[27]

> Christ's human officers, led by His apostles, are now especially alerted to the possibility of demonic wickedness in all those who try to oppose them by supernatural means. Put in another way, humans who manifest objectionable traits and behaviour may now be *expected* to have demonic helpers…" [28]

The demon versus the sons of Skeva

God was doing uncommonly powerful works through Paul's hands, so that when handkerchiefs and aprons that had touched his skin [29] were placed upon the sick, they were set free from their diseases and the evil spirits came out of them. Some of the itinerant Jewish exorcists [30] pronounced the name of the Lord Jesus over those having evil spirits, [31] saying, "I command you by the Jesus Paul proclaims…"

There were seven sons of Skeva the Jewish high priest doing this. The evil spirit said to them by way of reply, "I know Jesus and I am well aware of Paul, but who are you?" With that, the man in whom the evil spirit was leaped upon them, overcoming them all, and so overpowered them that they fled from the house naked and wounded.

This became known among all the Jews as well as Greeks who were living in Ephesus and fear fell on all of them and the name of Jesus was exalted. Many of those who had believed came forward, confessing and publicly disclosing their practices. A good number of those who were dabbling in such matters[32] collected their books together and burned them before everyone and when their value was calculated, it came to fifty thousand silver coins.[33]

Acts 19:11-19

The Lukan account of the fictitious "seven sons of Skeva" —seven was a well known magical number— is a reverse exorcism of sorts: rather than the exorcists driving out the demon, the demon drives out the exorcists.[34] The point of the story seems to be that even in Ephesus, a city famous for its association with magic,[35] even the demons have learned to distinguish between those with authority —Jesus and his apostles!— and interlopers.

It was essential that the apostles distinguish themselves early and clearly from the other wonder-workers of the day: "The external appearance of the itinerant Christian missionaries was very similar to the 'men of God' of every shade who wandered from place to place, and they risked being evaluated against this background and absorbed into this spectrum."[36] They are everywhere at a disadvantage compareed to professional orators —"of rude speech" as the church historian Eusebius freely admits— and they "proclaimed the knowledge of the kingdom of heaven only by the display of the divine spirit working in them and by what the wonderworking power of Christ accomplished through them."[37] In short, Eusebius attributed the success behind Christian preaching to *thaumaturgy*, not doctrine.

In the lifetime of Paul, Ephesus was the capitol of Asia Minor and the site of the temple of Artemis,[38] the ever virgin goddess of childbirth. In Asia, however, Artemis was patterned after the ancient Mother Goddess, Cybele, a fertility deity. It was here that Christian converts, "many of those who had believed," came forward with their books of magic and burned them. With magic, as with all life's endeavors, success is copied, and given the cultural context, one might fairly ask if the Ephesian Christians regarded themselves as having truly *discarded* magic along with their books, or instead to have "traded up." *shows the difference between magic e Jesus's spiritual abilities.*

Public manifestations of repentance notwithstanding, Christian miracles and pagan magic would exist in an uneasy alliance for centuries to come. As late as the mid-4th century, the church council of Laodicaea prohibited the practice of magic by the Christian clergy, a prohibition repeated in 398 at the council of Carthage, and in 667 the council of Toledo threatened to excommunicate clergy who said requiem masses for the living to induce "death by sorcery." Indeed, Christians used passages from the gospels themselves as incantations.[39]

SATOR
AREPO
TENET
OPERA
ROTAS

171

The talismanic SATOR-AREPO magic square, believed to have originated as an anagram of the opening words of the Lord's Prayer, first came to light in a Christian house in Pompeii, and it was in Ephesus — where else?— that an ecumenical council, convened in 430 to decide the status of Mary in the Christian pantheon, declared that "the Holy Virgin is the Mother of God."[40]

Notes

1 Acts 5:1-11. Compare the response of James and John in Luke 9:54.

2 As at 1 Corinthians 5:5: **παραδουναι** τον τοιουτον τω σατανα εις ολεθρον της σαρκος: "**to hand over** such a person to Satan for the destruction of the flesh." 1 Timothy 1:20: Υμεναιος και Αλεξανδρος ους **παρεδωκα** τω σατανα: "Hymenius and Alexander, whom **I handed over** to Satan..."

3 εις **αωρου** μνημα: "to the tomb **of one dead before his time...**"

4 **παραδιδωμι** σοι τον δεινα: "**I hand** X **over** to you..."

5 *Papyri Graecae Magicae*, I, 192 (V:332).

6 *Light from the Ancient East*, 302.

7 *Ancient Christian Magic*, 185.

Matthew 10:11-15, Luke 9:5, 54, 10:13-15, Acts 18:6. Ritualistic behavior is everywhere present: "shake the dust from your feet," and "he shook out his clothing."

"Occasionally the bargain was explicit: acknowledge God or be punished. So an ascetic of Hermoupolis in Egypt reduces a procession of non-Christian worshippers to frozen immobility, right in the middle of the road, through spells; and they cannot regain the use of their limbs until they 'renounce their error.' Or you might defy the ascetic–in this case, Aphraates, in a Syrian city–and by no mere coincidence, straightway you died a horrible death. From that, people 'realized the strength of Aphraates' prayer.'" *Christianizing the Roman Empire*, 62.

8   μαγευω (mageuô), *to practice magic*, the only occurrence of this verb in the New Testament.

Klauck: "When systems competed against each other, this accusation regularly provided a handy instrument: one party would accuse the other of black magic, hurling its entire available arsenal of abuse and polemics. As for one's own group, it practiced magic of the older, unreservedly positive kind –unless one preferred a priori to avoid the risk of even the remotest connection between one's own side and the concept of magic." *Magic and Paganism in Early Christianity: The World of the Acts of the Apostles*, 17.

9   μαγεια (mageia), *magical art*, the only occurrence of this noun in the New Testament.

Samaria's connection with magic leads the Jews to accuse Jesus of being a Samaritan (John 8:48).

Simon Magus versus Simon Peter, magic versus miracle. The distinction was essential particularly to Christians who "either made or presupposed one central, crucial point: that magic is the work of demons, while miracles are the work of God. What this amounted to, of course, was the claim that the Christian God is true and the pagan gods are false...unlike the pagans and the Jews, Christians had no ethnic cohesion, and they asserted their group identity not only by using mysterious rituals (like the mystery religions) but also by emphasizing strongly the distinctiveness of their God and their teachings about him...for them it was first of all a truth and secondly the sole basis for their existence as a group." *Magic in the Middle Ages*, 35-36.

Hull: "The argument is simply: God works miracles, demons work magic...Magic may look the same but (because it is done by devils) it cannot possibly be the same. The only conclusion is that it is deceptive. The similarity is a fraud." *Hellenistic Magic and the Synoptic Tradition*, 61.

10 **επιθεσις** των χειρων: the '**laying on** of hands,' the technique of passing the spirit from believer to believer (1 Timothy 4:14, 2 Timothy 1:6, Hebrews 6:2). This is a set phrase in the Christian vocabulary, pointing to an early ritual that may go back to the person of Jesus.

Of the application of hands in Egyptian magic, Pinch notes, "The gesture of laying a hand on the patient is sometimes linked with sealing. One spell to safeguard a child promises, 'My hand is on you, my seal is your protection.' In another spell, the goddess Hathor is described as laying her hand on a woman suffering in childbirth. Ivory rods ending in hands represented the divine hand and were part of a magician's equipment. A figure wearing an animal or Bes mask seems to be holding such a hand rod in a relief dating to the twenty-fourth century BC." *Magic in Ancient Egypt*, 84.

The implication is that Phillip did not have the authority to bestow supernatural gifts, therefore the intervention of apostles becomes necessary, a detail designed to support the emerging "apostolic fiction."

11 "The power can be passed from one person to another. It is not a moral quality nor a learned skill but an acquisition, a property which can be conveyed either with the will of the donor, as in Luke 9.1, or without it, as in 8.46." *Hellenistic Magic*, 107.

12 Klauck: "an objective consideration will note a suspicious similarity between the public appearance and working of Philip and of Simon; it is to some extent a question of interpretation, whether a successful healing is attributed to a miracle or to sorcery...most religious phenomena were ambiguous and required interpretation. Without interpretation, the phenomena have no value; this is what makes it so difficult to distinguish the working of miracles from magical activity." *Magic and Paganism*, 18-19.

There are wonderworkers everywhere, the circumstance that motivates the temple rulers to ask, "By what power or *by what name* did you do this?" (Acts 4:7) to which Peter replies, "in the name of Jesus Christ of Nazareth." (4:10). There are obviously *other* effective names.

13 "The twelve are the bearers of personal continuity, guaranteeing and handing on to future generations everything that had happened from the baptism of Jesus until his apparitions after Easter. In this special function, they are irreplaceable..." *Magic and Paganism in Early Christianity*, 7.

Naomi Janowitz: "Irenaeus, the fractious and always combative bishop of Lyons, did not waste much ink on pagans as magicians because his real battles were with other Christians. He yoked 'heretic' and 'magician' together in order to marginalize his Christian opponents and their followers, including Simon, Menander, Carpocrates and Basilides." *Magic in the Roman World*, 17.

14 μαγος (magos), *magician*, like the Magi in Matthew's infancy narrative.

15 ψευδοπροφητης (pseudoprophêtês), *false prophet.* False prophets were hardly the end of problem for the early church which is also plagued by false brothers (Galatians 2:4), false teachers (2 Peter 2:1), false apostles (2 Corinthians 11:13), and even false Christs (Mark 13:22).

16 "It is of some significance that the author of Acts can take it for granted that his readers will not have been puzzled by the presence of a Jewish magician and seer in the entourage of a high Roman official. That suggests that Jewish magicians and magicians who were part of the court of Roman administrators were in their eyes familiar figures." *Magic and Magicians in the Greco-Roman World*, 223.

17 Luke hastens to assert that Sergius Paulus is astonished by the teaching of Paul lest we assume that it is Paul's power alone that

has "overwhelmed" him. However, it is "primarily as a miracle worker" that Jesus attracts attention, and his disciples' success "arose from their deeds, above all, in healing." *Christianizing the Roman Empire*, 22. All the more reason to distinguish miracle from magic.

18 *Biblica* 85: 65-87.

19 *Magika Hiera*, 196.

20 "The narrator wants it understood that the charismatic power of miracle is in danger of being hijacked, as much as those who covet this force from the outside, as by the followers of Jesus." *Magic in the Biblical World*, 122-123.

As Strelan notes, "false prophets" arise from the *Christian* ranks (Matthew 7:15, 24:11, 24, 2 Peter 2:1, 1 John 4:1), as do "false brothers" (2 Corinthians 11:26, Galatians 2:4).

"Luke insults [Bar-Jesus] by describing him as a magician, because he sees his Christian preachers confronted with a situation of acute competition. There existed a wide spectrum of religious 'special offers,' often with a whiff of the exotic. The external appearance of the itinerant Christian missionaries was very similar to the 'men of God' of every shade who wandered from place to place, and they risked being evaluated against this background and absorbed into this spectrum." *Magic and Paganism*, 51-52.

21 My translation of: "Chaque parti est représenté visiblement sur terre par une série d'hommes-lieutenants. Aux prophètes respondent de faux prophètes, aux apôtres, de faux apôtres, au Christ l'Antéchrist. Et comme Dieu donne à ses 'saints' d'accomplir des miracles accréditant leur mission, Satan et ses satellites donnent à leurs suppôts de faire des prodiges qui sont, ou du moins paraissent, equivalents. Ces 'fils du diable' qui opèrent des merveilles sont les magiciens." *Ephemerides Theologicae Lovanienses* 15: 455.

22 παιδισκην τινα εχουσαν πνευμα **πυθωνα**: "a certain servant girl who had a spirit **of divination**"

176

23 Ἀπολλων, *Slayer.* .

24 πυθολnπτος (putholêptos), *seized by the python,* like the επιλnπτος (epilêptos), *seized* by the god like the young prophet (2 Kings 9:11).

25 Dodds, *The Greeks and the Irrational,* 72.

There were male "pythons" as well, but regardless of sex, possession was held to occur most readily in the "young and somewhat simple." *Pagans and Christians,* 208.

Spirit possession leading to oracular speech, i.e., "speaking in tongues," was recognized even by pre-Christian pagans as easiest to induce in those unencumbered by education and developed faculties of reasoning, an observation completely in keeping with the character of most early Christian converts as well as most modern enthusiasts of glossolalia.

26 "The prime model for witchcraft is the female practitioner in Exodus 22:18. In other instances the charge of witchcraft is combined with charges of prostitution and illicit sexuality. Prophetic texts associate harlotry and magical charms (Nah. 3:4) while historical texts denounce women as harlots who engage in sorcery (Jezebel in 2 Kings 9:22)." *Magic in the Roman World,* 87.

"A few personal letters from the late second millennium BC preserve references to women who were called *rekhet* –'knowing one'. These wise women were consulted as seers who could get in touch with the dead." *Magic in Ancient Egypt,* 56.

"...*only when she has gone into her trance* (for she, not Saul, sees the ghost of Samuel), is she able to *see through* Saul's disguise." *The Rotting Goddess: The Origin of the Witch in Classical Antiquity,* 128.

Daniel Ogden also notes the "tendency to associate a specialization in necromancy with aliens—Persians, Babylonians, and Egyptians—and with women or witches," a tendency which may reflect "cultural distancing." *Greek and Roman Necromancy,* 95.

27 1 Corinthians 14:32, Galatians 1:8.

28 Valerie Flint, *Witchcraft and Magic in Europe: Ancient Greece and Rome*, 298.

29 "Such cloths were indeed amulets (φυλακτηρια), and though not engraved with magic words, there is little to detract from the prospect that the cloths, once used effectively, would have been deployed again and again. These magically-charged reliquaries would have no doubt been reapplied with the necessary prayers or incantations: the young Christian community at Ephesus, it seems, adhered tenaciously to their magical beliefs, in some cases for up to two years after conversion (Acts 19:10)." *Ancient Magic and Ritual Power*, 244.

Regarding the "apostle's laundry," Klauck observes, "it appears that the miraculous power is thought of in material terms, so that it can be 'tapped' from the person of the wonderworker and stored for subsequent use. The cloths take on the function of amulets and talismans which were so common in the magic of antiquity." *Magic and Paganism*, 98.

φυλακτηριον (phulaktêrion), *safeguard* or *outpost*, from whence *phylactery* or *tefillin*, a small leather box containing scriptural passages worn by Jewish men during prayer, formerly used as amulets.

30 εξορκιστης (exorkistês), *exorcist*, the only occurrence of the word in the New Testament. The related verb εξορκιζω (exorkizó), *to put under oath*, is used of the high priest putting Jesus under oath to answer his question (Matthew 26:63).

Garrett notes that exorcist occurs nowhere else in the New Testament "perhaps because it too had magical connotations, as did the closely related verb 'adjure.'" *The Demise of the Devil*, 92.

31 τους **εχοντας** τα πνευματα τα πονηρα: "those **having** evil spirits…" (Acts 19:13). In this case the context indicates that "to have" an evil spirit is to be possessed by one.

Jesus' name is also featured in the magical papyri, where it is deemed efficacious for exorcism: ορκιζω σε κατα του θεου των Εβραιων Ιησου: "I cast you out by the god of the Hebrews,

178

of Jesus…" *Papyri Graecae Magicae*, I, 170 (IV:3019).

32   ικανοι δε των τα **περιεργα** πραξαντων: "a good number of those who were dabbling in such **matters**…"

Περιεργος (periergos), "pert[aining] to undue or misdirected curiosity," *Greek-English Lexicon of the New Testament*, 800.

"Concerning the burning of the magical books at Ephesus, described in Acts 19.19, Deissmann points out that τα περιεργα and πρασσειν are technical terms in the vocabulary of magic and that the papyrus codices may in general be similar to those burnt by the Christians." *Hellenistic Magic*, 17.

Regarding the charges brought up against Simon Magus by the church father Irenaeus, Dickie notes, "The list begins with exorcisms and incantations and moves on to amatory spells and spells that draw a person and ends with the use of familiar spirits and the sending of dreams and whatever other curious and excessive practices (*periergia*) they pursue…Now excessive or curious practices in this context mean interfering in what ought to be left undisturbed, which is to say, practicing magic." *Magic and Magicians*, 231-232.

33   "Lots of magic was practiced in the early churches: Acts 19.19 suggests the extent of it in Ephesus (the magical books of those Christians who could be persuaded to burn them were valued at about $320,000)." *Jesus the Magician*, 94.

34   The seven sons of Skeva is yet another piece of Lukan pseudohistory; there was never any Jewish high priest by this name.

35   Famous in particular for the *Ephesia grammata*, the "Ephesian letters," six words used on amulets and in spells: ασκιον (askion), κατασκιον (kataskion), λιξ (lix), τετραξ (tetrax), δαμναμενους (damnamenous), αισον (aison). Ogden suggests that "most of them were initially corruptions of things recognized as the names of deities or demons in some or other mortal language." *Witchcraft and Magic in Europe: Ancient Greece and Rome*, 47.

36   Klauck, *Magic and Paganism*, 52.

"The manhandling of demons–humiliating them, making them howl, beg for mercy, tell their secrets, and depart in a hurry–served a purpose quite essential to the Christian definition of monotheism: it made physically (or dramatically) visible the superiority of the Christian's patron Power over all others." *Christianizing the Roman Empire*, 28.

37 και τη δι' αυτων συντελουμενη **θαυματουργω** του Χριστου δυναμει: "and what the **wonder-working** power of Christ accomplished through them." *Ecclesiastical History*, III, 24, 3.

38 One of the seven wonders of the ancient world, some 260 feet wide, 430 feet long, and 60 feet high, with 127 columns. The central cella, or sanctuary, contained the famous Διοπετης (Diopetês), *fell-from-Zeus*, in all probability a meteorite seen as a heavensent cultic object. Likewise, "the primary image of Aphrodite was aniconic. It was…a black meteoric stone kept in her temple at Kouklia (Old Paphos), Cyprus." *A History of Pagan Europe*, 21.

39 *Witchcraft and Magic in Europe: The Middle Ages*, 181.

Priscillian of Avila, 2-3.

The Latin *Iesus autem transiens per medium illorum ibat*: "Jesus passed through their midst" (Luke 4:30) and *Et verbum caro factum est*: "And the Word became flesh" (John 1:14) were used as talismans. *Magic in the Middle Ages*, 77-78, 102-103.

40 θεοτοκος (theotokos), *god-bearing*. Madonna and child icons are still called *theotokos* icons in the Greek Orthodox Church.

Chapter Ten:
The Ecstatic Inner Circle

When Paul spoke of wanting to share "some spiritual gift," [1] he was referring to a miraculous manifestation of divine power for which early Christians used the word χαρισμα (charisma), a word absorbed into English unchanged in form but altered in meaning. To the early Christians the word had nothing to do with personal magnetism; it described gifts bestowed by God, the supernatural gifts of the spirit. For the Greeks the gifts of the gods were music and dance, theater and oracular utterance, poetry and love, for the Christians, healing and exorcism, tongues and prophesying, visions and discernment of spirits. *spiritual science*

I will pour out my spirit..."
Among the earliest Christians the spirit manifested its power through portents, signs, and miracles:

> Men, Israelites, hear these words: Jesus the Nazarene, a man attested to you by God through powerful works and portents

and signs which God performed through him in your midst, just as you yourselves know…"

Acts 2:22

The New Testament uses a number of words for powerful works: δυναμις (dunamis), *power*, from which *dynamite* was coined, and by extension, *powerful work*, *miracle*. Δυναμις is what flows like current from Jesus when a miracle is performed: "I felt the power leaving me…"[2]

There is also τερας (teras), *portent*, *omen*, or *prodigy*, the basis for our medical term *teratology*, the study and classification of birth defects. The ancient Mediterranean cultures considered the birth of deformed animals and humans to be ill-omened and employed priests —the τερατοσκοπος (teratoskopos), *omen inspector*— who specialized in the interpretation of such dark events. Regarding the impending plagues upon Egypt, the *Septuagint* has Yahweh say to Moses, "Behold all the portents I have placed in your hands!" [3]

The most common word for a work of wonder in the gospel of John is σημειον (sêmeion), *sign*, of which there are a magical *seven*: water into wine, healing a fever, a healing at Bethzatha, feeding a multitude, the translocation of a boat, healing a blind man, and the raising of Lazarus. [4] Interestingly, *exorcisms*, which are central to Jesus' miracle working in the synoptics, are completely ignored by John.

Other terms include αποδειξις (apodeixis), *display*,[5] and θαυμα (thauma), *wonder*.[6] The apparent avoidance of *thauma* and its cognates may signal a reticence to associate Jesus with *thaumaturgy*, or "wonder-working" which was common in the pagan world.

182

Paul's first letter to the Corinthians, which contains the single most complete account of the charismatic gifts, is a book written early in the history of the church. The nearness of Jesus' return is everywhere assumed in this letter:

> ...so that you are not lacking any of the gifts while you eagerly await the revelation of our Lord Jesus Christ...therefore do not judge anything before the appointed time, until the Lord comes, who will shine a light on the things hidden by the darkness and expose the motives of men's hearts...consequently, because of the impending tribulation, I consider it desirable for a man to remain just as he is... the appointed time is growing shorter...the ways of this world are passing away...on whom the end of the ages has arrived...if anyone does not love the Lord, let him be cursed. Lord, come!
>
> 1 Corinthians 1:7, 4:5, 7:26, 29, 31, 10:11, 16:22

For the early Christians, the gifts of the spirit are proof that the world is about to end:

> "It will be in the last days," God says, "that I will pour out my spirit on all flesh and your sons and daughters will prophesy and your young men will see visions...the sun will be turned to darkness and the moon to blood before the great and glorious Day of the Lord comes."
>
> Acts 2:17, 20

The primitive church was both apocalyptic and charismatic. In his letter to the church in Corinth Paul enumerates the major charismatic gifts:

> To each is given the manifestation of the spirit for the common good. To one, speech of wisdom is given through the spirit, but

to another, speech of knowledge according to the same spirit. To another, faith by the same spirit, but to another gifts of healing[7] in the spirit, but to another, works of power.[8] To another, prophecy, but to another, distinguishing between spirits,[9] to yet another, kinds of tongues, and to another, interpretation of tongues.[10] But all this operates through one and the same spirit, apportioned to each as it chooses.

1 Corinthians 12:7-11

The term translated "works of power" in the passage above — ενεργημα (energêma), "miraculous powers"[11] —is also used in the magical papyri where it means *magical powers*:

> The mighty assistant[12] will gladly accomplish these things. But impart them to no one except your own true and worthy son when he asks you for the magical powers.[13]

> However often you want to command the greatest god Ouphora, speak and he will comply. You have the ritual of the greatest and most divine magical working.[14]

Paul's discourse on the gifts of the spirit is specifically directed to people who had once worshipped the pagan deities —"You know that when you were serving speechless images"— and who were therefore already familiar with such manifesttations of spirit possession as ecstatic oracular speech, particularly during rites accompanied by music.[15] Regarding such ecstatic speech, Paul adds:

> …for tongues are a sign, not for believers, but for unbelievers, and prophecy, not for unbelievers, but for those who believe. In the same way, if the whole church comes together and all speak

in tongues, and strangers or unbelievers enter, will they not say you are possessed? [16]

1 Corinthians 14:22-23

Tongues are a sign for unbelievers because ecstatic speech, already familiar to pagans, is proof —even if no one can understand what they are saying— that Christians have the spirit. The pagan who enters a Christian gathering and finds a house full of agitated Christians all raving incomprehensibly will come to the conclusion that the speakers are *possessed*, the meaning of μαινομαι (mainomai) in this context. That something exactly like this was going on Paul makes explicit when setting out rules that will rein in the wild enthusiasm of the Corinthian church:

> So if anyone speaks in a tongue, do so two at a time, or three at most, and in turn, and let one interpret. But if there is no interpreter, keep silent in church. Let each speak to himself and to God. Let two or three prophets speak and let others evaluate what they say. But if another receives a revelation while seated, let the first person be silent. For all can prophesy in turn so that all may learn and all be encouraged. The spirits of the prophets are subject to the prophets, [17] for God is a God, not of rioting,[18] but of harmony.

1 Corinthians 14:27-32.

Although Paul chides former pagans for having worshipped "speechless images," he conveniently forgets that unless the God of the church speaks through the mouth of some intermediary,[19] he is just as speechless as the idols Paul despises.

Indeed, in earliest Christianity we find another strong parallel with pagan practice: as the apostles attempt to select a replacement for the traitor Judas, they engage in a séance. They first pray to Jesus to designate a successor and then cast lots —κληρος (klêros), *lot*— which fall to Mathias.[20] This is a straightforward example of necromantic sortilege:

> Sanctuaries where divination was exercised regularly, as part of the cult of the god, are known as oracles (L. *oracula*, Gk. *manteia* or *chresteria*). But as noted earlier, an oracle is also the response of the god to a question asked by a visitor to the shrine.
>
> The method of divination varied from shrine to shrine. Sometimes the will of the god was explored by the casting or drawing of lots (*kleroi, sortes*) —for example, dice or sticks or bones. The word *sortilegus* originally designated a soothsayer who practiced this particular method of divination (*sortes legere* 'to pick up lots'); later by extension, it referred to any type of prophecy or sorcery. [21]

Given the ecstatic visions and séances of the early church, what need had it of a written gospel? In this turbulent spiritual milieu, in the living presence of the Lord's first associates, and the expectation that Jesus might return at any moment to exalt his followers, what possible interest could there have been in compiling a record of the Lord's doings? The Christians had no more interest in Jesus' personal history than a toddler has in assembling a photo album of its parents.

> ...but regarding visions and revelations of the Lord, I know a man in Christ who, fourteen years ago, whether in the body I do not know, or out of the body I do not know —God knows— such a man was snatched away to the third heaven. And I know such a man, whether in the body or out of the body I do not know —God knows— that was snatched up to paradise and heard ineffable words which are not permitted a man to speak.
>
> 2 Corinthians 12:1-4

From mystery of the kingdom to secret of state

The Epicurean and Stoic philosophers who encountered Paul and listened to his arguments regarded him as a σπερμολογος (spermologos), a *seedpicker*, a person who, like a bird randomly gathering seeds, picks up scraps of information and terminology here and there and cobbles them together in an unsystematic, extemporaneous way that everywhere betrays a lack of understanding.[22] There is much in Paul's confirmed writings to support such an assessment: not only does Paul contradict himself, his style of argumentation is often a scatterbrained mixture of clashing metaphors and illogical rhetorical flourish. When it suits him —and it often does— Paul becomes suddenly vague about details. His correspondence veers erratically from boasting, to accusing, to cajoling, to pious condemnation. Paul embodied fundamentalism: he was fanatical, irrational, and *slick*, concerned only with convincing.

For better or worse, it was Paul and his school of followers who framed Christianity's "orthodox" theology, and it is preeminently their writings which survive —Paul's letters and those writing pseudonymously in his name account for over half the books in the New Testament. It should be pointed out that Paul's interpretation of Christianity was merely one of many, and that it was neither particularly persuasive nor understandable to many early Christians.[23]

Most scholars have noted within the New Testament both the terminology of the mystery religions and of Gnosticism. It was inevitable that in their travels Christian missionaries came into contact with multiple cults and philosophical systems, and that they haphazardly borrowed terms and phrases that had cultural currency. As we have

187

seen, Paul does not commit to a particular position even in regard to the *parousia*; like all religious opportunists, his explanations change to fit circumstances.[24] To seek a clear correspondence, therefore, between primitive Christianity and another, equally amorphous, system like Gnosticism is mostly an exercise in futility. It is not my purpose to draw attention to the many ways in which the language of the Pauline school mirrors that of Gnosticism, a project which has been carried forward to great effect by Elaine Pagels. [25]

It is, however, pertinent to note that Christianity bears several remarkable similarities to both the language and theory of the mystery religions, and it is Paul himself, one of the "assistants of Christ and stewards of the mysteries of God," [26] who everywhere employs such language:[27]

> We speak wisdom among the initiated[28] ...the wisdom of God in a mystery that has been hidden away[29] ...
>
> 1 Corinthians 2:6

Samuel Angus:
> Common to the Mysteries and Gnosticism were certain ideas, such as pantheistic mysticism, magic practices, elaborate cosmogonies and theogonies, rebirth, union with God, revelation from above, dualistic views, the importance attaching to names and attributes of the deity, and the same aim at personal salvation. As Gnosticism took possession of the field East and West, the Mysteries assumed an increasingly Gnostic character. The dividing line is sometimes difficult to determine.[30]

Christian metaphors such as rebirth,[31] being a new creation,[32] the importance attaching to the name of Christ[33] and claims of special

188

revelation —including being snatched away to heaven[34] — are common knowledge and certainly need no reiteration here.

By the end of the first century, the apocalyptic belief of the first generation was rapidly fading into a harsh austerity that would soon lead to an ascetic condemnation of the world, a state of mind predicted by Paul's declaration:

> May I never brag except about the cross of our Lord Jesus Christ through which the world has been crucified to me, and I to the world.
>
> Galatians 6:15

Hand in hand with that retreat from the early apocalyptic expectation, the initial charismatic ebullience becomes muted, and the Christian mystical experience is increasingly described in the terms of the mystery cult:

> For it was not by following cleverly contrived tales that we revealed the power and the presence of our Lord Jesus Christ to you, but by becoming witnesses of that majesty.[35]
>
> 2 Peter 1:16

The word I have translated *witness* in this passage, επoπτης (epoptês), is a technical term borrowed from the vocabulary of the mystery cults. It refers specifically to "those who have been initiated into the highest grade of the mysteries."[36] Pagan writers described from three to five stages in the initiatory process, the final on of which was the επoπτεια (epopteia), the *ecstatic vision* or *visio beatifica*.

In fact, the true vision of the new sect was near to fruition, nearer

189

indeed than anyone living in the 1ˢᵗ century could have guessed. Within the space of a few centuries the majesty of Christ would supplant the majesty of Rome itself. *God's Plan*

Notes

1   **χαρισμα**...πνευματικον: "spiritual...**gift**" (Romans 1:11).

2   Luke 8:46.

3   Exodus 4:21.

4   John 2:1-11, 4:46-54, 5:1-48, 6:1-14, 6:15-21, 9:1-41, 11:1-57.

    In addition to its seven signs, the gospel also records seven witnesses that say Jesus has been sent from God or is "the Son of God": John the Baptist (1:34), Nathanael (1:49), Peter (6:69), Jesus himself (10:36) Martha (11:27), Thomas (20:28), and the author of the gospel (20:31).

    There are also seven "I am" sayings: "I am the bread of life" (6:35), "...the light of the world" (8:12), "...the good shepherd," (10:11), "...the resurrection and the life" (11:25), "...the way, the truth, and the life" (14:6), "...the true vine" (15:1), and "before Abraham, I am. (8:58).

    Obviously these groupings are not coincidental: they mark the gospel as studiously crafted missionary literature that records historical details only coincidentally.

5   Not common: "in a *display* of spirit and power" (1 Corinthians 2:4).

6   Used only once in the New Testament in an exclamation: "And no *wonder!*" (1 Corinthians 11:14).

    The related adjective, θαυμασιος (thaumasios), is used once as a collective noun: "When the chief priest and scribes saw *the wonderful things* that he did..." (Matthew 21:15).

7   **χαρισματα** ιαματων: "**gifts** of healing." The *charismata* may also refer to the spiritual gifts collectively.

8 αλλω δε **ενεργηματα** δυναμεων: "but to another, **works** of power…"

9 **διακρισεις** πνευματων: literally, "**discernment** of spirits," the *ability to differentiate* (διακρισις) between works done through the power of God and those done through the power of demons.

Note, for example, 1 John 4:1 on testing the spirits.

10 In this instance, there is scant difference between the Christian and pagan oracles: "The Greeks were accustomed to ecstatic outpourings that had to be translated into intelligible Greek by trained interpreters." Luck, *Arcana Mundi*, 284.

"The methods of imparting oracles are almost as varied as the cult forms; attention is attracted first, of course, to the most spectacular mode, that in which the god speaks directly from a medium who enters the state of *enthousiasmos*." Burkert, *Greek Religion*, 114.

11 Danker, *Greek-English Lexicon*, 335.

12 ο κραταιος **παρεδρος**: "the mighty **assistant**," i.e., a magical assistant.

13 τα…ενεργηματα: "the magical powers…" *Papyri Graecae Magicae*, I, 12 (I, 193-194).

14 την τελετηον του μεγιστου και θειου **ενεργηματος**: "…the ritual of the greatest and most divine **magical working**." *Papyri Graecae Magicae*, II, 79 (XII, 316-317).

15 1 Corinthians 12:2. Note the mention of the flute and lyre in the same letter (14:7).

16 ουκ ερουσιν οτι **μαινεσθε**: "will they not say **you are possessed?**"

Elsewhere Paul mentions his own spiritual transports –"if we are in ecstasy, it is for God, if in our right mind, for you" (2 Corinthians 5:13)– and reminds the blabbering mass that he speaks in tongues more than all of them (1 Corinthians 14:22).

17 πνευματα προφητων προφηταις **υποτασσεται**: "the spirits of the prophets **are subject** to the prophets" as are the demons: τα δαιμονια **υποτασσεται** ημιν εν τω ονοματι σου: "the demons **are subject** to us in your name" (Luke 10:17).

18 ακαταστασια (akatastasia), *disorder* or *insurrection* as in Luke 21:9, where it is paired with "war." Given the context of its use in 1 Corinthians, one is sorely tempted to translate it *pandemonium.*

Hoffman: "Paul is gentle, but not uncritical of the babbling contests that threaten to displace the gospel in Corinth (1 Cor. 14:2-4)." *Jesus Outside the Gospels*, 33.

19 As at Acts 2:16-17, for example, where Yahweh is said to speak through angels, prophets, visions, and dreams –pretty much like any other deity.

20 Acts 1:23-26.

21 Luck, *Arcana Mundi*, 244.

22 Acts 17:18.

"Paul's contempt for 'human' standards of wisdom and authority is deepseated: His unsystematic theology, arising mainly from self defensive diatribes against rival preachers, is characterized by a dislike of learning and philosophy that blends ill with the legend that he was a pupil of the famous Rabbi Gamaliel." *Jesus Outside the Gospels*, 32.

23 2 Peter 3:15-16.

24 Nowhere is this more evident than in Paul's treatment of the parousia: "Behold! I tell you a mystery: we will not all fall asleep, but we will all be changed in an instant, in the blink of an eye at the sound of the last trumpet. For the trumpet will sound and the dead will be raised incorruptible and we will be changed." (1 Corinthians 15:51-52). The language is still very much apocalyptic, as at 1 Thessalonians 4:15-17, but Paul is now trying to integrate the Jewish apocalyptic vision of the resurrection of the body with the pagan belief in the immortality of the soul by conjuring

up spiritual bodies.

Burton Mack: "The argument is only a bizarre assortment of metaphors strung together by ad hoc associations, this time in order to create the impression of 'spiritual body.'" *Who Wrote the New Testament?* 133.

In a subsequent letter, Paul mixes metaphors of shelter and clothing: "For we know that if our earthly house, our tent, be destroyed, we have a building from God, a house not made by hand, everlasting in the heavens… for while we are still in this tent we sigh because we do not want to be unclothed, but to put on an additional garment so that what is mortal may be swallowed up by life." (2 Corinthians 5:1-4). At no point does Paul succeed in explaining himself in any consistent way. *I understand what he is saying* *I dont understand the author* Remarking on Paul's slippery exegesis, the Emperor Julian noted, "He changes his ideas about God according to his situation — just as a polypus changes his colors to match the rocks." *Julian's Against the Galileans*, 101.

25 See particularly *The Gnostic Paul: Gnostic Exegesis of the Pauline Letters.*

From the response of some of Pagel's Bible college detractors, one might conclude that she has simply hallucinated the remarkable similarity between Paul's language and that of gnosticism. However, regarding the vocabulary of Colossians, the eminent grammarian A.T. Robertson, whose Christian credentials I would assume are impeccable, remarked (in 1934!): "The Christians did not shrink from using these words in spite of the debased ideas due to emperor-cult, Mithraism, or other popular superstitions. Indeed, Paul (cf. Col.2:1 f.) often took the very words of Gnostic or Mithra cult and filled them with the riches of Christ…The mass of the N.T. vocabulary has been transfigured." *A Grammar of the Greek New Testament*, 116. To what extent the vocabulary of Gnosticism had been filled with riches, transfigured, or otherwise improved by Christians would have been debatable even in Paul's day, but that Christians plagiarized terminology and ideas from the Gnostics there is no disputing.

26 1 Corinthians 4:1.

27 Hans Dieter Betz: "Expansion of mystery cult terms and ideas is evidenced also by the early Christian literature. Paul frequently employs μυστηριον (mystery) as a term designating the revelation of the transcendental realities of the divine world and of wisdom, prophecy, history, the afterlife and, by implication, the sacraments of baptism and the eucharist as well. Ephesians extends the usage, calling the Gospel itself μυστηριον (mystery), something Paul himself did not do. The *agape* relationship between the heavenly Christ and his church on earth is called το μυστηριον μεγα (the great mystery). In all probability, Ephesians received this language from Colossians, which more closely reflects Paul's usage. 1 Timothy (3:9, 16) speaks of το μυστηριον της πιστεως (the mystery of faith) and το της ευσεβιας μυστηριον (the mystery of religion)." *Magika Hiera*, 251.

28 εν τοις **τελειοις**: "among the **initiated**..."

29 θεου σοφιαν **εν μυστηριω** την αποκεκρυμμενην: "the wisdom of God **in a mystery** that has been hidden away..."

30 *The Mystery Religions*, 54.

31 As at John 3:3.
    Angus: "Every serious mystes [initiate into a mystery cult, *my note*] approached the solemn sacrament of Initiation believing that he thereby became 'twice born,' a 'new creature,' and passed in a real sense from death unto life by being brought into a mysterious intimacy with the deity." *The Mystery Religions*, 95-96.

32 2 Corinthians 5:17, Galatians 6:15.

33 For example Ephesians 1:20-21, Philippians 2:9.

34 Galatians 1:11-12, for example.

35 **εποπται** γενηθεντες: "by becoming **witnesses**..."

The reference is to the transfiguration of Jesus, of which Mark says και **μεταμορφωθη** εμπροσθεν αυτων: "and **he was transformed** before them" (Mark 9:2). In Mark's version, Jesus' clothing becomes dazzlingly white, Moses and Elijah appear, and a voice from a cloud identifies Jesus as the beloved Son of God. Matthew's account characterizes the transformation as "the vision" (Matthew 17:9).

36   *The Mystery Religions*, 77.

Chapter Eleven:
The Christian Mysteries

Some hint of the inner workings of primitive Christianity can be gleaned from the writings of its earliest defenders. Two such apologists, Clement of Alexandria and Origen, are the subject of this chapter. Two others, Irenaeus and Justin Martyr, will be discussed in the following chapter in connection with the *Secret Gospel of Mark*.

Titus Flavius Clemens, known as Clement of Alexandria, (died circa 215 CE) was almost certainly initiated into one or more of the mystery cults before converting to Christianity. One of the first Christian writers to attempt a synthesis of Christian theology with pagan philosophy, Clement reveals how easily Christian doctrine could be expounded in the imagery of the mysteries, as well as how closely magic and mystery cults must have intertwined.[1]

> Let us sweep away then, sweep away forgetfulness of the truth, the ignorance and the darkness, the obstacle which like a film[2] slips down over our sight. Let us see a vision[3] of what is really and truly divine, first of all singing out to Him this cry, Welcome,

Light! Light for us from heaven![4] For us who lie buried in darkness and have been wrapped up in the shadow of death![5] If, on the one hand, those who have trusted in the sorcerers[6] receive amulets and enchantments[7] merely purported to bring deliverance, do you not rather resolve to put on the heavenly [amulet], the Word that saves, and trusting in the enchantment of God,[8] be delivered from passions...[9]

O the truly holy mysteries![10] O pure light! Holding my torch aloft,[11] I am initiated into the highest mysteries of the heavens and of God![12] I become holy by being initiated![13]

The Lord reveals the mysteries[14] and places his seal upon the initiate when he has believed,[15] and lighting his way, conducts him to the Father, where he is protected for all ages.

These are my mysteries, my Bacchic revelries![16] If you desire, be initiated yourself and you will dance with angels around[17] the unbegotten and undying and only true God as the Word of God chants along with us.[18]

Clement quite ingenuously refers to the heavenly Christ as an *amulet* and the salvific process as an *enchantment*, describing his Christian faith in the ecstatic terms of a mystery celebrant. Although Clement, the head of the catechetical school in Alexandria, Egypt, was no minor figure, during the 16th century his feast day, December 4th, was dropped from the calendar after his writings came to be viewed as doctrinally tainted, an event which reflected the tendency of the Catholic Counter-Reformation to distance itself from anything that emitted the slightest whiff of heresy or magic.

Origen, whose name means "son of Horus," (185-254 CE) was a controversial figure both in life and death. While still in his late teens he replaced Clement as chief catechist in Alexandria, and sometime early in his adult life, according to the historian Eusebius, he castrated himself. Although regarded as one of the most important pre-Nicene Christian intellectual figures, his teachings included several ideas that were clearly heretical.

Of Origen's extensive writings, I have reproduced two short sections from his apologetic magnum opus, *Contra Celsum*,[19] a paragraph-by-paragraph refutation of an extensive critique of Christianity by Celsus, an early pagan opponent of Christianity. *Contra Celsum* had the unintended consequence of preserving Celsus' arguments nearly in their entirety as well as recording some very interesting admissions for posterity.

> After these things, through what motivation I do not know, Celsus says that Christians appear to exercise powers by using the names of demons and by incantations, hinting, I presume, at those who drive out demons by incantations. For not by incantations do Christians appear to have power over demons, but by the name of Jesus, combined with recitals of the accounts about him,[20] for recitation of these things has often succeeded in having driven the demon from men, and especially so when those reciting them speak with a healthy attitude and a believing frame of mind. Indeed, the name of Jesus is so powerful against the demon that now and then it is effecttive even when named by unworthy men, just as Jesus taught when he said, "Many will say to me in that day, we cast out demons and performed powerful works in your name." [21] Whether Celsus overlooked this from intentional malice or lack of understanding, I do not know.
>
> Next he even accuses the Savior of having performed wonders by practicing sorcery [22] and, foreseeing that others are destined to acquire the same knowledge[23] and brag about doing the same things by the power of God, Jesus banishes such men from his kingdom. Celsus' accusation is that if such men are justly

banished, while Jesus himself does the same things, then he is morally base and subject to the same punishment, but if Jesus is not evil for performing such works, neither are they who do as he does. On the other hand, even if it is conceded to be beyond demonstration how Jesus did these things, it is clear that Christians reject the practice of using incantations. Rather they accomplish it by the name of Jesus together with other words in which they have faith[24] according to the divine Scripture.

Contra Celsum, I, 6

Even from this brief passage it is clear that Christian exorcists used the name of Jesus *together with other words in which they had faith,* which included "recitations of accounts about him." Although Origen did not consider such performances as magical, the present day scholar would almost certainly classify such "recitations" as examples of *historiolae* —what Origen calls ιστορια (historia)— "short stories recounting mythical themes" [25] that were a part of the ancient magical repertoire.

My point is that these "recitations," undoubtedly accompanied by prayers, gestures —which may have included the laying on of hands [26]— would have been indistinguishable from incantations, for Celsus and other pagans at any rate, regardless of how the actions were interpreted by Christians.

By quoting Matthew 7:22, Origen tacitly admits that the performance of exorcism was considered knowledge —μαθημα (mathêma), "that which is learned," from which we derive *math*— and that such knowledge not only could, but would *inevitably* be acquired by others: "foreseeing that others are destined to acquire the same knowledge." The "others" in question are those "unworthy men" who Origen admits were even then using Jesus' name to perform exorcisms. One might fairly ask why, *if even unworthy men could learn to perform successful exorcisms using Jesus' name*, such exorcisms should not be considered magical rather than miraculous since their performance did not depend on religious merit.

> Moreover, seeing that [Celsus] often speaks of "the secret doctrine,"[27] in this also he stands accused —nearly everyone in the world knows the preaching of the Christians better than those things that tickle the fancy of the philosophers. For who does not know that Jesus was born of a virgin, and was crucified, and that his resurrecttion has been believed by many, and that the judgment of God has been proclaimed in which the wicked will be punished in keeping with their sins, but the righteous correspondingly rewarded? Yet not having discerned the mystery of the resurrection, it is chattered around derisively among unbelievers.
>
> So on this basis, to speak of "the hidden doctrine" is entirely out of place. But that certain doctrines not revealed to the majority are attained after the public ones [28] is not unique to the teaching of Christians only, but also to that of the philosophers for whom some things were public teachings, but others private.[29] Even some of Pythagoras' listeners accepted his statements without proof, whereas others were taught about those things not to be spoken[30] to profane and insufficiently worthy ears. All the mysteries everywhere, the Greek and the non-Greek, although being secret have not been slandered, therefore it is in vain that Celsus misrepresents what is secret in Christianity.
>
> *Contra Celsum* I.7

Origen nowhere denies that the Christianity of his day —in common with the Greek mystery cults to which he alludes— had *inner teachings*, esoteric doctrines not for public consumption, and though he condemns Celsus for misrepresenting what was secret about Christianity, he leaves unrevealed just what those secrets were.

In short, our earliest extracanonical writers on Christian doctrine use the language of the mystery cults to describe their faith, and concede that secret doctrine was taught privately to an inner circle. A probable reference to such private revelations survives in the text of Colossians where the ambiguous phrase α εορακεν εμβατευων (ha heoraken embateuôn), which from the evidence of ancient inscriptions should be translated "entering an oracle for interpretation of what he has seen,"[31] is more often rendered "taking his stand on visions,"[32] thus saving early Christianity from an overt association with mystery cults.

Notes

1   Betz: "Information about and relics from the Greek mystery cults definitely suggest that magic was a constituent element of the rituals of the mysteries...magic was a constituent element of the mystery cults from their inception." *Magika Hiera*, 250.

2   αχλυς (achlus), *mist*, or if the reference is to Homer –for Clement was exceedingly well read– the *film* that forms on the eyes of the dying.

3   **εποπτευσωμεν**: **"let us see a vision,"** from εποπτευω, *to be admitted* into the highest grade of the mysteries, to become an εποπτης (epoptês), one who has achieved the final grade of the mysteries and seen all that is to be revealed. The same term is used in 2 Peter 1:16.

4   χαιρε φως φως ημιν εξ ουρανου: "Welcome, Light! Light for us from heaven!" The Light/Darkness dichotomy was central to the mystery cults as it was to Christianity (John 1:5).

5   *Clement of Alexandria: The Exhortation to the Greeks*, XI (Loeb, 242).

6   ειθ' οι μεν τοις **γοησι** πεπιστευκοτες: If, on the one hand, those who have trusted in the **sorcerers**..." As noted elsewhere,

the term γοης also meant *deceiver*, a double meaning Clement clearly intended.

7   τα **περιαπτα** και τας **επαοιδας**...αποδεχονται: "receive **amulets** and **enchantments**..." An amulet, περιαπτον (periapton) –the term was derived from the fact that it was suspended from or hung around the neck.

Kotansky's "Greek Exorcistic Amulets," in *Ancient Magic and Ritual Power*, 243-277, is highly recommended.

8   τη **επωδη** του θεου πιστευσαντες: "trusting in the **enchantment** of God..."

9   *Clement of Alexandria: The Exhortation to the Greeks*, XI (Loeb, 244-246).

Johnston: "In accord with theurgy's Platonizing tendencies, these demons were interpreted by the theurgists as the inflictors of corporeal passions that would lure the soul away from its proper pursuits..." *Restless Dead*, 137.

10 Ω των αγιων ως αληθως **μυστηριων**: "O the truly holy **mysteries!**"

11 δαδουχουμαι: "Holding my torch aloft..." The δαδουχος (dadouchos), *torch bearer*, was an official in the Eleusinian mysteries.

Burkert: "The celebration of the mysteries [of Eleusis] was in the hands of two families, the Eumolpidai, who provide the hierophant and Kerykes who provide the torch bearer, *dadouchos*, and the sacred herald, *hierokeryx*. In addition there is a priestess of Demeter who lives permanently in the sanctuary." *Greek Religion*, 285.

12 τους ουρανους και τον θεον **εποπτευσαι**: "**I am initiated into the highest mysteries** of the heavens and of God!"

13 αγιος γινομαι **μυουμενος**: "I become holy **by being initiated!**"

14 **ιεροφαντει** δε ο κυριος: "the Lord **reveals the mysteries**..."
To be the ιεροφαντης (hierophanttês), the *hierophant*, the revealer of the mysteries, derived from ιερος (hieros), *holy*, and φαινειν (phainein), to *show, bring to light*. The hierophant is an initiator who reveals what is holy as Clement's next words make clear.

15 Compare the wording of "an amulet intended to provide protection against illness and the power of evil": "for the seal of Jesus Christ is written upon my forehead…" *Ancient Christian Magic: Coptic Texts of Ritual Power*, 113, 115.

16 ταυτα των εμων **μυστηριων** τα **βακχευματα**: "These are my **mysteries**, my **Bacchic revelries!**" The βακχευμα (bakcheuma), the frenzied nocturnal rites of Bacchus.

17 και **χορευσεις** μετ᾽ αγγελων: "and **you will dance** with angels **around**…" From χορευω (choreuô), *dancing in the round*, used of religious rites, particularly of the Bacchic chorus.

MacMullen discusses the difficulty the church faced in banning dancing from ritual: "Ambrose of Milan…witnessed his congregation dancing during times of worship. (He seems to mean right inside the churches, but he does not supply details.) He was shocked. Such conduct was pagan." *Christianizing the Roman Empire*, 74.

18 *Clement of Alexandria: The Exhortation to the Greeks*, XII (Loeb, 256)

συνυμνουντος ημιν του θεου λογου: "as the Word of God **chants along with** us." To chant a υμνος (humnos), *hymn* or *festal song* in honor of the god *with*, συν (sun), the rest of the Bacchic chorus.

19 Written around 248 CE, years after Celsus, who wrote the Αληθης Λογος (*True Doctrine*), had already died. The contents of Celsus' polemic have been reconstructed by Joseph Hoffman, *Celsus On the True Doctrine*.

20 της απαγγελιας **των** περι αυτον **ιστοριων**: "recitals **of the accounts** about him…"

21 Origen quotes from the form of the saying recorded at Matthew 7:22. The parallel saying in Luke 13:27 has Jesus call the miracle workers "workers of wickedness."

22 ως **γοητεια** δυνηθεντος α εδοξε παραδοξα πεποιηκεναι: "of having performed wonders by practicing **sorcery**…"

23 μελλουσι και αλλοι **τα αυτα μαθηματα** εγνωκοτες: "others

are destined to acquire **the same knowledge...**"

24 μετ' **αλλων λογων** πεπιστευμενων: "together with **other words** in which they have faith..."

25 Kotansky, *Magika Hiera*, 112. The author elsewhere mentions "the problem that one faces when presented with prayers for salvation that seem embedded in an indisputable magical context." (123)

26 The church historian Eusebius (3rd century) has the disciple Thaddeus tell the mythical Abgar, **τιθημι την χειρα μου** επι σε εν ονοματι αυτου: "**I lay my hand** on you in his name..." *Ecclesiastical History*, I, 13, 17. The implication is that the laying on of hands was not uncommon.

27 ονομαζει **κρυφιον** δογμα: "speaks of the **secret** doctrine..."

28 μετα **τα εξωτερικα**: after **the public ones...**" εξωτερικος (exoterikôs), from whence *exoteric*, pertaining to *the outer*, i.e., those teachings revealed to those *outside* the inner circle, the public.

29 ετεροι δε **εσωτερικοι**: "but others **private...**" εσωτερικος (esôterikos), *esoteric*, pertaining to *the inner*, i.e., the teachings revealed to insiders.

30 **εν απορρητω** διδασκομενοι: "taught about those things **not to be spoken...**" απορρητος (aporrhêtos), *secret*. The neuter form of the adjective can mean "state secret."

31 Danker, *Greek-English Lexicon*, 321.

Lane Fox: "Among the Colossians, by contrast, there were people who trusted other visions, worshipping angels and 'vaunting the things which they have crossed the threshold and seen' ...Paul's word for 'crossing the threshold' is the word for visitors who 'entered' a temple like Claros and penetrated its tunnels." *Pagans and Christians*, 380.

Claros was an oracular shrine of Apollo.

32 Colossians 2:18, *Revised Standard Version*.

Chapter Twelve:
The *Secret Gospel* of Mark

The saga of the *Secret Gospel of Mark* is as fascinating as it is complex, but the principle claim advanced is simple: the gospel of Mark that we possess is an expurgated version of an original which contained potentially shocking content. If this claim is true, the *Secret Gospel* becomes *the* case study of New Testament textual manipulation, providing both a clear example of suppression of details of Jesus' life as well as a convincing motive. However, to attempt even a partial reconstruction of what that suppressed content may have consisted, we must compare the canonical gospel of Mark with the gospel of John and with a recently discovered letter written by the early Christian theologian, Clement of Alexandria. We will start with Clement's letter.

As the stories of the centurion's boy and the post-resurrection appearances of Jesus illustrate, the content of the gospels underwent an extensive editing process during which material was added, subtracted, moved, or rephrased according to the needs and whims of various redactors. It is clear that a primitive written tradition, of which Q is an example, coexisted with an oral tradition, and that these early forms of "the text" influenced one another for a minimum of several decades before and after the gospels as we know them were penned.

Naturally the oral tradition did not simply stop once written gospels appeared. To the contrary, it would have continued to flourish, providing one of the driving forces behind the fantastic elaborations of Jesus' story that are typical of the apocryphal gospels of the 2nd century and beyond. Within this mélange of sayings and stories elements were added, deleted, and displaced from their original context while the oral tradition continued to interact with the written text. Narrative seams and contradictory details of time and place within the text of our present gospels indicate where material has been excised, leaving a lacuna in the text, the verbal equivalent of an empty frame with no picture.

Such processes appear to have taken place in many of the New Testament documents. Textual analysis suggests that the present 1 and 2 Corinthians may be composed of fragments of several letters that have been combined into two,[1] as well as containing non-Pauline interpolations. It is quite likely that the present chapters of the gospel of John were originally in a different order, and that John 18:1 originally followed John 14:31 —the intervening material being an insertion that predates any existing manuscript.[2]

> …During the first period of their transmission, all gospel texts were very unstable. The text of the canonical gospels later enjoyed a certain degree of protection, beginning with the process of canonization in the 3rd and 4th centuries CE…In our

discussion of the process of the formation of the gospel tradition, two observations applied to all relevant materials: (1) the oral tradition continued for many decades and remained an important factor, influencing even later stages of the written records; (2) the earliest written materials were relatively small compositions of specific materials which paralleled the oral use of traditional materials, such as collections of wisdom sayings or of miracle stories, which were assembled for very practical purposes

...It does not appear that the text of the Gospel of John as it is extant in the oldest manuscripts has preserved the text of the autograph without changes. John 21, though belonging to the older stages of the transmission of the text, is certainly a later appendix.[3]

The scribal tradition centered in Alexandria, Egypt, produced the most reliable copies of the New Testament documents, the Alexandrian text type, but as the most superficial comparison of Matthew and Luke with Mark reveals, Matthew and Luke both made significant changes when quoting Mark, changes that altered the sense of the passages they reproduced. At times Matthew and Luke simply omitted details or whole stories with which they were uncomfortable. Clearly if material has been *deleted* from a document during its composition, the accuracy of subsequent copying becomes nearly moot: *the original itself is a corrupted text.*

The reader should be aware that even a partial reconstitution of the *Secret Gospel of Mark* involves painstaking literary detective work that restores passages suppressed early in the history of Christianity and reestablishes the continuity of a story —certainly the most revealing story pertaining to Jesus' personal life— that has been dismembered and its parts scattered.

The Mar Saba letter of Clement

The story of the lost letter of Clement begins with the controversial figure of Morton Smith, who, in 1958, was a history professor specializing in patristics, the study of the writings of the earliest leaders of the church. As a part of his investigations, Smith was cataloging the books of the library at the Greek Orthodox monastery of Mar Saba, a hermitage located 12 miles south of Jerusalem, a place he had visited previously in 1941 as a graduate student.

In the process of examining a copy of Isaac Voss' 1646 edition of the letters of Ignatius, Smith noticed three pages of Greek that had been written by hand on blank pages at the end of the printed book. The Greek text appeared to be part of a previously unknown letter of Clement of Alexandria[4] Excited by his discovery, Smith took photographs of the handwritten pages and at the end of his stay, returned the volume to the shelf. His subsequent studies were done from his photographs.[5] Smith spent years carefully analyzing his findings and published the results in two venues, one scholarly, the other popular, in 1973.[6] The popular version, *The Secret Gospel: The Discovery and Interpretation of the Secret Gospel According to Mark*, was reissued by Dawn Horse Press in 1982, 1984, and 2005.

The text[7] of Clement's letter reads as follows (the citations from *Secret Mark* are italicized).

> From the letters of the Most Holy Clement of the *Stromateis*:
> To Theodore:
> You did well to silence the unmentionable teachings of the
> Carpocratians, for they are the wandering stars which were
> foretold. They stray from the narrow path of the commandments

toward the bottomless pit of sins of the flesh embodied, for having been inflated with the knowledge[8] —as they call it— of the deep things of Satan, they fail to notice that they are plunging themselves into the outer darkness of falsehood, and while bragging about being free, they have become slaves of despicable cravings. Such men are always to be resisted in all ways, for even if they speak truthfully, even so, a lover of truth should not agree with them, for neither are all true things truth, nor should what appears to be true according to human opinions take precedence over the true truth which is in accord with faith.

Now concerning the things they keep chattering about regarding the divinely inspired Gospel according to Mark, some are complete lies, and others, even if they contain some truth, are not accurately represented, for the truth, having been mixed up with inventions, is thereby falsified so that —as the saying goes— even the salt loses its flavor.

As for Mark, during Peter's stay in Rome, he wrote down the things the Lord did, not, however, revealing everything,[9] much less hinting at the mysteries,[10] but selecting what he considered advantageous for increasing the faith of those being instructed.[11] When Peter suffered martyrdom, Mark came to Alexandria, preserving both his own recollections and those of Peter, from which he carried over into his first book[12] what was suitable for those progressing step by step[13] toward knowledge.

He composed a more spiritual gospel [14] for the use of those having attained perfection.[15] Nevertheless, he never betrayed the ineffable mysteries,[16] nor did he write down the hierophantic teachings of the Lord,[17] but to those things already written, he added yet other deeds and still other sayings, the interpretation with which he was familiar, to initiate the hearers into the forbidden sanctuary of the truth seven times veiled.[18] In this manner, in my opinion, he prepared them neither grudgingly nor carelessly, and dying, he bequeathed his writing to the church in Alexandria, where even now it is most carefully guarded, being read only before those who have been initiated into the great mysteries.[19]

Since the unclean demons are always scheming the destruction of the race of men, Carpocrates, having been taught by them and employing deceptive arts, enslaved by those means a certain presbyter of the church in Alexandria and obtained from him a copy of the secret gospel[20] and interpreted it according to his blasphemous and carnal opinion. Moreover, he defiled the spotless and holy words, mixing them with shameless lies. The teachings of the Carpocratians are drawn out of this mixture.

Just as I have previously said, one must never yield to them as they expound their lies, nor concede that the secret gospel was written by Mark, but rather deny it even under oath. For everything that is true is not spoken to all men. The wisdom of God declares through Solomon, "Answer the fool according to his foolishness," teaching that the light of truth is to be hidden from those who are mentally blind, and it also says, "from he who has not, it shall be taken away," and "let the fool walk in darkness." But we are sons of light, having been illuminated by the sunrise of the spirit of the Lord, for it says, "where the spirit of the Lord is, there is freedom."

To the clean, everything is clean. Therefore I will not hesitate to answer what you have asked, exposing their lies from the very words of the Gospel. For instance, after "And they were in the road going up to Jerusalem," and what follows until "after three days he shall rise," it next says, word for word, *"And they came to Bethany, and a certain woman whose brother had died came out and threw herself before Jesus and said to him, 'Son of David, have mercy on me.' But the disciples rebuked her. Becoming angry, Jesus went off after her into the garden where the tomb was and suddenly there was heard coming from the tomb a loud voice. Approaching, Jesus rolled away the stone from the door of the tomb and immediately going into where the young man was, he stretched out his hand and raised him, holding his hand. And gazing at him, the young man loved him and began to plead with him that he might be with him. And going from the tomb, they went into the young man's house, for he was rich. After six days, Jesus summoned him and when evening came, the young man went to him wearing a linen cloth over his naked body and he stayed with him that night, for Jesus taught him the mystery of the kingdom of God.*[21] *And then, arising, he went to the far side of the Jordan.*

After this, it adds, "James and John went to him," and all that section, but "naked man with naked man" and the other things about which you wrote, are not found. After "he goes into Jericho," it adds only, "*and the sister of the young man who Jesus loved and his mother and Salome were there, but Jesus did not agree to see them.*" But the many other things about which you wrote appear not to be, and are not, true. According to the true philosophical explanation…"

[handwritten: Jesus turned his back on the magic of the day e went straight to God quote. His mother father were devoutly religious quote Against our Gospel. P 31]

At this point the text breaks off.

The scholars answer the letter

Smith's analysis of his discovery and the conclusions he drew were very different from the understanding of Jesus in mainstream New Testament studies, and they provoked a firestorm of invective and denial from mostly Catholic and evangelical quarters, a reaction which has been well summarized by Shawn Eyer.[22]

Most of the response was of little or no factual consequence; the majority of reviewers, writing for the most part in sectarian publications, were intensely antagonistic to Smith's conclusions and were simply venting their displeasure. One of the few writers who attempted a point-by-point refutation strongly implied that the Clement letter and the lost gospel fragments it preserved were forgeries.[23] The clear implication was that Smith himself had forged the letter, and Smith so interpreted it in his rebuttal, concluding "…one should not suppose a text spurious simply because one dislikes what it says."[24] Since Smith's death, occasional articles and even books appear that reject the authenticity of the Clement letter, at times on such grounds

211

as statistical analysis of the vocabulary of the text.[25]

In a recent exchange of opinion on the merits of Smith's discovery, Charles Hedrick observed:

> Thirty years later, the reviews of Smith's books are almost embarrassing to read —not embarrassing to Smith, though I am sure they must have bothered him immensely at the time, but embarrassing to the academy. From my later perspective, the personal attacks on Smith were entirely unwarranted.[26]

It is not my purpose to rehearse the complex and varied arguments for or against the authenticity of the Clement letter, a valuable summation of which has thankfully been written.[27] I would, however, offer several reasons why I find the Clement letter and the gospel fragments it preserves to be ultimately persuasive.

First and foremost is the way in which the Markan passages from the letter fit back into the text of canonical Mark, an observation also made by Helmut Koester, who was quoted by Smith: "The piece of Secret Mark fits the Markan trajectory so well that a forgery is inconceivable."[28] The language of the gospel fragments preserved in the letter fits perfectly with the language of the canonical gospel: when an isolated piece makes a seamless fit with a larger body, the logical assumption is to regard them both as having once formed a unity.

Consistent with Koester's remark, several plausible interpretations based on the restored text —solutions *not* envisioned by Smith— have been advanced. The ways in which the expanded text of Mark clears up longstanding exegetical aporia will be explored in the next chapter. However, seeing that the full implications of the letter do not seem to

212

have been appreciated, and were therefore not pursued by Smith reinforces my conviction that he did not forge the Clement letter. One would at least expect a self-aggrandizing forger to fully understand and exploit the product of his deceit. To the contrary, the full explanatory force of Smith's discovery had to wait for others to develop.

It must also be asked what Smith had to gain by forging such a document. Regardless of the answer one gives —and some of the answers border on the bizarre— it is certainly clear how much he stood to lose. Had the letter proven to be a forgery perpetrated by Smith —the letter was available for inspection for some time after Smith published his conclusions[29] — it seems impossible that his teaching career at Columbia would have survived the dustup. Nor must we neglect to mention the acute embarrassment to his department and university had forgery been proven, or the negative reflection that would have fallen on Harvard University Press and Harper and Row who published the scholarly and popular accounts of the discovery respectively. To this must be added the betrayal of the confidence of the legendary voices in the academic community with whom Smith shared his findings and to whose judgment he appealed, to say nothing of the miserable repayment for the hospitality of the monks of Mar Saba who opened their library to Smith and entrusted him with its contents. It is impossible that these considerations would not have occurred to Smith had he contemplated faking a letter by Clement of Alexandria.

Confronted with the hurdles of producing a spurious letter of Clement that duplicates the style of Clement, inserting into it fake fragments of Mark which exactly copy the style of authentic Mark, and then producing the letter flawlessly by hand in 18th century Greek script in the back of an irreplaceable book, champions of the forgery hypothesis were forced to accuse Smith of being *fiendishly* clever, a backhanded compliment of which Smith himself made light. Impressive though his erudition was, I fail to find in Morton Smith a latter day reincarnation of Professor Moriarty. *or (Carpocrates?*

The daunting technical and scholarly difficulties involved in forging such an ancient letter have led Bart Ehrman, who believes that Smith had the skills to commit the deed, but has never claimed he actually did so, to observe:

> It is true that a modern forgery would be an amazing feat. For this to be forged, someone would have had to imitate an eighteenth-century Greek style of handwriting and to produce a document that is so much like Clement that it fools experts who spend their lives analyzing Clement, which quotes a previously lost passage from Mark that is so much like Mark that it fools experts who spend their lives analyzing Mark. If this is forged, it is one of the greatest works of scholarship of the twentieth century, by someone who put an uncanny amount of work into it.[30]

Elsewhere Ehrman has stated, "I don't think we can say whether or not Smith forged the letter. We won't know until, if ever, the manuscript is found and subjected to a rigorous investigation, including testing of the ink."[31] But at least one other recently published scholar has gone so far as to flatly deny the possibility that the Clement letter was faked: "Morton Smith did not forge the manuscript... Smith simply could not have pulled off a forgery under the conditions at the monastery in 1958."[32]

By 1977 the Voss book had been removed from the monastery and the handwritten pages separated from it. Both book and pages have since disappeared, presumably due to carelessness on the part of the Greek Orthodox library staff. At any rate, the manuscript has done what its detractors no doubt wished from the very beginning: it has conveniently gone away. Even if the pages were rediscovered — something I seriously doubt will ever happen— the authenticity of the letter might still never be established. A forger clever enough to have done the work attributed to Smith might also have produced ink using an old recipe and of the age of the paper there was never any doubt since the book itself is from the 17th century. The argument would then spin on the flimsy axle of handwriting analysis, which given the nearly unlimited idiosyncrasies of a given writer —hand tremor due to disease or age, for example— could never be unquestionably conclusive. *Why is the author dragging Jesus down to his level of thinking.*

Nevertheless, it is truly remarkable that the last living scholar to have seen the Clement letter *in situ* waited *27 years* after the fact to publish.[33] In the meanwhile, members of the academy have engaged in a decades long food fight over the authenticity of the letter, hurling reckless accusations of forgery and fraud, while making the most feeble efforts imaginable to verify either the existence or the reliability of the evidence. Given the admitted implications of the discovery, one can only imagine how the course of the controversy might have changed if some group of scholars had had the spine to pull its boots on, board a plane, and go check. In the end, the bookish lethargy of the Jesus studies community is perhaps the most bizarre feature of the *Secret Gospel* saga.

215

Unable to finally establish that the words of the letter are the true words of Clement, or that the quotations from Mark are the true words of Mark, we are left to put the quotes back into the gospel and see if the amplified text changes our understanding, and in the next chapter that is what we will do.

Carpocrates and his heresies

The claims of Carpocrates and his coreligionists, the Carpocratians, are one of the principle subjects of Clement's letter to Theodore. Very little is known about Carpocrates, and what little information we have comes to us from his enemies. Aside from a brief mention in Clement, the church father Irenaeus is our only other original source.[34]

The Clement letter mentions the *Secret Gospel of Mark* in connection with Carpocrates, but apart from that we do not know what other Christian books the Carpocratians may have used. Irenaeus lumps Carpocrates together with the Gnostics, but the teachings he attributes to him, reincarnation and reminiscence of previous lives, are derived from Platonism.[35] And though Irenaeus considered him to be a Christian heretic, we don't know how Carpocrates might have defined himself; the church saw to it that none of his writings survived.[36]

Like Clement himself, Carpocrates taught in Alexandria, Egypt, his career overlapping the reigns of Hadrian (117-138) and Antonius Pius (138-161). His teachings are awarded six paragraphs in the polemic *Adversus Haereses* (*Against Heresies*), written about 180 by Irenaeus (130-202), the bishop of Lyon, considered to be the most important theologian of the 2nd century.[37]

216

Subtracting the venom and libel, Irenaeus' sketch of the Carpocratians leaves us with a picture of a dualistic antinomian philosophy that regarded the material world as fallen and escape from the cycle of reincarnation as possible only by experiencing all human conditions, which apparently included all sexual behaviors. Pansexuality, whatever its value for any given individual, was justified as *ritually* necessary to escape the prison of the lower world and gain the reward of ascent *?* into heaven.

A certain amount of evidence for primitive Christian antinomianism survives in quotations from pagan critics. Hoffman's explanation for a tendency toward libertine behavior merits an extended quote:

> Eschatological thinking thus seems to have bred both an ascetic form of piety, best represented in Paul's letters and stemming from the conviction that, as the present order is corrupt, one ought to defy the world through self-mortification and disregard the flesh, and an antinomian enthusiasm, one aspect of which was sexual self-indulgence. These responses to the eschaton, in turn, correspond to rival theological outlooks in the early church: the antinomian emphasis, favored especially by some of Paul's converts, took its cue from Paul's (and doubtless other missionaries') stance against the law. Without the constraints of the Jewish law, such Christians reasoned, anything is possible; and as the Christian is saved by grace and faith rather than by works, anything is permissible.[38] *not true today works are what you are judged on.*

Two characteristics of Carpocratian practice really pertain to our discussion: the elements of mystery and magic. On these two points at least, Irenaeus is clear: the Carpocratians taught that Jesus "spoke privately in mystery to his disciples"[39] and performed various types of magic.

217

If Irenaeus was vague about what "speaking in mystery" involved, he is much more specific about magic. Fortunately for us, the pertinent section is preserved not only in Latin, but also in Greek in the form of quotations by other church officials:

> They also perform magical arts and enchantments,[40] potions and erotic spells,[41] use magical assistants and messengers of dreams,[42] and other such evil works, alleging they already have authority to be the masters of the princes[43] and creators of this world...

> *Against Heresies*, I. 25, 3

Irenaeus thus confronts us with clear evidence for varied magical practice in the primitive church, with a sexual component being preserved among some factions. It is against this background that Justin Martyr's *Apology* must be read, and it is to that early document we now turn.

Justin, a student of several schools of philosophy, was born in Samaria (present-day Palestine) around the year 100 and was executed early in the reign of Marcus Aurelius, probably about the year 165. He converted to Christianity around 130 and wrote his protest against the persecution of Christians shortly after 150 CE. Justin's work, although poorly and incompletely preserved, is nevertheless a valuable window into the practices of early Christians, particularly as perceived by their pagan contemporaries. Justin's writings are of particular relevance because he was a near contemporary of Carpocrates and his followers.

Justin's argumentation is muddled and his writing discursive in the

218

worst sense. There are two overriding assumptions in the *Apology*: the mere antiquity of the Old Testament is its guarantee of truth and that because Jesus fulfilled the prophecies of the Old Testament —which Justin quotes exhaustively— he must be the promised Messiah. I have reproduced only those portions of his discourse that deal with charges that Jesus and his disciples practiced magic. In fact, it is not until the thirtieth section of his tract that Justin finally manages to come to the crux of this issue, posing the question much as pagans undoubtedly did:

> What prevents him we call Christ, a man born of men, having performed what we call powerful works by magical art[44] and by this means appear to be a son of God?

Like his Christian contemporaries, Justin is not only familiar with magicians and their practices, but apparently includes many of his coreligionists as formerly among their number:

> …and we who once employed magical arts have now consecrated ourselves to the good and unbegotten God…
>
> *Apology* 14.2

> For even necromancy and haruspexy using uncorrupted children,[45] and calling up human souls, and those who among the magicians are called senders of dreams and familiars, and all things done by those with such skills, may these persuade you that even after death souls are sentient and men seized and thrown down by souls of the dead, who everyone calls demon-possessed[46] and madmen, and which is known to you as "prophesying," Amphilochus and Dodona and Pytho and whatever others there are…
>
> *Apology* 18.3-4

219

It would appear that many Christians were still practitioners of magic. Justin says as much, citing the sect of Simon the Samaritan, who "by the art of working with demons performed feats of magic" and noting that "all who belong to his sect are, as we have said, called Christians." It is against this sect that the following accusations are leveled:

> Whether those legendarily evil works they perform — overturning the lamp,[47] unrestrained intercourse, and feasting on human flesh— are true we do not know, but they are neither persecuted nor put to death by you on account of the doctrines they hold...

Apology 26.2,6,7.

Justin returns to the subject of sexual license to reiterate that "promiscuous intercourse is not a mystery of ours."[48] From the foregoing it is plain that Justin not only knew of accusations that Christian ritual included sexual free-for-alls, he joins in with the chorus of accusers by stipulating which sects he thought engaged in such practices.

Are such charges to be taken seriously? Christians charging other Christians with gross sexual indecency was certainly not new in Justin's day: the later books of the New Testament claim that nonconforming Christians behaved like "irrational animals"[49] and generally portray the members of competing Christian sects as prisoners of unbridled lust. To these charges later writers added cannibalism and the ritual ingestion of semen and menstrual blood.[50] Given antiquity's passion for overstatement, the charges involving debauchery and murder are probably in the main false, whereas those of dabbling in magic are almost certainly true.

220

Notes

1   Burton Mack, *Who Wrote the New Testament*, 126-127.

2   See Koester, *Ancient Christian Gospels*, 246-250, for a more complete enumeration of problems of this type. The very earliest manuscripts of the gospels already contain divergent forms of the text, and most authorities in the field of New Testament studies agree that in its earliest period the text was unstable.

It bears reiterating that none of the writers of the gospels were eyewitnesses of Jesus' life. Mark's authority traditionally derives from being an associate of the apostle Peter. As shown in a previous chapter, even a superficial examination of Matthew and Luke proves they did not witness the events they recorded. The gospel of John is known with near certainly to have used previous sources as can be demonstrated by the presence of narrative seams. *The New Testament: A Historical Introduction to the Early Christian Writings*, 164-167. *Why accuse Jesus of these things.*

3   Koester, 219, 246.

4   Titus Flavius Clemens, died c. 215 CE, known as Clement of Alexandria. Aside from Smith's discovery at Mar Saba, no letter attributed to Clement is known to exist. Some scholars have expressed surprise that a letter of Clement should be discovered, but this is a transparent reaction to the unwelcome contents of the letter, not to the possibility of its preservation. Clement was a prolific writer and it is hardly incredible that a letter of his could have survived the centuries and that it might turn up in – of all places!– a monastery. Clement's understanding of the mysteries is discussed in the previous chapter.

"It is known that Clement of Alexandria wrote letters. But not one of these letters had survived, although quotations from Clement's letters appear in the *Sacra Parallela* attributed to John of Damascus who stayed at the Mar Saba Monastery from the beginning of the 8th century to his death (ca. 750 CE). The first question was, therefore, whether this letter was indeed the copy of a genuine letter of the Alexandrian Father. There are a number of scholars who have expressed doubts with respect to its authenticity. However, vocabulary, style, syntax, and manner of presentation in the letter are either identical with, or similar to, that of Clement's genuine writings. Skepticism is hard to justify." *Ancient Christian Gospels, 293-294.*

5   Photographs of the letter can be viewed online: www.earlychristianwritings.com/secretmark.

Father Kallistos Dourvas of the Greek Orthodox Patriarchate library in Jerusalem took additional color photographs of the Clement letter in 1976. *The Secret Gospel* (2005 reprint), 149.

6   *Clement of Alexandria and a Secret Gospel of Mark,* Harvard University Press, 1973, and *The Secret Gospel: The Discovery and Interpretation of the Secret Gospel According to Mark,* Harper & Row, 1973. The simultaneous release was coincidental; the scholarly edition, which would normally have preceded the popular edition, was held up in the editorial process.

7   This is my translation of the letter. Several other translations, including Smith's, are available on the *world wide web.*

8   γνωσις (gnosis), *knowledge* supernaturally revealed.

9   ου μεντοι πασας **εξαγγελλων**: "not, however, **revealing** everything..." The verb εξαγγελω (exangelô), to *betray* a secret. Εξαγγελος (exangelos), *informer.*

10   ουδε μην **τας μυστικας** υποσημαινων: "much less hinting at **the mysteries...**" τας μυστικας (tas mustikas), *the mysteries,* a term not used in the New Testament, whose writers favor a related word, μυστηριον (mustêrion), but used of the mystery rites by pagan authors.

11   των κατηχουμενων: "of those being instructed," *the catechumens,* from κατηχουμενος (katêchoumenos), *the one being instructed.*

Valerie Flint: "The rite of baptism was full of echoes of an older world. Catechumens were exorcized several times as they approached the sacrament at which, finally, the Devil, father of the demons, was renounced." *Witchcraft and Magic in Europe: Ancient Greece and Rome*, 335.

12 μεταφερων εις **το πρωτον αυτου βιβλιον**: "he carried over into **his first book**…"

13 **καταλληλα** (katallêla), "step by step," or *one after another, in a row, in good order*, reflecting the rites and rituals through which the initiate passed progressively toward γνωσις. Liddell and Scott, *A Greek-English Lexicon*, 899.

14 συνεταξε **πνευματικωτερον** ευαγγελιον: "He composed a **more spiritual** gospel…" Several experts on early Christian gospels believe that the *Secret Gospel* was the original gospel of Mark and that text was *subtracted* from it, arriving at the present form of the gospel. Which was chicken and which egg need not detain us here.

Clement contrasts "the more spiritual gospel" with Mark's *initial* composition, "his first book," making a claim that Mark wrote more than one gospel. Clement, who taught in the catechetical school in Alexandria, had some interesting things to say about the origin of the gospels. The 4th century historian Eusebius cites one of Clement's lost writings, the *Hypotyposeis*, on the composition of the gospels: **προγεγραφθαι** ελεγεν των ευαγγελιων τα περιεχοντα τας γενεαλογιας: "he said of the gospels that those **first published** included the genealogies." *Ecclesiastical History*, VI, 14, 5.

The verb in question, προγραφω, has generally been understood to mean *written before*, but also frequently means *to display publicly* and is used in exactly that sense in Galatians 3:1 where Jesus' crucifixion is described as a *public display*. Stephen Carlson has made an excellent case that Clement was not claiming that the genealogic gospels were *written* first, but that they were *published* first, i.e., that Matthew and Luke were the first *official, public,* biographies. *New Testament Studies* 47: 118-125.

This reading of the evidence is strongly supported by the context of Eusebius' report which says of Mark's gospel that το ευαγγελιον μεταδουναι **τοις δεομενοις** αυτου· "the gospel was shared **by those who requested** it." The implication is that Mark was not a public gospel, but that it initially circulated hand to hand. *Ecclesiastical History* VI 14 6

The earliest manuscript of Mark is part of the Chester Beatty papyrus which dates from the early to mid-3rd century. An almost comically flimsy case has been advanced that a tiny papyrus fragment, 7Q5, recovered with other papyrus fragments from a cave at Qumran, may in part at least affirm writing as to Mark, but as the fragment contains only nine complete words — ten (10), and with a grand total of *ten additional letters* that can be positively identified, this claim can be dismissed outright. The fact that the earliest gospel is not better represented by manuscripts may reflect its originally private nature.

15   εις την **των τελειουμενων** χρησις: "for the use **of those having been perfected**..." from   τελειος (teleios), the *perfected* or *fully initiated* whom Clement contrasts with the *catechumens*, those still in the process of having the secrets revealed.

16   ουδεπω ομος αυτα **τα απορρητα** εξωρχησατο: "Nevertheless, he never betrayed the ineffable mysteries...," things which were either *forbidden* to be spoken, or *unspeakable*. The term could encompass *ineffable mysteries* as well as *unmentionable vices*, and in some of the mystery rites, both meanings might have applied.

Samuel Angus: "An awful obligation to perpetual secrecy as to what was said and transacted behind closed doors in the initiation proper was imposed —an obligation so scrupulously observed through the centuries that not one account of the secrets of the holy of holies of the Mysteries has been published to gratify the curiosity of historians." *The Mystery Religions*, 78.

17   ουδε κατεγραψε την **ιεροφαντικεν** διδασκαλιαν: "nor did he write down the **hierophantic** teachings...," from ιεροφαντες (hierophants), *hierophant*, the expounder of the sacred mysteries.

18   **το αδυτον** της επτακις κεκαλυμμενης αληθειας: "the **forbidden sanctuary** of the truth seven times veiled..." The

αδυτος (adutos), is the *sanctum sanctorum* of the mystery religions, that which is forbidden to be entered except by the initiated.

"Seven times veiled:" the verb is formed off καλυμμα (kalumma), *veil*, either bridal veil or the cloth covering the face of a corpse, possibly containing an echo of marrying Christ and dying to the world through (seven?) steps of initiation. Seven was much loved number: in the gospel of John, for example, Jesus performs seven signs.

Gershom Scholem: "Among the most important objects which Metatron describes to Rabbi Ishmael is the cosmic veil or curtain before the throne, which conceals the glory of God from the host of angels. The idea of such a veil appears to be very old; references to it are to be found already in Aggadic passages from the second century. The existence of veils in the resplendent sphere of the aeons is also mentioned in a Coptic writing belonging to the gnostic school, the *Pistis Sophia*." *Major Trends in Jewish Mysticism*, 72.

19   προς αυτους μονους τους μυουμενους **τα μεγαλα μυστερια**: "only before those who have been initiated into **the great mysteries**..." The image is that of a secret book being read before (προς) a group of initiates who face the reader.

The *greater mysteries* were a feature of the Eleusinian rites.

20   του **μυστικου** ευαγγελιου: "of the **secret** gospel..." Μυστικος (mustikos), like the English *mystical* directly derived from it, means "pertaining to mysteries."

The *Secret Gospel* was a text used in mystery rites as the reference to αδυτος and ιεροφαντες, discussed in previous notes, clearly shows. Nevertheless, Scott Brown, a recent writer, has denied that μυστικος means *secret*, claiming instead that Clement uses the term to mean *symbolic* or *allegorical*. *Journal of Biblical Literature* 122: 89. However, Clement not only uses the language of the mysteries, but stipulates that the gospel was carefully guarded, read only before initiates, and that the copy obtained by Carpocrates was obtained by means of deception, all of which, to my mind, would qualify it as a *secret* gospel.

21 The gospel of Mark (4:11) in referring to a *singular* "mystery of the kingdom" where the other synoptics have "mysteries" (Matthew 13:11, Luke 8:10)

22 Alexandria: *The Journal for the Western Cosmological Tradition* No. 5, 129.

The conclusion which most enraged the religious establishment was that the individuals are sanctioned may have murdered physical union between Jesus and his disciple following a much baptismal ritual. The offending passage, quoted from the Dawn House Press reprint (pages 106-107), reads as follows:

"It was a water baptism administered by Jesus to chosen disciples, singly and by night. The costume, for the disciple, was a linen cloth worn over the naked body. This cloth was probably removed for the baptism proper, the immersion in water, which was now reduced to a preparatory purification. After that, by unknown ceremonies, the disciple was possessed by Jesus' spirit and so united with Jesus. One with him, he participated by hallucination in Jesus' ascent into the heavens, he entered the kingdom of God, and was thereby set free from the laws ordained for and in the lower world. Freedom from the law may have resulted in completion of the spiritual union by physical union. This certainly occurred in many forms of gnostic Chrisitianity; how early it began there is no telling."

23 Quesnell, *The Catholic Biblical Quarterly* 37: 48-67.

24 Smith, *The Catholic Biblical Quarterly* 38: 196.

25 As, for example, Eric Osborn in *The Second Century: A Journal of Early Christian Studies* 3: 219-244 and A. H. Criddle in *Journal of Early Christian Studies* 3: 215-220.

The gist of the statistical argument appears to be that the Clement letter contains too many words *peculiar to Clement* to actually have been written by Clement, a claim which seems to cast the modern critic in the role of mind reader. Claims based on vocabulary analysis have the advantage of being impossible either to entirely substantiate or refute.

26   *Journal of Early Christian Studies* 11: 136.

27   See Ehrman's "The Forgery of an Ancient Discovery? Morton Smith and the Secret Gospel of Mark," a chapter in *Lost Christianities*, 67-89.

Marvin Meyer's essays represent another valuable source of analysis of both the contents and controversies surrounding the *Secret Gospel* (see references), and Crossan's *Four Other Gospels* contains additional valuable commentary (see references).

Ten years after the publication of the Mar Saba letter, Smith noted that 25 experts attributed it to Clement, 4 did not, and 6 had no opinion. *Harvard Theological Review* 75: 449-461.

28   *Harvard Theological Review* 75: 459.

29   The last living Western scholar to have seen the letter *in situ*, Guy Stroumsa, published an open letter to that effect (*Journal of Early Christian Studies* 11: 147-153) in which he says (148), "...the idea of a secret gospel in the Alexandrian Church never really surprised me."

Others have seen the pages in question. Marvin Meyer quotes Thomas Talley, "as witness to its existence I can cite the Archimandrite Meliton of the Jerusalem Greek Patriarchate who, after the publication of Smith's work, found the volume at Mar Saba and removed it to the patriarchal library, and the patriarchal librarian, Father Kallistos, who told me that the manuscript (two folios) has been removed from the printed volume and is being repaired." *Secret Gospels: Essays on Thomas and the Secret Gospel of Mark*, 110.

30   *Lost Christianities*, 82.

31   *Journal of Early Christian Studies* 11: 162.

32   *Journal of Early Christian Studies* 11: 140.

33   *The Secret Gospel* (2005 reprint), 148.

34   Hippolytus (2nd century) and Eusebius (early 4th century) refer to Carpocrates, but they are almost certainly using Irenaeus as their source.

35   Cf. *Gnosticism, Judaism, and Egyptian Christianity*, 205-206.

36   Clement records a small portion of a philosophical tract written by Carpocrates' son, Epiphanes, who died at age 17. Aside from its radical egalitarianism, there is nothing particularly scandalous about it.

37   *Against Heresies* was originally composed in Greek –Ἐλεγχος και ανατροπη της ψευδονομον γνωσεως– *Detection and Refutation of Falsely-called Knowledge*, but largely survived in the form of an early Latin translation. Some Greek fragments of the original survive in the form of quotations.

38   *Celsus on the True Doctrine*, 14.

39   Iesum dicentes in mysterio discipulis suis et apostolis seorsum locutum…: "saying Jesus spoke privately in mystery to his disciples and apostles…" *Against Heresies* I, 25, 5.

40   τεχνας…μαγικας…επαοιδας: "magical arts…enchantments…"

41   φιλτρα και χαριτησια: "potions and erotic spells…"

      A φιλτρον (philtron) is a spell for controlling the actions or emotions of others, used of horses it means *the bit*. In the magical papyri, a φιλτροκαταδεσμος (philtrokatadesmos) is an erotic binding spell. In the magical papyri as –or so it would appear– in Carpocratian Christianity, spells and prayers combined: "religion and magic, at least with regard to prayer, are coterminus." *Magika Hiera*, 194.

      "A philtron or amatorium [the Latin equivalent, *my note*] may then be the substance put into food or drink to induce sexual passion in the person who consumes or imbibes it; it may be a substance used as an ointment; it may be a substance accompanied by a spoken spell designed to elicit the same result; and it may be a spoken spell intended to provoke sexual desire." *Magic and Magicians in the Greco-Roman World*, 17.

The term χαριτησιον (charitêsion) "covered not only prayers and amulets but more directly material technologies for stimulating and managing sexual feelings, such as penis ointments and love potions...if you can throw your handkerchief over lizards copulating it will be a χαριτησιον μεγα (a great spell to produce charm); the tail worn as an amulet promotes erection..." *Magika Hiera*, 220.

That the Greek terms had become technical terms in magic is suggested by the fact that the Latin version simply transliterates them.

42   παρεδρους και ονειροπομπους: "magical assistants and messengers of dreams..."

The Greek word for magical assistant is also carried over into Latin as *paredros*. "The 'assistant,' as one of the many spirits or stellar angels or daemons of the dead, may contribute anything, including dream transmissions and revelations by dreams." *Magika Hiera*, 180.

Oneiropompos, "dream sender," also a technical term, is simply transposed into Latin.

The complex interrelationship between sex magic and dreams is briefly discussed by Winkler who notes Celsus' charge that "Mary Magdalene's encounter with the risen Jesus was only the ονειρωγμος [dream-working, *my note*] of a sexually excited woman." *Magika Hiera*, 230.

"Sorcerers offered spells for conjuring up prophetic dreams and considered the arts of 'dream-seeking' and 'dream-sending' to be a central part of their business." *Pagans and Christians*, 151.

The ritual of dream sending, ονειροπομπεια (oneiropompeia), is well attested in the Greek magical papyri. *Léxico de magia y religión en los papiros mágicos griegos*, 94.

43   φασκοντες **εξουσιαν** εχειν...των αρχωντων: "alleging

they…have **authority**…of the princes…"

The princes over which the Carpocratians had authority were demonic entities as at Mark 3:22 where the scribes accuse Jesus of expelling demons by his authority over "the prince of demons."

44 **μαγικη τεχνη** ας λεγομεν δυναμεις πεποιηκεναι: "having performed what we call powerful works by **magical art**…? *Apology* 30.1.

45 και αι αδιαφθορων παιδων **εποπτευσεις**: "and **haruspexy** using uncorrupted children…"

Munier, whose Greek text I have used, translates this phrase "les divinations faites sur les entrailles d'enfants innocents…" i.e., "divination using the entrails of innocent children…" *Saint Justin Apologie pour les Chrétiens*, 60.

Since Justin is adducing the evocation of souls of the dead as proof of a conscious afterlife, this translation, which imputes the murder of children to pagan magicians, is probably correct. The verb Justin uses, εποπτευω, is used (as previously noted) in the mystery cults for revelation of ultimate truth, and if by such usage Justin implies that the ultimate revelation for pagans was to be glimpsed in the guts of dead children it comes as little surprise that he finally managed to get himself executed.

46 δαιμονοληπτος, literally "demonseized." Justin is arguing that the pagan oracles are possessed by the souls of dead humans.

47 "Overturning the lamp" so that the participants could engage in evil under the cover of darkness.

48 *Apology* 29.2.

49 2 Peter 2:1-2, 12-14, Jude 10, 18.

50 *Lost Christianities*, 197-202.

Eusebius reports that Christians were repeatedly accused of cannibalism: *Ecclesiastical History* IV, 7.11, V, 1.14, 52.

Chapter Thirteen:
The Beloved Disciple

*A certain young man had gone along with him, wearing nothing but a
linen cloth over his naked body, and they seized him, but he ran away
naked, leaving them holding the linen cloth.*

Mark 14:51-52

Carpocrates and his gospel

From reading Clement's letter to Theodore, it appears that the
Carpocratians believed Jesus' relationship with his disciples —or at
least *one* of his disciples— was sexual in nature. Carpocrates may have
been among the first known to us to pose the poisoned question of
Jesus' sexuality, but he was far from being the last. However, given the
hysterical reaction in the New Testament academy, one could be
forgiven for thinking that Smith's discovery had raised some ridiculous
notion previously uncontemplated in the history of the world.[1]

Clement's dismissal of the Carpocratians as evil men misled by the
Devil is a bit too *pro forma*. It was, as we know from other contexts, the
conventional Christian response to all with whom they disagreed. The
obvious solution to the problem of Carpocrates' version of Mark
would have been to deny its authenticity, to claim —as have some
modern churchmen— that it was a forgery. We can only wonder why
Clement did not resort to that explanation. Did Theodore already

know the *Secret Gospel* to be authentic? Was there some factual basis for the Carpocratian's interpretation of the relation between Jesus and the young man of *Secret Mark*?

No answer to those questions can be attempted without first putting Clement's missing verses, italicized for ease of identification, back into the relevant section of canonical Mark:

> As he set out on the road, a man came running up to him and fell on his knees before him and asked him, "Good Teacher, what must I do to receive eternal life?" But Jesus said to him, "Why do you call me good? No one is good except God alone. You know the commandments: do not murder, do not commit adultery, do not steal, do not give false testimony, do not commit fraud, honor your father and your mother."
>
> He said to him, "Teacher, I have observed all these things since my childhood." Gazing at him attentively, Jesus loved him[2], and said to him, "You're missing one thing. Go sell everything you have and give it to the poor and you will have treasure in heaven. Come follow me." But he was appalled by Jesus' words and he went away offended, for he owned many possessions.
>
> Then Jesus looked from person to person and said to his disciples, "How hard it will be for those who have wealth to enter the kingdom of God!"
>
> The disciples were astounded by his words, but Jesus said to them again, "Children, how hard it is to enter the kingdom of God! It is easier for a camel to go through the eye of a needle than for a rich man to enter the kingdom of God!" They were overwhelmed with amazement and began saying to one another, "Who can be saved?" Looking at them intently, Jesus said, "Impossible for men, but not for God! For God, anything is possible."
>
> Peter began to say to him, "Look, we have given up everything and followed you!"

Jesus answered, "Truly I say to you, there is no one who has left house or brothers or sisters or mother or father or children or fields on my account and on account of the good news who will not receive a hundred times as much now in this present time, houses and brothers and sisters and mothers and children and fields —with persecutions— and in the age to come eternal life. But many who are first will be last, and the last will be first."

They were on the road going up into Jerusalem and Jesus was going ahead of them. They were amazed, and those who followed were afraid. He took the twelve aside again and began to tell them about the things that were soon to happen to him. "Look, we are going up to Jerusalem and the son of man will be handed over to the chief priests and the scribes and they will condemn him to death and they will hand him over to the Romans. They will ridicule him and spit on him and whip him and kill him, and after three days he will rise."

And they came to Bethany³ and a certain woman whose brother had died came out and threw herself before Jesus and said to him, "Son of David, have mercy on me." ⁴ But the disciples rebuked her. ⁵ Becoming angry, Jesus went off after her ⁶ into the garden where the tomb was and suddenly there was heard coming from the tomb a loud voice. Approaching, Jesus rolled away the stone from the door of the tomb and immediately going into where the young man was, he stretched out his hand and raised him, holding his hand. And gazing at him, the young man loved him and began to plead with him that he might be with him.

And going from the tomb, they went into the young man's house, for he was rich. After six days, Jesus summoned him, and when evening came, the young man went to him wearing a linen cloth over his naked body and he stayed with him that night for Jesus taught him the mystery of the kingdom of God. And then arising, he went to the far side of the Jordan.

James and John, the sons of Zebedee, approached him and said to him, "Teacher, we want you to do whatever we ask you."

He said, "What do you want me to do for you?"

They said to him, "Let us sit, one at your right hand and one at your left in your glory."

But Jesus said to them, "You don't know what it is you're

asking for. Can you drink from the cup I drink or be baptized with the baptism with which I will be baptized?"

They said to him, "We can."

So Jesus said to them, "The cup from which I drink, you will drink, and the baptism with which I am baptized, you will be baptized. But to sit at my right or at my left is not for me to give, but for those for whom it has been prepared."

Now when the ten heard, they became incensed at James and John. Calling them all before him, Jesus said to them, "You know that those who appear to rule over the Gentiles lord it over them, and their great men exercise authority over them, but that is not how it is among you. Whoever wants to become great among you will be your servant, and whoever wants to be first among you will be a slave to everyone, because the son of man came not to be served, but to serve and to give his life as the price paid for many."

They came to Jericho, *and the sister of the young man that Jesus loved and his mother and Salome were there, but Jesus did not agree to see them.* [7] And as he was leaving Jericho with his disciples and a large crowd, a blind beggar, Bartimaeus, [8] the son of Timaeus, was sitting by the road. When he heard that it was Jesus of Nazareth, he began to shout out, saying, "Son of David, Jesus, take pity on me!" Many sternly warned him to shut up, but he shouted out even louder, "Son of David, take pity on me!"

So Jesus stopped and said, "Call him over." So they summoned the blind man, saying, "Take heart! Get up, he's calling you!"

Throwing aside his coat, he got to his feet and went toward Jesus and Jesus said to him, "What do you want me to do for you?" The blind man said to him, "Rabbouni, restore my sight!"

Jesus said to him, "Go. Your trust has healed you." And immediately his sight was restored and he followed him down the road.

Mark 10:17-52

The restoration of the verses quoted by Clement results in a more coherent story, but one which is still incomplete. At least with the missing verses back in place, we are now able to detect a *frame*, a parallel construction *Secret Mark* has used to identify a single character, the young man beloved by Jesus. The frame consists of looks of mutual love, and the parallelism between the two passages is too obvious to miss:

ο δε Ισους εμβλεψας αυτω ηγαπησεν αυτον...

(Mark 10:21)

ο δε νεανισκος εμβλεψας αυτω ηγαπησεν αυτον...

(*Secret Mark*)

Jesus looked at him (the young man) and loved him...

(Mark 10:21)

the young man looked at him (Jesus) and loved him...

(*Secret Mark*)

While it is true that the *canonical* gospel of Mark does not specify the age of the man who met Jesus on the road to Jerusalem, the parallel account in Matthew *twice* specifies that he was a young man [9] —it is clear that both *Secret Mark* and Matthew preserve the earliest tradition in this case, namely that the man who met Jesus on the road was both *young* and *rich*.

There is, however, in addition to Matthew and *Secret Mark*, another witness who will testify to both the youth of the rich man of Mark's gospel, as well as the purpose of Jesus' invitation to become his follower, and this third witness is none other than Clement of Alexandria.

Still preserved among Clement's writings is a sermon on the Christian attitude toward wealth, *The Rich Man's Salvation*. In the course of his extended discussion, Clement expounds on many biblical passages, particularly on the encounter on the road between Jesus and the rich young man.

It is clear that Clement's letter is directed toward a wealthy spiritual upperclass, and his argument correspondingly concerns spiritual truths to be understood "not in a clumsy way, nor like common people, nor in an unenlightened way," [10] for "in fact there are already some, the most elite of the elite, [11] and all the more so for being less noticeable…who in the depth of their mind conceal the inexpressible mysteries," [12] "the spirit of the Savior and the secret of his thought." [13] Of the common run of mankind he baldly states "for those uninitiated in the truth, I care little." [14]

It is plain that Clement has in mind a *young* rich man, a man subject to the "lusts born from youth…in youthful exuberance and the burning of youthful passions,"[15] but who has nevertheless obeyed the commands "from childhood."[16] Such a man is invited, "Behold the mysteries of love, and then you will see a vision of the bosom of the Father[17] whom the only begotten God alone revealed" —the only begotten God is in the bosom of the Father, even as Lazarus is in the bosom of Abraham, and the beloved disciple is in the bosom of Jesus.[18] The salvation of such a man, like the raising of Lazarus, would be "a notable example of regeneration, a monument of a resurrection seen."[19] As is evident from the language of his sermon, Clement understood that the rich man who met Jesus on the road was *young*. So

Lazarus, the rich young ruler

Other elements of the story now make more sense. The apostle Peter —who is repeatedly associated with the beloved disciple[20] — tells Jesus, "We have given up *everything* and followed you," and is told by way of reply that he will receive eternal life. The rich young man asks Jesus what he must do to obtain eternal life and is told, "Sell *everything* you have." When the rich young man goes away angry, Jesus observes how difficult it will be for a rich man to enter the kingdom —what rich man could he have had in mind except the rich young man he has gazed upon and loved— but follows up this remark with the pregnant observation, "For God, anything is possible."

In point of fact, the rich young man gives up his possessions, not by selling them, but by dying. But Jesus is not thwarted. He raises the young man from the dead, and at that moment the youth gazes upon the face of the Good Teacher and loves him. The young man will enter the kingdom after all, but in the way a camel might pass through the eye of a needle, by a miracle. This stunning reversal of fortune illuminates the saying, "Many who are first will be last, and the last will be first." Who better to exemplify this situation than the *last* of the disciples Jesus personally selects, who ranks *first* in Jesus' affection, called by him from the grave only days before Jesus' own death, and initiated by Jesus personally into the kingdom of God?

The theme of the beloved disciple is developed most completely by the gospel of John,[21] and it is to that source we must turn next in search of the identity of the rich young man.

It is curious that the gospel of Mark, widely regarded as the first of the canonical gospels to be written and therefore the most primitive record of the early tradition, should share much of its structure with the gospel of John, the last to be written and certainly the most developed theologically. On the basis of these similarities, Koester concludes,

> The similarities of the Johannine and Markan passion narratives suggest that the author of the Fourth Gospel used a written narrative source also for the second part of his writing. This assumption is confirmed by several agreements between John and the Gospel of Peter, the third independent witness of this passion narrative and its development on the basis of scriptural exegesis.[22]

It is probable that Mark and John were both drawn independently from a preexisting written source since neither Mark nor John shows any sign of familiarity with the other's gospel. If that is the case, we would expect to find important similarities between the accounts of the beloved disciple in John and the young man beloved by Jesus in Mark. Bearing that in mind, consider the story of the raising of Lazarus:

> A certain Lazarus from Bethany, from the village of Mary and Martha, his sister, was sick. This was the Mary who anointed the Lord with perfume and dried his feet with her hair. Her brother Lazarus fell sick. So the sisters sent for him, saying, "Listen, Lord, the one you love is sick."[23]
> But when Jesus heard, he said to her, "This sickness will not result in death, but for the glory of God, so the son of God may be glorified because of it. For Jesus loved Martha and her sister and Lazarus even though when he heard he was sick he stayed in the place he was for two days. After that, he said to his disciples, "Let's go into Judea again."
> The disciples were saying to him, "Rabbi, the Jews were just

now seeking to stone you and you're going there again?"

Jesus answered, "Are there not twelve hours of daylight? Whoever walks in the daylight does not trip because he sees the light of this world. But whoever walks at night trips, because the light is not in him." [24] He said these things and after this he said to them, "Lazarus our friend[25] has fallen asleep, but I am going there and I will wake him."

Therefore the disciples said to him, "Lord, if he has fallen asleep he will recover."

Jesus had spoken about his death, but they thought he was speaking about the repose of sleep. Then Jesus spoke to them plainly, "Lazarus has died, and for your sake I'm glad that we were not there so that you may believe. But let's go to him."

When Jesus arrived, he found him already four days in the tomb. Bethany was near Jerusalem, about two miles away. Many of the Jews had come out to Martha and Mary to console them about their brother.

When Martha heard that Jesus was on his way, she went to meet him, but Mary sat at home. Martha said to Jesus, "Lord, if you had been here, my brother would not have died, but even now I know that whatever you ask of God, God will grant you."

Jesus said to her, "Your brother will be raised."

Martha said to him, "I know he will be raised in the resurrection on the last day."

Jesus said to her, "I am the resurrection and the life. The one who believes in me will live even if he dies, and everyone who lives and believes in me will not die for all ages. Do you believe this?"

She said to him, "Yes, Lord. I have believed that you are the Christ, the Son of God, the One coming into the world."

And when she said this, she went and called Mary her sister and told her privately, "The Teacher is here and is calling you." And when she heard that, she got up quickly and went to him. Jesus had not come to the village yet, but was still in the place where Martha met him. The Jews who were with her in the house, and those comforting her, saw Mary get up suddenly and leave. They followed her, thinking that she was going to the tomb to cry there.

When Mary came to where Jesus was and saw him, she fell at his feet and said to him, "Lord, if only you had been here, my brother would not have died."

When Jesus saw her crying and the Jews who came with her crying, he was deeply moved by the spirit and disturbed within himself[26] and he said, "Where have you laid him?"

They said to him, "Lord, come and see." Jesus began to cry.

The Jews said, "See how he loved him!" [27] But some of them said, "Couldn't he who opened the blind man's eyes have done something so he might not have died?"

Then Jesus, again deeply moved within himself,[28] came to the tomb. It was a cave and a stone was laying over it. Jesus said, "Take away the stone!"

Martha, the sister of the dead man, said to him, "Lord, by now he stinks, for it is four days!"

Jesus said to her, "Did I not tell you that if you believed you would see the glory of God?" So they removed the stone and Jesus raised his eyes and said, "Father, I thank you because you heard me. I knew that you always hear me, but for the sake of the crowd standing here I said it so they may believe that you sent me."

And when he had said these things, he called out with a loud voice, "Lazarus! Out here!" The dead man came out, his hands and feet wrapped with bindings and his face wrapped up in a cloth. Jesus said to them, "Unwrap him and let him go."

John 11:1-44

The account of Lazarus shares a remarkable number of similarities with the story of the rich young man recounted in Mark.[29] Both stories are set at the same point in Jesus' career, a time of increasing hostility between Jesus and the temple officials,[30] a circumstance which provokes high anxiety among the disciples.[31] The healing of blind

Bartimaeus, completely described in Mark, is alluded to in John.[32] The man who meets Jesus on the road is evidently young and in good health —he *ran up* to Jesus— and Lazarus is evidently young and in good health, for the implication is that he is expected to recover from his illness.[33] The young man of Mark is rich; Lazarus is also a man of means: he owns a house, is buried in a tomb, his funeral is well-attended, and his sister Mary anoints Jesus' feet with perfume worth 300 denarii, the equivalent of a year's wages for a common laborer.[34] Lazarus and his sisters know Jesus as *The Teacher*, the rich man of Mark addresses Jesus by the same title.[35] Both the rich man of Mark and Lazarus are pious. Mark specifies that he is observant, and the fact that "many of the Jews" came down from Jerusalem to console Lazarus' sisters indicates that the family is both well-known and of good reputation within a devout community.[36] In Mark, Jesus says that anything is possible for God, in John's account Martha says that whatever Jesus wants, God will grant him.[37]

In a series of recently published essays, Marvin Meyer notes a number of additional parallels between *Secret Mark* and the gospel of John: the youth is from Bethany, his sister greets Jesus, a loud voice is mentioned, the stone sealing the tomb is removed, after which Jesus raises the youth.[38]

The notion that there might have been *two* separate youths, both raised at the same point in Jesus' career, and both sharing so many characteristics and circumstances, verges on the absurd. The conclusion is obvious: *the rich young man of both the gospel of Mark and of* Secret Mark, *and Lazarus of the gospel of John are one and the same.*

Having established Lazarus' identity and the circumstances of his discipleship with a high degree of certainty, let us consider his role in the week preceding Jesus' arrest as described in the gospel of John:

> Many from among the Jews who had come to console Mary and witnessed what he did believed in him, but some from among them went to the Pharisees and told them what Jesus had done.
>
> Therefore the chief priests and the Pharisees assembled the High Council and they said, "What will we do? This man is performing many signs! If we tolerate him like this, everyone will believe in him and the Romans will come and take over both our holy place and our people!"
>
> But one of them, Caiaphas, being the High Priest that year, said to them, "You don't understand anything! You don't even take into account that it is more advantageous for you that one man die for the people than to have the whole nation destroyed!"
>
> He did not say this of his own accord, but being High Priest that year, he prophesied that Jesus was about to die for the nation, and not only for the nation, but to gather together God's dispersed children into one.
>
> So from that day forward they planned how they might kill him.
>
> Therefore Jesus no longer went around publicly among the Jews, but went from there into the district adjoining the wilderness, into a town called Ephraim, and stayed there with his disciples.
>
> The Passover of the Jews was near and many went up to Jerusalem from the surrounding country so they could purify themselves. They were looking for Jesus and were saying to one another as they stood in the temple, "What do you think? Will he dare come to the festival?" For the chief priests and the Pharisees had issued orders that anyone who knew where he was should reveal it so they could arrest him.[39]
>
> Consequently, six days before Passover, Jesus came to Bethany, where Lazarus was, [40] who Jesus had raised from the dead. They

made a feast for him there. Martha served and Lazarus was one of those reclining with him. Mary took a litra[41] of ointment, unadulterated spikenard —very valuable— and anointed Jesus' feet with it and wiped his feet dry with her hair. The house was filled with the fragrance of the ointment.

A great multitude of the Jews found out he was there and came out, not only because of Jesus, but also that they might catch sight of Lazarus, who he had raised from the dead. So the chief priests planned on killing Lazarus as well, for because of him many of the Jews were breaking ranks and were beginning to believe in Jesus.

For the crowd that had been with him when he called Lazarus from the tomb and raised him from the dead kept attesting to the event. That is why the crowd went out to meet him, because they heard that he had performed the sign. Then the Pharisees said to each other,[42] "You see! It's no use! Look, the whole world has gone off after him!" [43]

John 11:45-12:3, 9-11, 17-19

From this account it is evident that Lazarus has become the main exhibit of Jesus' claim to miracle working, and by extension, the entire content of Jesus' message. Not discounting Jesus' true feelings for Lazarus which, as I have noted, are multiply attested, his resurrection is an occasion for belief —"so the son of God may be glorified because of it."[44]

Unfortunately for the temple authorities, word spread rapidly among the Passover crowds, a multitude that numbered in the hundreds of thousands, so that many who did not see the resurrection of Lazarus were thronging to Jesus, hoping to catch sight of Lazarus, who, *dressed in a burial shroud*, publicly announced the reality of the miracle, and, if they were lucky, perhaps witness another wondrous sign. The Jewish authorities feared that from the agitation over Jesus would spring disorder, from disorder, rioting, and from rioting, open rebellion.[45]

The identity of Lazarus as the rich young man, the disciple Jesus loved, also clears up a particularly enigmatic passage in the gospel of Mark —a passage which Marvin Meyer has described as "an interpretive nightmare" [46] — the mention of an event that happened during Jesus' arrest by the temple police:

> And they all fled, deserting him. A certain young man had gone along with him,[47] wearing nothing but a linen cloth over his naked body, and they seized him, but he ran away naked, leaving them holding the linen cloth.
>
> Mark 14:51-52

More parallels now appear between Jesus and the young man who flees naked at the time of his arrest, parallels noted with particular insight by Albert Van Hoye, who pointed out that the same verb, κρατεω (krateô), *seize*, is used both of the arrest of Jesus and the attempted arrest of the young man in the garden. This confirms the identity of the young man in the garden as Lazarus: Jesus and Lazarus are the two marked for death by the temple authorities (John 11:53, 12:10), and are therefore the two seized by the temple police in the garden. Jesus is retained, Lazarus escapes.

The young man leaves behind a *linen cloth* as he flees naked; the same word, σινδων (sindôn), is used of the young man's clothing in Mark —as well as in *Secret Mark*— and of Jesus' burial garment.[48] Van Hoye also noted the similarity between the young man, νεανισκος (*neaniskos*), in the garden of Gethsemane and the young man in the empty tomb.[49]

244

The same verb, περιβαλλω (periballô), *wrap up in*, is used to describe the wearing of the linen garment by the youth in the garden, and the wearing of the white robe by the youth in the tomb.[50] Van Hoye concluded, "There is therefore reason to think that the numerous verbal correspondences which we have noted are not the result of pure chance, but manifest an intention." [51]

Indeed the numerous verbal correspondences point to a specific individual —well known to the primitive community— who remains unnamed in Mark, but identified by name in John: Lazarus. The young man in the garden is Lazarus, still dressed in a linen burial shroud. To my knowledge, both Miles Fowler and Michael Haren have separately suggested this identification. Fowler asks,

> How would a crowd recognize which person standing among the numerous followers of Jesus is Lazarus? Mark 14:51 provides the answer that there could be no more impressive identification of Lazarus, nor any more vivid symbol of his resurrection, than his wearing a burial shroud.[52]

To this Haren adds,

> The question must arise whether the manifestation of the glory was to be confined to Bethany or whether it was contemplated presenting Lazarus, dramatically and dressed so that he would instantly proclaim the miracle, in Jerusalem itself. Alternatively or concurrently, if, as the Gospels insist, Jesus was reconciled to or intent upon his own sacrifice, the prospect that Lazarus would be presented in Jerusalem as a sign of God's power might have been a central part of the mechanism by which the Jewish authorities were utterly drawn to act.[53]

245

The σινδων (*sindôn*), or *linen shroud*, worn by Lazarus in the garden is the same garment worn by the young man of *Secret Mark* who comes to Jesus by night, and by Jesus himself at the time of his burial according to Matthew 27:59.[54] Following Morton Smith, Marvin Meyer associates the shroud with a secret baptismal rite,[55] but as pointed out by Paul Achtemeier in a critique of Smith's interpretive methodology, baptism is never mentioned in *Secret Mark*,[56] and for whatever it's worth, John's gospel appears to claim that Jesus himself did not baptize anyone.[57] Early Christians were baptized *nude*, not while wearing shrouds.

The drinking of the cup and sharing in the baptism mentioned in Mark 10:38-39 is unlikely to have been meant literally. If those who would share in Jesus' heavenly glory must expect to share in his earthly fate, then *baptism* in that context is a metaphor for plunging into death so as to be raised to life, not a baptism in water —"John's baptism."[58]

That the believer will share Jesus' fate *in its totality*, both his agony and its reward, seems to be the clear message of such passages as Romans 6:5 and 2 Corinthians 4:10-11, and may go far to explain why early Christians sought martyrdom. In Paul's words, "What you sow is not made alive unless first it dies."[59] Be that as it may, it seems unlikely that the linen garment of Lazarus —who is both the young man of Mark 14:51-52, and the young man of *Secret Mark* who came to Jesus by night— had anything at all to do with baptism. In my opinion, the reconstruction of events proposed by Fowler and Haren makes infinitely more sense: the wearing of the shroud publicly announced the reality of the miracle of Lazarus' resurrection.

According to the gospel of John, Peter and the beloved disciple are the first men to witness the empty tomb, but the beloved disciple, who by now has given ample evidence that he is limber and fleet of foot, beats Peter to the tomb, becoming the first male witness of the resurrection.[60] It is an impossible coincidence that the women who first arrive at Jesus' tomb find there "a *young man* clothed in a white robe" who announces to them, "He has been raised. He is not here."[61]

It seems likely that the raising of Lazarus was seen by the inner circle as an enacted parable of Jesus' own resurrection. The observation that our texts reveal so many parallels between the raising of Lazarus and the resurrection of Jesus suggests that the first disciples were eager to find and record such correspondences. The eventual death of Lazarus is the raison d'être for the composition of the second ending of the gospel of John: his death is thought by some to put the post-resurrection life of Jesus himself in question.

> Turning around, Peter saw the disciple Jesus loved following them, the one who leaned against Jesus' chest during the supper and said, "Lord, who is the one betraying you?" When Peter saw him, he said to Jesus, "Lord, what about him?"
> Jesus said to him, "If I wish for him to remain until I come, what do you care? You follow me." Therefore the word went out among the brothers that that disciple would not die. But Jesus did not say of him, "He will not die," but "If I wish for him to remain until I come, what do you care?"
>
> John 21:20-23

It is likely that it was Peter himself who put the word out that the beloved disciple would not die, and possibly based his own faith on that belief. When the beloved disciple identified the stranger on the shore as the risen Lord, Peter "heard that it was the Lord," threw on some clothes, jumped into the sea, and swam to shore rather than wait for the boat.[62] Peter himself is the most likely candidate for the formulation and preservation of the story of Jesus and his beloved disciple. As Miles Fowler notes, "John 21:23a suggests that there is speculation within the earliest Jesus movement —especially by Peter— regarding the mortality of this disciple, whoever he is...if, perhaps even in historical fact, Peter went around saying that a certain youth would never die, and that youth did die, such an embarrassment might explain why the synoptic gospels omit stories about Jesus raising his friend from the dead."

Clement is probably accurate when he says that Mark wrote down Jesus' activities "while Peter was in Rome." The *Secret Gospel* likely contained a complete recounting of the story of Jesus and Lazarus, part of which —a love story perhaps?— was subsequently deleted to protect the sensibilities of the church. Later writers, unfamiliar with the story or uncomfortable with its details, ignored it. It has no doubt struck many as strange that the story of Lazarus, one of the most emotionally resonant of all the gospel stories, appears only in John, and even there it is incompletely told.

Notes

1   John Dominic Crossan: "...canonical Mark is a censored version of Secret Mark...it was probably used in the nude baptismal practice of his community and thereby received an erotic interpretation among some believers. The second century Carpocratians known to Clement were not, in other words, the only or even the first early Christians with homosexual understandings of such baptisms. Proto-Carpocratians existed, as it were, within the immediate time and place of Mark's first composition...and for that reason, the story was excised

completely from the second edition, the one we call canonical Mark." *The Historical Jesus*, 329.

2   ο δε Ιησους εμβλεψας αυτω **ηγαπησεν** αυτον: "Gazing at him attentively, Jesus **loved** him…"

The verb αγαπαω can also mean *caress*; a possible alternate translation would be, "Gazing at him attentively, Jesus *caressed* him…" Compare the note in Danker's *Greek-English Lexicon*, 5. A consensus of Sunday school scholarship has long held that αγαπη (agapê) and its cognates refer to a pure and ethereal *love-of-God-for-man*, a platitude that has been repeated for so long and so often that it has become an *idée fixe* which fairly begs to be demolished.

A closely related word, αγαπημα, means *darling*. John Boswell's trenchant observation on the Greek vocabulary of love may well apply here: "Only a naïve and ill-informed optimism assumes that any word or expression in one language can be accurately rendered in another…" *Same Sex Unions in Premodern Europe*, 3.

3   Canonical Mark mentions Bethany at 11:1, 11-12. Matthew omits any mention of Bethany (21:1) and Luke rephrases the passage while retaining a mention of the village (19:28-29).

4   See **Appendix A** for a discussion of "son of David."

5   Compare the rebuke at Mark 10:13.

6   **οργισθεις** ο Ιησους απηλθεν μετ' αυτης εις τον κηπον: "**Becoming angry**, Jesus went off after her into the garden…"

As Meyer notes, οργιζω, *become angry*, is a synonym of εμβριμαομαι, *become disturbed*, the verb used in the gospel of John (11:33) of Jesus' emotional reaction to Lazarus' death. *Secret Gospels*, 139.

As is well known, John has Jesus buried in a garden tomb (John 19:41), establishing yet another verbal parallel in the story of Jesus and the rich young man of *Secret Mark*.

7   John Dominic Crossan, who has published a valuable analysis of

Secret Mark, believes the restored text is still deficient at this point: "After Jesus refused to see the women something *else* must have been included –there is no narrative point to the text as it stands…I conclude that Mark 10:46 knew a more original text in which there was mention of something which happened to Jesus at Jericho. But that means that Mark 10:46 is an even more expurgated version of that censored event than is present in S[ecret] G[ospel of] M[ark] 5." *Four Other Gospels*, 74-75.

8 Luke has the miracle occur as Jesus is *approaching* Jericho (Luke 18:35).

Matthew, who characteristically multiplies the numbers of healed (compare Mark 7:31-37 with Matthew 15:29-31), has *two* blind men (20:29).

9 λεγει αυτω **ο νεανισκος** παντα ταυτα εφυλαξα: "**the young man** said to him, 'I have observed all these things…'" (Matthew 19:20), ακουσας δε **ο νεανισκος** τον λογον απηλθεν λυπουμενος: "when **the young man** heard what [Jesus] said, he went away offended…" (Matthew 19:22).

10 μη σκαιως μηδε αγοροικως μηδε **σαρκινως**: "not in a clumsy way, nor like common people, nor **in an unenlightened way**…" (306) Literally "in a fleshly way," as at 1 Corinthians 3:1, where it is the opposite of "spiritual," i.e., *enlightened* by the spirit. The text of *The Rich Man's Salvation* I have used is the accessible Loeb library version. The relevant page numbers are indicated.

11 των εκλεκτων **εκλεκτοτεροι**: "**the most elite** of the elite," literally *the most elect of the elect* spiritually (344).

12 τα ανεκλαλητα **μυστερια**: "the inexpressible **mysteries**…" (344)

13 **το** της γνωμης **απορρητον**: "**the secret** of his thought…" (282) Απορρητος, *that which is not to be spoken.* The neuter form, το απορρητον can mean *state secret.*

14 **των δε αμυητων** της αληθειας ολιγον μοι μελει: "for those

uninitiated in the truth, I care little" (274).

15   επιθυμιαι τικτουσι **νεανισκαι**...εν σκιρτηματι **νεοτησιω**...:
     "lusts born **from youth**...in **youthful** exuberance..." (286)

16   εκ νεοτητος: "from childhood," (286) Clement is quoting from
     Mark 10:20 where the rich man assures Jesus that he has observed
     the commandments "from my childhood."

17   τοτε **εποπτευσεις** τον κολπον του πατρος: "then **you will
     see a vision** of the bosom of the Father..." (346) From
     εποπτευω, *to see a vision*, a term familiar in the mystery cults and
     much beloved by Clement.

18   The passage is a concatenation of New Testament references:
     μονογενης θεος ο ων **εις τον κολπον** του πατρος: "the only
     begotten God who is **in the bosom** of the Father" (John 1:18),
     Lazarus is carried by angels to Abraham's bosom (Luke 16:22),
     the beloved disciple leans on Jesus' bosom (John 13:23).

19   μεγα γνωρισμα παλιγγενεσιας τροπαιον αναστασεως
     βλεπομενης: "a notable example of regeneration, a monument
     of a resurrection **seen**." (364) Clement's immediate reference is
     to the legend of John and the salvation of the robber, a story
     repeated by Eusebius, but contains a reference to Lazarus, whose
     resurrection was *seen*, is contrasted with that of Jesus, who no
     one (according to the canonical gospels) directly witnessed.

20   As at John 13:23-24, 21:7, 20-22.

21   There are six references to the beloved disciple, all occurring late
     in the gospel: John 13:23, 19:26, 21:7, 20 in which he is ον **ηγαπα**:
     "the one **he loved**," and John 20:2 in which he is ον **εφιλει**: "the
     one **he loved**." These are the verbal equivalents of αγαπη, *love*,
     and φιλια, *affection* or *devotion*.

The first identification of the apostle John as the "beloved
disciple" occurs well into the 2nd century; it is an attempt by the
early church to validate the gospel as apostolic, and takes no
precedence over the internal evidence of the texts. Bart Ehrman:

"...sometime in the second century, when proto-orthodox Christians recognized the need for *apostolic* authorities, they attributed these books to apostles (Matthew and John) and close acquaintances of apostles..." *Lost Christianities*, 235. I will expend no further ink or effort to debunk the myth that John was either the author of the fourth gospel or the beloved disciple. Neither legend enjoys any factual support.

22　*Ancient Christian Gospels*, 253.

The *Gospel of Peter* is a fragmentary early Greek gospel, discovered in Akhmim, Egypt, in 1886, and published in 1892. It recounts a passion narrative covering the trial, crucifixion, death, and burial of Jesus. It contains numerous parallels with the canonical gospels as well as some fantastic elaborations, the most famous of which is a speaking cross that follows the risen Jesus out of the tomb.

23　The *first* time Jesus' love for Lazarus is specified.

24　The implication seems to be that those with the inner light can walk without tripping day or night. Perhaps Jesus and the disciples went to Bethany under cover of darkness.

25　The *second* reference to Lazarus as beloved: Λαζαρος ο **φιλος** ημων: "Lazarus our **friend**..."

Φιλος (philos) is more intimate than our *friend*; it refers to one *beloved, dear,* to whom one is *devoted*. Aristotle's definition was "one soul inhabiting two bodies," i.e., "soulmates." The related verb, φιλεω, means not only to *love*, but to *kiss* as at Mark 14:44: ον αν **φιληςω** αυτος εστιν: "whoever **I kiss**, that's him..." The related noun, φιλημα, means *kiss*, as at Romans 16:16: "Greet one another with a holy kiss."

The idea that the verb refers always to platonic love is belied by its use in the Septuagint where the demon Asmodeus' feelings for the woman Sara cause him to kill her suitors οτι δαιμονιον **φιλει** αυτην: "because the demon **loves** her."

26　ενεβριμησατο τω πνευματιχ και **εταραξεν** εαυτον: "he was **deeply moved** by the spirit and **disturbed** within himself..."

Campbell Bonner's suggested translation: "the Spirit set him in a frenzy and he threw himself into disorder" emphasizes one of the "familiar features of the ordinary wonderworker's manner of operation." Of εμβριμαομαι, which means *snort* when applied to horses, Bonner notes, "when used of the behavior of a prophet, magician, or wonderworker, there is a strong presumption that they [εμβριμαομαι and ταρασσω, *my note*] imply frenzy or raving." *Harvard Theological Review* 20: 171-181.

27   The *third* time Jesus' love for Lazarus is noted. Lazarus' family, Jesus himself, and even strangers recognized a special relationship between Jesus and Lazarus.

28   **εμβριμωμενος** εν εαυτω: "**deeply moved** within himself" or as Bonner would have it, "in suppressed frenzy."

29   Miles Fowler: "...the echoes of Secret Mark within canonical Mark help tell a coherent tale, and, what is more, tell one that is not merely parallel to but continuous with the story of Lazarus in John." *Journal of Higher Criticism* 5: 3.

30   Mark 10:33, John 11:53, 57.

31   Mark 10:32, John 11:16.

32   Mark 10:46-52, John 11:37.

33   Mark 10:17, John 11:4. Matthew 19:20, 22, as already noted, specifies that the man on the road is a νεανισκος (neaniskos), a *young man*. In John, the beloved disciple outruns Peter, arriving first at Jesus' tomb (John 20:4), behavior consistent with youth.

34   Mark 10:22, John 11:19, 31, 38, 12:3-5.

35   Mark 10:17, John 11:28.

36   Mark 10:20, John 11:19.

It has been suggested that Lazarus was the disciple known to the High Priest –possibly through family connections– who accompanied Peter during Jesus' hearing before the Jewish authorities (John 18:15). If Lazarus' family was of the Judean priestly caste, it may have been deemed expedient to release him and concentrate on Jesus instead, the *Galilean* ringleader of the opposition. To have delivered over a family member to the Roman authorities could have been seen as implicating the Jewish leadership in subversion at precisely the time the temple leadership was most anxious to distance themselves from such accusations –compare John 19:15, "We have no king but Caesar."

It should also be noted that in Luke's account (18:18) the young man, who according to John would have been Lazarus, is described as an αρχων, a *leader*. Miles Fowler, in the article referenced above, speculates that "the political connections of the young aristocrat" protected him from arrest by the temple authorities.

Josephus associates Galileans with revolt in the *Antiquities* (20.120-121).

37 Mark 10: 27, John 11:22.

38 John 11:1, 20, 39, 43, 44. *Secret Gospels: Essays on Thomas and the Secret Gospel of Mark*, 139.

39 Mark's account specifies that the authorities planned to arrest Jesus by stealth (11:18, 12:12, 14:1-2).

40 In canonical Mark, the account has been changed to make the house belong to Simon the leper (Mark 14:3).

41 A Roman pound. Quite a lot, in other words.

42 The block of text in John chapters 7-9 belongs to this part of the story. It both records the dispute over Jesus' authority as well as the story of Bartimaeus (9:1-41).

43 Compare "this damned crowd" in John 7:45-49 which has been dispatched to a different site in the gospel.

44 John 11:4, 15, 26-27, 42.

45 Matthew 27:24 specifies that Pilate washed his hands of *l'affaire Jesus* because he feared a riot was imminent.

According to John 11:47-48, fear of Roman intervention was the reason the Jewish authorities were finally moved to action.

46 *Secret Gospels*, 117.

47 και νεανισκος τις **συνηκολουθει** αυτω: "and a certain young man **had gone along with** him…"

The verb συνακολουθεω (sunakoloutheô), *to go along with*, is used also in Mark 5:37 in the following passage: ουκ αφηκεν ουδενα μετ' αυτον **συνακολουθησαι** ει μη τον Πετρον…: "he allowed no one but Peter…**to go along with** him…" That the verb marks an inner circle of disciples is shown by the fact that it is again Peter, James and John who accompany Jesus to the garden (Mark 14:33). Lazarus has joined this inner circle: he is the beloved who at Peter's behest asks who will betray Jesus (John 13:23-25), the one to whom Jesus entrusts his mother (John 19:26-27), and the first to identify the risen Jesus in Galilee (John 21:7).

The presence of Lazarus in the garden also solves the problem of the "missing witness": Jesus did not write the gospels, and the disciples who went with him into the garden on the night of his betrayal repeatedly fell asleep. Who saw that Jesus prayed and returned to find his disciples sleeping? *Lazarus*, the beloved disciple who stayed awake to keep vigil with him.

48 Mark 14:51: καταλιπων **την σινδονα** γυμνος εφυγεν: "he ran away naked, leaving them holding **the linen cloth**." Mark 15:46: αγορασας **σινδονα** καθελων αυτον ενειλησεν τη **σινδονι**: "he bought a **linen cloth** and took him down and wrapped him in the **linen cloth**…"

49 Mark 14:51, 16:5.

50 Mark 14:51, 16:5.

51 My translation of: "Il y a donc lieu de penser que les nombreaux contacts verbaux que nous avons relevés ne sont pas un pur effet du hazard, mais manifestent une intention" in "La fuite du jeune

homme nu (Mc 14,51-52)," *Biblica* 52:406.

52 Fowler, *Journal of Higher Criticism* 5/1: 3-22.

53 Haren, *Biblica* 79: 525-531.

54 λαβων το σωμα ο Ιωσεφ ενετυλιξεν αυτο εν **σινδονα** **καθαρα**: "taking the body, Joseph wrapped it in a clean **linen shroud**…"

55 "…the neaniskos participates in baptism as an experience of sharing in the suffering and death of Christ, and wears ritual clothing appropriate for such an experience." *Secret Gospels*, 124.

56 *Journal of Biblical Literature* 93: 625-628.

57 John 4:1-2.

Crossan: "Jesus, unlike John, was not a baptizer but a healer. The tradition, therefore, had no baptism-by-Jesus stories that could be used in their baptismal liturgies. But a story about a miraculous or physical raising from death could be used or created as a symbol for baptismal or spiritual raising from death." *The Historical Jesus*, 330.

58 Mark 11:30.

59 1 Corinthians 15:36. Paul's argument clearly indicates that Christians expected to share in the nature of Jesus' post-resurrection life (15:22-23, 42-53) as a reward for sharing in his suffering.

60 John 20:2-4.

61 Mark 16:5-6.

62 John 21:7-8.

Chapter Fourteen: On the Use of Boys in Magic.

After six days, Jesus summoned him and when evening came, the young man went to him wearing a linen cloth over his naked body and he stayed with him that night, for Jesus taught him the mystery of the kingdom of God.

Secret Gospel of Mark

It is possible, if not likely, that this intriguing passage from the *Secret Gospel of Mark* alludes to a rite of magical initiation, although given the poverty of the evidence any attempt to reconstruct such an event is obviously speculative. That said, the account contains the following telltale elements: (1) the *nocturnal* timing of the visit, (2) the *youth* of the subject, (3) the *linen* garment, (4) the *nakedness* of the subject, and (5) the connection with *mystery*.

The artificial distinction between religion and magic long maintained in New Testament studies has already been mentioned. New Testament scholars are traditionally loath to see any connection between Jesus' miracles and magical techniques, the unambiguous evidence of the gospels notwithstanding, but over the past several decades those arbitrary barriers have significantly eroded, a process both anticipated and hastened by Smith's *Jesus the Magician.*

The only specifically magical documents roughly contemporaneous with the time of Jesus are the magical papyri, preserved in Egypt by the vicissitudes of geography and weather, and brought to light by excavations over the past century or so. These documents, written in Greek or Coptic, or a mixture of both, are handbooks of magical technique that consist mostly of spells and instructions for casting them. Against the argument that the papyri were written too late to truly reflect the time of Jesus, I would offer this observation by Joshua Trachtenberg:

> However unorthodox in principle, magic is perhaps the most tradition-bound of cultural forms…As we have had occasion to note, magic is the most conservative of disciplines —like the law it clings to archaic forms long after they have lost currency.[1]

To posit a connection between Jesus of Nazareth and the magicians of Egypt and their techniques might seem at first to be the pursuit of an exegetical phantom, but it will be recalled that it is the New Testament itself that connects Jesus both with *magicians* and with *Egypt*.[2] It is also clear from the New Testament that early Christian converts far from Egypt possessed quantities of magical books,[3] in all probability not unlike the magical papyri known today, and Coptic Christians are known to have practiced magic into late antiquity.[4] Although the infancy narratives, discussed in Chapter Two, are clearly pious confabulations, the details of these stories obviously came from somewhere and it is likely that Matthew's account of magicians and Egypt reflects distant echoes of historical facts, namely early speculation about the source of Jesus' extraordinary power, a power which was being attributed by some to Egyptian magic.

The facticity of Jesus' miracles are not the concern of this book; I have taken the miracles at face value, neither tentatively accepting them as psychological aberrations, nor altogether denying them as quaint relics of an ignorant age. In any case, the fact remains that *there is no Jesus apart from miracles*: they are by far the best attested feature of his life —not even his opponents tried to deny their reality. [5] A Jesus with no wonders to perform is a historical perversion, as much a reflection of the materialist philosophy of our culture as of the superstition of his. Had Jesus no fame for performing wonders, it is doubtful whether there would be any such religion as Christianity or that the world would even recall his existence.[6]

In the excerpts from the magical papyri produced below, readers may judge for themselves how closely the contents of these texts match the elements identified above in the *Secret Gospel of Mark*.

And when evening came...

It is plain from the frequent mention of lamps in the papyri that much magical ritual took place at night. On this feature of the magician's work, the late Samson Eitrem noted,

> Lamp or lantern magic (Lampenzauber) plays a major role here as generally in Egyptian magic —for light, the nocturnal sun, was something to be exploited. The night with its horde of dead spirits and eerie ways —the night through which the sun god navigated in his vessel to reach the east through the dark kingdom of the underworld while the moon shone or the heavens were starry— offered the magician the best opportunity for exercising his art or arts.[7]

Nicodemus also came to Jesus by night and the subject of his inquiry was also how one entered the kingdom of God.[8]

The nocturnal workings of the magician are, in part, a simple reflection of human physiology: "In general the association between sleep, death, dreams, and night was tight."[9] The author of Matthew's gospel clearly considered dreams to be supernatural in origin.[10] The world of the New Testament, the world before artificial light, was literally a darker place, a place where night and the dreams that haunt it held a larger place in life.

The young man went to him wearing a linen cloth...

Another [invocation] to Helios:

Wrap a naked boy in linen from head to foot, clap [your hands] and ring a bell. Put the boy directly opposite the sun, and standing behind him, say the spell... [11]

Solomon's Seizure [which] works on both boys and men:

I adjure you by the holy gods, the heavenly gods, not to share the ritual of Solomon with anyone, nor to use it for trivialities...

...

Spell to be recited:

...Obey my holy voice because I call upon your holy names and make clear to me what I want [to know] through this X man or boy[12] ...inspire the X man or boy about that which I inquire...Come to me through the X man or boy and explain [everything] clearly and precisely to me because I speak the names which thrice-greatest Hermes wrote in Heliopolis in hieroglyphic symbols... [13]

...First of all, unite yourself to Helios in this manner: on whatever sunrise you wish —provided it is the third of the month— go to the highest part of the house, spread a clean linen cloth on the floor —do it with a mystagogue— but as for you, crowned with dark ivy, when the sun reaches the midpoint of the sky, at the fifth hour, while looking upward, lie down naked on the linen cloth and command that your eyes be covered around with a black band, and wrapping yourself up in the manner of a corpse, close your eyes, direct your face toward the sun, and begin the recitation of these words... [14]

Oracle of Serapis by means of a boy, a lamp, a bowl, and a seat:

...

Release:

Be gone, Lord, to your own world and your own thrones, and your own vaults, and keep me and this boy safe from harm in the name of the highest god... [15]

Divination by means of a boy:

Having laid him on the ground, speak, and a black-colored boy will appear to him.

Spell:

I invoke you Chaos and Erebos of the deep, of the earth, inhabitants of heaven, masters of the deepest unseen mysteries, guardians of things concealed, sovereigns of the chthonic spirits, rulers of infinity, *etc*... [16]

Divination by a lamp:

In a clean house, put an iron lamp stand in the direction of the rising sun, and having put a lamp not colored red on it, light it. Let the wick be of new linen...the boy must be uncorrupt, pure...

Spell:
...I beseech you this very day, in this very hour, to reveal to this boy the light and the sun...Isis, Anubis...make the boy be taken into a trance and see the gods... [17]

...you may use [these names] for the boys who are not seeing [visions] so that he may see without fail, and for all the spells and [other] necessities: questionings, prophecies of Helios, divination by mirrors... [18]

Over his naked body...

The connection between magic —"powerful works"— and nakedness is everywhere assumed in antiquity.[19] Jesus' command to heal, raise the dead, and perform exorcisms is directed to his *shoeless* disciples, even as Moses is commanded to remove his sandals in the presence of God, and Saul, in an ecstatic frenzy, strips off his clothing. [20] Nudity is associated with transitional states, changes in cultic or social status. [21] The nakedness of boys used for divinatory purposes has been noted in the preceding excerpts.

For Jesus taught him the mystery of the kingdom...

As for the connection between *mystery* and *magic*, it is plain from the papyri that the two fields were, if not for all practical purposes synonymous, certainly overlapping. Comparing the vocabulary of the papyri with that of the mystery cults, Graf identifies three links between the two: "magic and mystery involve secrecy, they seek direct contact with the divine, and they are reached by a complex ritual of initiation."[22] All authorities agree that the two were intimately linked: "The tradition of magic and that of the mysteries have coexisted for a long time, with multiple contacts and mutual interrelations, especially at the level of charismatic craftsmanship." [23]

Was there a *sexual* Jesus?

None of Morton Smith's claims enraged his opponents more than his claim that Jesus was a sexual being, possibly a *homosexual* being. Most scholars, fixated on the image of the Sunday school Jesus, could apparently not even imagine such a thing. The very notion repelled them. But Jesus was a man, and barring some physical or psychological failure in his development, he would have had normal male genitalia and normal male sexual urges. Every normal adult is capable of falling in love and expressing that feeling through sexual activity. So why *not* Jesus?

Of course the vast majority of Christians would categorically deny that Jesus had homosexual feelings, and no amount of proof would ever be sufficient to overturn that opinion —the possibility of arriving at such a conclusion depends more on one's susceptibility to even consider it than it does on what the New Testament may have to say. As various recent detractors have noted, Smith himself was apparently gay, a circumstance that undoubtedly contributed to his seeing the homoerotic implications of *Secret Mark*. Charles Hedrick has pointedly noted that "homophobia may well have contributed to the disappearance of Clement's letter," citing the "practical problem for religious institutions rejecting homosexuality as a sin, but promoting communal monasteries and convents." [24]

Of course *Smith's* sexual orientation never had anything to do with the question of Jesus' sexuality, but making an issue of Smith's emotional life has proven a useful ploy for those anxious to avoid the real subject. Was Jesus sexual? Was Jesus possibly homosexual?

The relevant facts are these: at thirty years of age, Jesus appears to have been a single man, a feature of his life that would have been remarked upon in his time and culture: "Singleness —an unmarried lifestyle— was exceptional, even suspicious among the Jews, because it was seen as an offense to the divine obligation to procreate (Gen. 1:28). Jesus, however, was apparently single." [25] Celibacy was not unknown in 1st century Judaism: the Essenes appear to have practiced celibacy as a part of their severely legalistic and isolationist religious movement, but there is no evidence that Jesus was particularly legalistic or isolationist, so one might fairly ask why he remained unmarried.

Jesus himself may have offered an oblique answer to that question in his saying regarding the self-made eunuch: "some made eunuchs of themselves for the sake of the kingdom of heaven."[26] The implication is that Jesus himself was indisposed to marriage, either physically, emotionally, or due to prophetic calling. Nevertheless, this is a curious saying given that castrated or emasculated men were specifically excluded by Jewish law from cultic participation.[27]

Jesus' most thoroughly attested emotional attachment was to another man, and a young man at that.[28] Close male relationships were probably not unusual in Jesus' day, particularly since the society in which he lived was sexually segregated and casual contact between the sexes was considered suspect.[29] There were women in Jesus' retinue, but speculation to the contrary, it is a man, not a woman, who is repeatedly designated as the disciple particularly loved by Jesus. As I have pointed

264

out along the way, the language used to describe Jesus' relationship with Lazarus everywhere points to intimacy, and it is hard to imagine why the story of the beloved young man was suppressed in whole or in part without some compelling reason. Could the reason be that Jesus *loved* him? [30] If the young man in the garden of Gethsemane is the young man in Jesus' empty tomb, as Mark seems to imply, then the intimacy that binds Jesus and Lazarus was seen by the narrator as even transcending death, rendering the question of genital intercourse almost —*but not quite*— beside the point.

Several other observations merit comment.

When asked by the disciples where he wanted to eat the Passover, Jesus told them to go into the city where they will be met by a man carrying a jar of water. [31] It was the duty of women to draw water and the prerogative of men to demand a drink as illustrated by Jesus' conversation with the Samaritan woman at the well. [32] As Morton Smith pointed out:

> When he sent a couple of disciples to make preparations for the Passover meal, he did not tell them the address, but told them to look for a man carrying a pitcher of water. (Carrying water was woman's work, so this was like saying, "Look for a man wearing lipstick.") [33] *Pukhtah* .

The disciples were to follow this man into the house he entered and speak to the owner, who would provide a room for the Passover celebration.

Like many cultures in modern times, the culture in which Jesus lived traditionally divided labor according to sex, making particular tasks marks of gender. Distinguishing gender extended to a religious prohibition against men and women wearing each other's clothing.[34] Among the curses David pronounced against Joab and his descendents, "one who holds a spindle," —presumably an effeminate man— was included along with venereal disease, leprosy, violent death, and hunger.[35] Given such cultural animosity toward those who bent gender, one might also fairly ask how Jesus knew a man who carried water, and why he directed his disciples to prepare Passover in his home.

A second point, raised by Theodore Jennings, concerns the ritual of foot washing.[36] John relates the story of Jesus washing the feet of his disciples, the point of which is that the servant is not above his master.[37] In the Greco-Roman world, the washing of feet as a gesture of hospitality was the work of slaves, and lacking slaves, the work of women.[38] In cases where men invite other men to stay for supper, the guests wash their own feet, otherwise it is the job of women.[39] In the New Testament it is the women who wash feet, and rather dramatically at that, drying them with their hair.[40] Although normally the work of slaves —and Jesus says as much— Jesus was certainly too poor to own slaves himself and none of his circle are mentioned as owning slaves.[41] Therefore, when Peter tells Jesus, "You will never wash my feet!" is he objecting to Jesus performing the work of a slave, the work of a woman, or both? [42]

It is in connection with the sort of devotion, "the likes of which not even a slave would do," that David Martinez notes "the close parallel between magical ερως θειος (erôs theios) and the exclusive devotion demanded by Jesus in Lk 14:26" where the oft-repeated demand to hate one's family members is stipulated as a requirement for discipleship.[43] The phenomenon of ερως θειος *the love due a god*, or φιλια μανικη (philia manikè), *maniacal devotion*, is a feature of the erotomagical spells in the papyri. The connection between nocturnal mystery rites and sexual acts is also well attested. [44] Is the similarity between Jesus' language as remembered in the gospels and the language of magical love spells merely coincidental?

Jesus relationship to his body of disciples is frequently likened to marriage, particularly in the apocalyptic passages of the New Testament, [45] and the 144,000 who are the collective "bride" of the Lamb are virgin males: "these are the ones who were not defiled with women, for they are virgins. These are the ones who follow the Lamb wherever he goes…" [46]

Samuel Angus:

> Another conception of communion with the deity in the Mysteries was a religious marriage —a conception the roots of which can be traced back to the Egyptian and Asiatic belief and practice of copulation with deity…Such *synousia* had a double underlying idea: first, an erotic-anthropomorphic, in which *synousia* has the character of an offering or sacrifice (of purity); secondly, the magical, whereby the worshippers participated in the god's *Mana* and secured life and salvation." [47]

Rubbish

Conclusions

One proposal of this book is that Mark and John shared a written source that told the story of Jesus and Lazarus, the beloved disciple, a story which may have been completely related by *Secret Mark*, reproduced in an expurgated version by canonical Mark, incompletely reproduced by John, and suppressed by Matthew and Luke. The very existence of *Secret Mark* is known only through the letter of Clement, and the two missing pieces provided by the Clement letter by no means restore its text —Clement, a self-acknowledged keeper of secrets in a society in which keeping the secrets of the mysteries was an ingrained taboo, was forced to divulge *some* information only in response to the threat posed by the Carpocratians. A partial reconstruction of the story of Jesus and Lazarus is possible by triangulating canonical Mark, *Secret Mark*, and John, but there is no reason to believe the resulting picture is complete.

No one doubts that the text of Mark has been manipulated: the existing manuscripts of the gospel record four different endings. Assuming that the Clement letter is genuine, we are presented with further evidence of textual tampering, either by a second hand or by the author himself. If, as Clement states, a *private edition* of the gospel, restricted reading for initiates, coexisted with a *public edition* available to the less enlightened, then we today clearly possess an incomplete book.[48] In response to the question regarding "naked man with naked man" as well as *"the many other things"* Theodore asked, Clement confessed to two excised passages, but there is little reason to doubt, given the cloak of secrecy that Clement describes as having been drawn around the unexpurgated edition, that a longer form of the gospel existed.

The texts as we have them establish two points: (1) the disciple Jesus loved was a particular person, a male, and (2) the story of the beloved disciple was incompletely preserved by Mark and John and suppressed by Matthew and Luke. The Carpocratian sect may have learned of a homoerotic element that those who preserved the *Secret Gospel* were unwilling to acknowledge. If so, Jesus would hardly be the first public figure to have had a homosexual relationship *en cachette*, and its recognition, or worse yet *celebration*, by the Carpocratians would have been more than adequate reason for the nascent church to suppress all mention of a certain rich young man named Lazarus.

In the magical papyri, as in *Secret Mark*, there is a powerful association between linen and death: the cultural context points to a ritual of initiation involving rising from the dead as well as union with the divine. The "mystery of the kingdom" that Jesus taught almost certainly involved some similar union —to be united with Jesus. There is a strong symbolic connection in the mystery cults between regeneration and sexuality, an association echoed in the New Testament with its metaphor of bride and bridegroom.[49]

In the mystery cults the attainment of spiritual ecstasy was often accompanied by physical ecstasy, as was apparently the case in some early Christian sects of which the Carpocratians were representative. Whether enactment of mystical union through physical union can be traced back to Jesus can no longer be known, but as Smith pointed out, the evidence at hand is suggestive, and it is pretty certain that *Secret Mark* was *secret* for a reason.

There is no way that any modern researcher could hope to establish the truth about Jesus' sexual orientation, a matter which is, in the final analysis, irrelevant. More interesting by far was the reaction of New Testament scholars to the question itself: the mood of hysterical denial that followed Smith's speculations reflected the phobias of society generally, proving once again that Jesus is for every age no more or no less than what that age construes him to be.

Notes

1   *Jewish Magic and Superstition*, 75, 81.

2   Matthew 2:1-2, 13, 19.

Of particular interest is Koester's observation that the concept of virgin birth, which is foreign to Judaism, "is Hellenistic and, ultimately, Egyptian. No other religious or political tradition of antiquity can be identified as its generator." *Ancient Christian Gospels*, 306.

Fritz Graf: "...those who accused Jesus of being a magician (they were not few among the pagans) argued that he, after all, had spent part of his youth in the homeland of magic, after the escape from Palestine..." *Envisioning Magic: A Princeton Seminar and Symposium*, 94-95.

Joseph Hoffman: "The Talmud knows Egypt as the center of the magical arts: 'Ten measures of sorcery descended in the world: Egypt received nine, the rest of the world one.' (Talmud b. Qidd. 49). Thus, to say that Jesus learned magic in Egypt is to say that he is more powerful as a worker of signs than the local variety of wonder-workers (see Matt. 9:33)." *Jesus Outside the Gospels*, 45.

3   Acts 19:18-19.

4   *Ancient Christian Magic: Coptic Texts of Ritual Power* is the definitive book on this subject.

5   John Hull: "The crucial point of inquiry into the miracles of Jesus, as of those of the early church, was not whether they had in fact happened but the nature and origin of the power used to perform them. By means of such as these 'the apostles gave witness with great power', i.e., not simply with great impact but the aid of a mighty force (Acts 4.33)." *Hellenistic Magic and the Synoptic Tradition*, 108.

6   As noted by Ramsay MacMullen, *Christianizing the Roman Empire*, 22.

7   *Magika Hiera*, 176.

8   John 3:1-5.

9   *Greek and Roman Necromancy*, 77.

     Nighttime was particularly associated with works of sorcery, and
     Greek preserves several relevant terms such as νυκτιπλανος,
     roaming by night, and νυκτοπεριπλανητος, *wandering around by night*,
     that refer to such activities.

     "Alongside public Dionysiac festivals there emerge private
     Dionysos mysteries. These are esoteric, they take place at night;
     access is through an individual initiation, *telete.*" *Greek Religion*,
     291.

     Georg Luck: "It seems that the magos had a little bit of everything
     –the bacchantic (i.e. ecstatic) element, the initiation rites, the
     migratory life, the nocturnal activities." *Witchcraft and Magic in
     Europe: Ancient Greece and Rome*, 104.

     "In modern languages the word *mystery* is mainly used in the sense
     of 'secret,' a usage that goes back to the New Testament. In fact,
     secrecy was a necessary attribute of ancient mysteries… Secrecy
     and in most cases a nocturnal setting are concomitants of this
     exclusiveness." *Ancient Mystery Cults*, 7-8.

10   Matthew 2:12, 19, etc.

11   *Papyri Graecae Magicae*, I, 70 (IV:89-91). All subsequent citations
     will be listed as *PGM*. In each case the volume and page number
     are given first, and the sections and line numbers in parentheses.

     σινδονιασις κατα κεφαλης μεχρι ποδων γυμνον: "**Wrap** a
     naked boy **in linen** from head to foot…" The verb is formed off
     σινδων (sindôn), *linen cloth*, the same clothing used by the beloved
     disciple and by Jesus. *Sindôn* is an Egyptian loan word (*A Grammar
     of the Greek New Testament in the Light of Historical Research*, 111).

     The reference in the magical papyri is probably to mummy cloth.
     The connection between linen and Egypt is fundamental and of
     long standing. Egyptian priests wore linen while performing
     religious functions, like the Hebrews were both circumcised and
     prohibited from eating certain foods, and underwent rites of

initiation prior to attaining higher offices. *Ancient Egyptian Magic*, 38.

12   "this *X* man or boy…" The name of the man or boy is to be inserted into the spell as appropriate.

13   PGM, I, 102 (IV:850-855, 870-879, 884-889).

Σολομωνος καταπτωσις: "Solomon's seizure," literally, Solomon's "falling-down" in a trance from which the man or boy speaks.

και επι παιδων και **τελειων**: "on both boys and **adults**…" Although the magicians had a clear preference for working with boys –who were thought to be uncorrupted– the possibility of working with *adults* is specifically included. The subject's virginal state was perhaps more important than the age, and virginity could not be assumed of any post-pubescent male.

14   *PGM, I, 76 (IV:169-179).*

συσταθεις προς τον Ηλιον τροπω: "**unite yourself** to Helios in this manner…" The rite aims to produce a συστασις (sustasis), *union*, or *fusion* of identity with Helios Apollo, the god of prophecy.

This is, as Meyer notes, "an example of the ritual specialist playing the role of, and being for that duration and purpose an embodiment of, the divine being or power" and cites the wearing of Anubis masks by embalmers and mortuary priests as a further "example of this phenomenon." *Ancient Christian Magic*, 17.

στρωσον επι της γης **σινδονιον** καθαρον: "spread a clean **linen cloth** on the floor…"

περικαλυπτεσθαι τους οφθαλμους **τελαμων** μελανι: "your eyes be covered around with a black **band**…" A τελαμων (telamôn), a *linen bandage* of the kind used for wrapping mummies, specifically, an *Isis band*.

"Cloth or material taken from the dresses of the gods, especially of Isis, was considered magically potent. Isis is the widow of Osiris and thus identified with the color black." *The Greek Magical Papyri in Translation*, 336.

15   *PGM*, 1, 180 (V:4-5, 44-46).

Divination by means of a bowl and a lamp: the boy sits holding the bowl in his lap, scrying by the aid of lamplight reflected in the surface of the water. A spell pronounced over the boy induces a trance. Rainwater summoned the heavenly deities, spring water, issuing from the earth, summoned ghosts. *Greek and Roman Necromancy*, 192.

Divination in bowls is *lecanomancy*, by lamps, *lychnomancy*. This rite combines both techniques.

16   *PGM*, II, 16 (VII:349-352).

φανησεται αυτω **παιδιον μελανχρουν**...: "**a black-colored boy** will appear to him..." The boy medium, who has been laid out in the posture of death, will see the ghost of a boy. Exorcised ghosts were frequently perceived as black. The necromantic nature of the evocation is obvious from the wording of the spell spoken over the recumbent boy. *Greek and Roman Necromancy*, 224.

The ghost of the boy is an αωρος, the spirit of one *untimely dead*, which will stir restlessly until it reaches the limit of what would have been its natural lifespan. *Witchcraft and Magic in Europe: Ancient Greece and Rome*, 16.

17   *PGM*, II, 25 (VII:540-544, 548-549).

ο δε παις εστω **αφθορος** καθαρος: "the boy must be **uncorrupt**, pure..." The boy is to be "unspoiled" by sexual relations. Presumably, the purity of the uncorrupted boy's soul allows it to separate from the body more readily during the trance state. The use of children, particularly boys, in magic is well-attested into the Middle Ages.

"New things, first actions, are innocent and virginal, like the boy or girl who were the best mediums in divinations, uncontaminated by use or repetition or by years and experience." *Jewish Magic and Superstition*, 122.

18   *PGM*, II, 121 (XIII:749-752).

19   *Priscillian of Avila*, 17-20.

On an Attic black-figure cup, the sorceress Circe –"naked as becomes a witch"– is seen offering a potion to Odysseus and his crew. *Looking At Greek Vases*, 83.

20   Matthew 10:3-10, Exodus 3:5, 1 Samuel 19:24.

21   "…young people sometimes exchange clothing for nakedness and then nakedness for clothing; nudity marks their marginality, whereas assumption of new clothing marks assumption of new status." *Restless Dead: Encounters Between the Living and the Dead in Ancient Greece*, 234.

22   *Magic in the Ancient World*, 99.

23   *Ancient Mystery Cults*, 68.

24   *Journal of Early Christian Studies* 11:136.

For the record, I believe that homosexuality is a normal developmental variant, and that it conveys no disadvantage apart from the various limitations on personal freedom that societies frequently impose.

25   *Homoeroticism in the Biblical World*, 119.

26   Matthew 19:12.

27   Deuteronomy 23:1.

As noted elsewhere, some early Christians took Jesus' words literally and castrated themselves.

28   Of νεανισκος (neaniskos), "a young man in his prime as a sexual object…A word with strong connotations of erotic desire." *Same Sex Unions in Premodern Europe*, 143-146.

In our own culture, the announcement that one is "seeing a young man" implies that sensations other than sight are in play.

29   Compare John 4:27.

30   Jesus' relationship with Mary Magdalene, the subject of so much recent speculation, is discussed in **Appendix B**.

Working within the framework of conventional scholarship which knows of but ignores the evidence of *Secret Mark*, Nissinen concludes, "The custom of a student resting against his teacher's chest manifests cultural conventions rather than homoeroticism; in this sense the relationship between Jesus and his favorite disciple evinces homosociability that tolerates also physical expressions of mutual attachment...Finally, there is the basic question of the historical authenticity of the Gospel of John. Even if this Gospel allows for some homosocial interpretations, this would not necessarily reveal anything about Jesus' actual life." *Homoeroticism in the Biblical World*, 122.

If the gospels do not "necessarily reveal anything about Jesus' actual life," then for all practical purposes they can be regarded as on par with fairy tales and historical inquiry be abandoned as foolish.

Marvin Meyer eludes the homosexual question by proposing that the beloved disciple is "the paradigmatic disciple" or "prototype disciple." *Secret Gospels*, 128.

The New Testament writers consistently shun the *other* Greek word pair for love: ερου and ερως, both of which have overtly sexual connotations. However, as previously noted, αγαπαω and φιλεω include to *caress* and to *kiss* as possible meanings and can hardly be regarded as limited to "spiritual" or "brotherly" love as frequently claimed.

31 Mark 14:13, Luke 22:10.

32 John 4:7.

33 *Secret Gospel*, 80.

34 Deuteronomy 22:5.

35 2 Samuel 3:29.

36 *The Man Jesus Loved*, 163-165.

37 John 13:1-16.

38 In their article, "La lavanda dei piedi di Giovanni 13,1-20," Pesce and Destro argue that the washing of the disciples' feet, which

takes place *during*, not before the meal, has ritual, even initiatory, significance, but slight the biblical evidence on foot washing, particularly its connection to women. *Biblica* 80: 240-249.

39 Genesis 18:4, 19:2, 24:32, 43:24, Judges 19:21, 2 Samuel 11:8, Song of Solomon 5:3, 1 Samuel 25:41, 1 Timothy 5:10.

40 Luke 7:38, John 12:3.

41 John 13:6.

42 John 13:8.

43 *Ancient Magic and Ritual Power*, 357, 358.
Compare Matthew 10:37, 19:29, Mark 10:29-30, Luke 14:26, 18:29.

44 "The modern use of the word 'orgies,' from *orgia*, reflects the puritan's worst suspicions about secret nocturnal rites. There is no doubt that sexuality was prominent in mysteries." *Ancient Mystery Cults*, 104.

The term οργια (orgia) referred to *worship* generally, rites and sacrifices, but when applied to the mystery cults, it meant the *secret rite* practiced by an initiate.

45 As at Matthew 9:15, 25:1-10, Mark 2:19-20, Revelation 18:23, for instance.

46 Revelation 14:4.

47 *The Mystery Religions*, 222-223.
Συνουσια (sunousia), *communion, social intercourse*, or even *unio mystica, mystical union*.

48 This is essentially the position of Helmut Koester: "In other words, the text of canonical Mark—it is the same text as the one known to Clement of Alexandria as Mark's public Gospel—is not the original Mark used by Matthew and Luke, but an abbreviated version of the *Secret Gospel of Mark*. It was only the latter that had survived, and in order to make this text suitable for public reading, the story of the raising of the young man and

his subsequent private initiation by Jesus as well as the reference to this young man's sister and mother and Salome after Mark 10:46b were removed." *Ancient Christian Gospels*, 302.

49 "A third and undeniable aspect of the mysteries is the sexual aspect: genital symbols, exposures, and occasionally veritable orgies, in the common sense, are attested. Puberty initiation, agrarian magic, and sexuality may unite in the great experience of life overcoming death." *Greek Religion*, 277.

"The magical and the mystical, the physical and the erotic merged in that initiation intimacy between master and disciple. That is the background against which an erotic reading of the baptismal rite must be understood." *The Historical Jesus*, 331.

Regarding the well known connection between the mystery cults and the agricultural cycle, Burkert notes "that the one occurrence of the word *mysterion* in the Gospels is in the context of allegory, the parable of the sower." *Ancient Mystery Cults*, 80.

Chapter Fifteen: Apocalypse, Magic, and Christianity

All is fair in love and war, and religious
domination is nothing if not love and war.[1]

The Salesmen of the Apocalypse

What if Jesus had been right? What if the Apocalypse had occurred as he predicted? There would be no world as we know it, of course, and no Christianity. There would be no magnificent gothic cathedrals, no Vatican, no Mormons on the doorstep, no Gideon Bibles in cut-rate motel rooms. But the generation Jesus promised would by no means disappear before the glorious return of the Son of Man died awaiting his return and so has every generation since.

The failure of the parousia to occur firmly established Christianity's credentials as a non-prophet organization, but the fledgling religion did not wither away or even appear to suffer any noticeable setback. Although this confounds rational expectations, a quick survey of Christian sects in America and elsewhere will prove that discredited predictions —and there have been many— almost never lead to the disappearance of the groups that make them. Despite the fact that every apocalyptic prediction made to date by Jesus and his followers has proven false, end-of-the-world preachers continue to flourish.

The scandal of the missing parousia and the potential for connecting false prophecy with magic provoked a *sauve-qui-peut* among the early Christians, the effects of which persist to the present. After noting that "Jesus was accused of sorcery," Garrett comments on the reluctance of Christian scholars to address the clear and varied evidence for magical practice in early Christianity:

> Perhaps embarrassment has been partly to blame for the scholarly inattention…Peter curses Simon Magus, and Paul inflicts blindness on Bar Jesus. It is Paul's own "sensationalist" miracles that provoke the antics of the seven sons of Sceva. The Christians' actions seem hardly to differ from those of the "magicians" whom they oppose! Such resemblances aggravate the interpretive problem faced by those persons in the academy and church who would prefer to leave Christianity's first-century mythological framework behind. [2]

But not all scholars have been reluctant to accept the evidence of the New Testament:

> Because of magic's position as subversive, unofficial, unapproved, and often lower-class religion, I have deliberately used the word *magic* rather than some euphemism in the preceding and present parts of this book. Elijah and Elisha, Honi and Hanina, were magicians, and so was Jesus of Nazareth. It is endlessly fascinating to watch Christian theologians describe Jesus as miracle worker rather than magician and then attempt to define the substantive difference between those two. There is, it would seem from the tendentiousness of such arguments, an ideological need to protect religion and its miracles from magic and its effects. [3]

It is difficult for modern people who have been taught the divinity of Christ from childhood to appreciate the distance the early church had to travel to enthrone its Messiah. The Council of Nicea, convened in 325CE, described the itinerant Galilean exorcist and apocalyptic prophet as follows:

> We believe in one Lord, Jesus Christ, the only Son of God, eternally begotten of the Father, God from God, Light from Light, true God from true God, begotten, not made, of one Being with the Father.[4]

Although Jesus eventually found his way from the insignificant village of Nazareth to the right hand of God, the New Testament writers were unclear about when Jesus became the Son of God, and this uncertainty apparently existed prior to the composition of any of the New Testament documents.

Paul, quoting from a pre-existing confession of faith, says of Jesus that he "was appointed" the Son of God "by resurrection from the dead."[5] The idea that Jesus did not become the Son of God until *after* he died may shock modern Christian sensibilities, but Paul says as much when he connects the bestowal of sonship —"You are my son, today I have begotten you"— with Jesus' resurrection —"when he raised Jesus."[6] These are hardly the only passages where such linkage occurs: Paul again says that God "appointed" Jesus to be the judge of the world and confirmed that appointment "by raising him from the dead."[7] *Read the masters to the from fast for the real Jesus this book no be no supposition,*

A different strand of the earliest tradition has Jesus become God's son at the moment of his baptism. In Mark's gospel, a voice from heaven announces, "You are my son" as Jesus comes up out of the water,[8] and the corresponding passage in Luke, according to several of the earliest manuscripts, says, "You are my son, today I have begotten you."[9]

Christians began to fight among themselves almost from the very beginning over the question of Jesus' divinity. The proto-orthodox eventually came to believe that he had always existed with God prior to his human incarnation, and had always been God's Son, but many rejected the idea both of his pre-existence and of his virgin birth. Some —known under the blanket term of *adoptionists*— taught that Jesus was a holy man who had been "adopted" by God at the time of his baptism, hence the announcement, "You are my son." Some Gnostics taught that a spirit entity, an *aeon* called "the Christ," entered Jesus at his baptism after descending in the form of a dove,[10] and abandoned his body prior to his death, provoking his well known cry of desperation on the cross.[11]

Jesus himself, who expected the world to end in his lifetime and may have believed that his confrontation with the temple authorities would trigger the apocalypse —his final and greatest feat of magic[12] — made no provisions for the transmission of his authority from generation to generation. After all, Jesus' generation was supposed to be the last. The sudden loss of its charismatic leader left a nearly fatal power vacuum in the emerging cult, but in the centuries after his death his followers noisily regrouped, formulated the beginnings of Christian theology, backtracked to produce quasi-historical biographies, and starting with the book of Acts, invented the "apostolic fiction," written to create the illusion of continuity between Jesus and the later community of believers. In the process the apostles became the eyewitnesses of Jesus' life, the putative authors of the New Testament books, the first missionaries, founders of the first churches, the first theologians, and the first martyrs.

> It is as important for the disciples to be apostles as it is for Jesus to be the Christ. Without the apostles, the story of Jesus would recede into the past like a tale told once upon a time without effect in shaping social history...Without the apostles the Christian church would not know how to connect its history with Jesus. The apostles are the church's guarantee that, as a social historical institution of religion, it started right and has its story straight.[13]

If the experience of Jesus and the first Christians proved anything, it confirmed that apocalyptic predictions based on religious belief are guaranteed to fail. Given that fact, it comes as no surprise that the orthodox mainstream has de-emphasized end-of-the-world theology, sparing itself the repeated embarrassment and negative publicity of failed prophecies. Nevertheless, apocalyptic belief lies at the core of Christianity, and though banished to its fringes, refuses to go away.

A recrudescence of apocalypse fever hit the United States during the socially tumultuous 1970s while the civil rights of blacks, women, and gays were being asserted and the war in Vietnam spiraled downward to stalemate and defeat —all to the dismay of reactionary whites living in the Bible Belt. This time the Second Coming was trumpeted by a folksy book, *Late Great Planet Earth*, which sold an estimated 35 million copies in 54 languages, spawned a dozen or so sequels, and galvanized fundamentalists who were panting for the end of the world and the extinction of unbelievers.

282

The same apocalyptic subculture is currently slurping up the pre-millennial pap of the *Left Behind* series of novels, the first of which appeared in 1995. The fact that none of the geopolitical maneuverings foretold by these books has actually happened —*LGPE* assured its readers that the Soviet Union would invade Israel— has barely cast a shadow over the salesmen of the apocalypse, who merely rewrite their prophecies of a Christian *tausandjahriger Reich* and scurry on. Like their Hollywood counterparts, evangelical celebs have made fortunes selling the end of the world.

Chills up and down my spine: repudiating that old black magic

By the end of the 1st century, Christians were in open, continuous verbal warfare with each other. Their writings speak of little else than doctrinal perversion and matters of internal discipline, and in keeping with well established apocalyptic style, the spats between the various sects are characterized as the final battle between Light and Darkness, between God and Satan:

> ...in the last times some will fall away from the faith,[14] misled by deceptive spirits and teachings of demons...for some have already turned away to follow Satan...having a sick craving for controversies and fights about words.
>
> 1 Timothy 4:1, 5:15, 6:4

> The one who sins is from the Devil because the Devil has been sinning from the beginning. That is why the Son of God was made manifest, to destroy the works of the Devil.
>
> 1 John 3:8

Even as there were false prophets among the people, so also there will be false teachers among you who will introduce destructive heresies.

2 Peter 2:1

The beleaguered flock, hemmed in on all sides by wicked powers, is warned "not to fight about words…to the utter ruin of those listening," "nor to be misled by Jewish myths," but to "reject the heretical man."[15] "Those who do not remain in the teaching of Christ do not have God. The one who remains in the teaching has both the Father and the Son," but of the man who deserts the fold: "This is the imposter and the Antichrist."[16] The Antichrist arises from the *Christian* ranks: "now there have come to be many Antichrists…they went forth from *us*." [17]

If for Jesus the apocalypse marks the rescue of the world *from* Satan, for the primitive church the failure of the apocalypse marks the abandonment of the world *to* Satan, who has become, in the words of Paul, "the god of this age."[18] The real tragedy of Christianity resides in its apocalyptic predisposition to see the world as inherently evil, to exchange the fantasy of the apocalypse for the equally delusional New Jerusalem, to declare that the citizenship of its members is in heaven, in a city built by God.[19] The Christian faithful confess "that they are strangers and temporary residents on the earth."[20] If the founding documents of a religion proclaim its adherents to be mere planetary tourists, can anyone be surprised when they behave accordingly?

There is a subtle irony here. In an important sense, a strong family resemblance exists between the world as viewed by those who see Divinity as utterly transcendent and the world as viewed by those who see Divinity as utterly irrelevant. In both cases,

284

the world is a collection of objects, devoid of intrinsic meaning. For many Christians, the world's value derives from its God-given utility to human beings in the process of carrying out His will and from the fact that God thought it worth his while to create it in the first place. For secular modern thinkers, the world is valuable solely because human beings value it. Both agree that there is nothing about the world that gives it intrinsic value.[21]

Christianity's overwhelming urge to find the demonic lurking behind every tree is too exhaustively documented to merit extended comment, but far from being a relic of the ignorant past, the tendency is as alive —and as bizarre— as ever. Gavin Baddeley points to several absurd fundamentalist claims, which he characterizes as "sorcery wrapped in a thin veil of pseudo-scientific gibberish": the "back-masking" myth, the once popular notion that occult messages could be heard when vinyl records were played backward, cattle mutilation —blamed variously on aliens *and* Devil worshippers— as well as allegations of ritual child abuse as part of an international Satanic conspiracy.[22]

Other recent targets of evangelical satanophobia have included the role-playing game, *Dungeons and Dragons*, the soap company Proctor and Gamble —accused of using a satanic logo— and the World Wild Life Fund, purported to be a front for pagan nature worship.[23] From time to time one hears of congregations gathering in church parking lots to burn Harry Potter books, using Acts 19:19 as their justification, thus joining in spirit with fundamentalist Islamic regimes in trying to ban the Rowling books from both shelves and culture. Many examples of similar idiocy enthroned could be cited if only for their entertainment value.

Two primary characteristics of Christianity, intolerance of opinion and the rejection of the world as flawed, have been mentioned. Contrary to the claims of Christian apologists, neither is inconsistent with Jesus' message which was emphatic in its claim that the world, particularly as embodied in the religious and social status quo, was soon to disappear.

Writing about the connection between what humans believe about the world and environmental devastation, philosopher Christian de Quincey notes, "there are also existential deserts —deserts of the spirit, of the soul, of the mind. Deserts of *meaning*."[24] If this book makes one overarching claim, it is that public understanding of what the New Testament says about primitive Christianity has *receded*, not advanced, and that this failure of comprehension is partly due to what passes for New Testament scholarship.

It is inevitable that the majority of students of the New Testament come to the subject armed with a previously established belief in the truth of Christianity and its founding texts, and that their course of study in religious schools is largely designed to reinforce that belief, prepare them to proselytize, and to serve as pastors. It should go without saying that the professoriate in such schools —which in the case of "Bible colleges" are nothing more than Christian madrassas— teach and interact within a shallow pool, an intellectually incestuous tendency that actively discourages investigation while promoting fundamentalist orthodoxy. Despite the superficially impressive strings of degrees such scholars award each other, critical study of the New Testament within their ranks is at best a prolonged Sunday school for overachievers. Indeed, at the beginning of the 21st century the primary purpose of such seminaries is the defense of the steadily eroding

286

subcontinent of literalist belief from the surrounding ocean of contrary fact and opinion.

There is little doubt that the answer to the fundamentalist theology of destruction currently sweeping the world must be a radical reorientation of human thinking, but to rescue humanity from its apparent death wish, that reorientation must move far beyond the revivalism of the Christian bestsellers or the current enthusiasm for befuddled New Age neo-gnosticism. More Christianity, whatever its stripe, is not an option.

Notes

1   *Lost Christianities*, 47.

2   *The Demise of the Devil*, 1.

Modern fundamentalists, like the church fathers before them, connect magic with the service of Satan, but that connection is peculiar to Christianity. "Pagan society knew of no 'Devil' with whom individuals could make a pact, and thus no torture and persecutions of 'false' prophets and prophetesses. These features were a consequence of Christianity." *Pagans and Christians*, 205.

Paul linked false prophecy and magic (Acts 13:6), as does Jeremiah, the Old Testament prophet Jesus quoted to such effect in his condemnation of the temple authorities (Jeremiah 27:9-10, 29:8-9).

3   *The Historical Jesus*, 305.

4   The Nicene Creed is usually considered the one universal statement of belief common to all true Christians. The several Christian sects, such as the Jehovah's Witnesses, that still preserve an Arian christology might beg to disagree.

5   Romans 1:4. The grammatically ambiguous εξ αναστασεως νεκρων: "by resurrection from the dead" could also mean

"starting from [his] resurrection from the dead."

6 αναστησας Ιησουν: "when he raised Jesus" (Acts 13:33-34).

7 Acts 17:31. Compare Acts 10:42.

8 Mark 1:10-11.

9 Luke 3:22.

Ehrman argues that the reading preserved in these ancient witnesses is the original. *Orthodox Corruption of Scripture*, 49, 62-67, 140-143.

10 Matthew 3:16, Mark 1:10, Luke 3:22.

11 Matthew 27:46, Luke 23:46.

12 *Ancient Magic and Ritual Power*, 335-359.

13 Burton Mack, *Who Wrote the New Testament*, 225.

14 **αποστησονται** τινες της πιστεως: "some **will fall away from** the faith…"

The verbal form of αποστασια (apostasia), *apostasy, defection* from the faith, the crime that will lead untold numbers to the rack and stake under the rule of totalitarian Christianity. As the last pagan emperor of Rome prophetically remarked, "no wild beasts are as dangerous to man as the Christians are to one another." *Julian's Against the Galileans*, 32.

15 2 Timothy 2:14, Titus 1:14.

By the end of the 1st century, Christianity had become rabidly anti-Semitic. As James Carroll, following Elaine Pagels, points out: "The Jews, which occurs 16 times in Matthew, Mark, and Luke combined, is found 71 times in John where *the Jews* has become synonymous with all that is in opposition to God." *Constantine's Sword*, 92.

In Revelation 3:9, the Jews are called "the synagogue of Satan" and by the Middle Ages a Christian woman who had sexual relations with a Jew could be burned alive as punishment. It is not coincidence that conventicles of witches were called *sabbaths* or even *synagogues*, "a sign of anti-Semitism" by which the church conflated the heresies of Judaism and sorcery. *Magic in the Middle Ages*, 197.

Christianity also spreads a new category of crime: **αιρετικον** ανθρωπον...παραιτου: "reject...the **heretical** man." *Heresy* – from αιρεσις (hairesis), *sect*, the nominal form of αιρετιζω, to *choose* [for oneself]– enters the Christian lexicon and seals the fate of millions.

16 2 John 7, 9.

17 1 John 2:18-19.

Or in the words of Pogo, "We have met the enemy and he is us."

18 2 Corinthians 4:4.

Jules Michelet on the Inquisitor: "This solid, stolid Schoolman, so full of words and so void of sense, sworn foe of Nature no less than of human reason, takes his seat with superb confidence in his books and his learned gown, in the dust and dirt and litter of his gloomy court. On the desk before him he has on one side the *Summa Theologiae*, on the other the *Directorium*. This is his library, and he laughs at anything outside its limits." *Witchcraft, Sorcery, and Superstition*, 134.

19 Revelation 3:12, 21:2, Philippians 3:20, Hebrews 11:10.

20 Hebrews 11:13: οτι ξενοι και **παρεπιδημοι** εισιν επι της γης: "that they are strangers and **temporary residents** on the earth." The term παρεπιδημος was used of civil servants on temporary assignment in foreign countries, and the term παροικια, from whence *parish* and *parochial*, meant *sojourn* in a foreign land.

21 *Pagans and Christians*, 6.

Pagan writers of antiquity voiced similar objections to Christian belief: "The Christians, Celsus complains, inherit from the Jews the notion that the world was made solely for the benefit of mankind. When it does not conspicuously serve this purpose, they immediately call for a new order that suits them, ascribing their failures to an increase of evil ordained by their god." *Celsus On the True Doctrine*, 40.

22 *Lucifer Rising*, 114, 117-120, 134-145.

23 *Witchcraft and Magic in Europe: The Twentieth Century*, 123.

24 *Radical Nature*, 16.

Appendix A:
The "Son of David."

Jesus is frequently called the "Son of David," a title usually interpreted as a reference to the kingdom of Israel of which Jesus is the promised heir.[1] However, a different explanation has been proposed.

It is notable that the term "Son of David" is very frequently used in the context of healing and exorcism, particularly in the formula, "Son of David, take pity on me!"[2] Jesus is so addressed by the Canaanite woman whose daughter he exorcises,[3] and after the exorcism of a blind and deaf man, which exorcism is characterized as a healing, the crowd asks, "Can this be the son of David?" In response to this question, the Jewish leaders reply that Jesus *casts out demons* by the power of Beelzeboul, the prince of demons.[4] The final occurrence of the title is part of the acclamation of the crowds in the temple at Jerusalem, "Hosanna, Son of David," which is said in recognition that Jesus is a prophet, a wonder-worker who cures the blind and lame.[5]

The context of the gospels firmly connects the "Son of David" with exorcism. As has been noted by various scholars,[6] the son of David was, in point of fact, *Solomon*,[7] and that in addition to his wisdom and ostentation,[8] Solomon had quite a reputation as a magician, particularly for his ability to control demons.

There is substantial evidence that Solomon's magical abilities were already celebrated in Jesus' lifetime. The *Wisdom of Solomon*, which was probably composed in the Jewish community in Alexandria, Egypt, a century or more prior to Jesus' birth, reflects the belief that Solomon's fabled wisdom consisted of both manifest and occult knowledge.[9]

> For he gave me faultless knowledge of the things that are, to know the structure of the world and the operation of elemental spirits,[10] the beginning, end, and midpoints of time, the manner of the change and transitions of the seasons of the year, the orbits and position of the stars, the natural qualities of animals and passions of beasts, the power of spirits[11] and designs of men, the varieties of plants and powers of roots, both that which is hidden and visible I know.
>
> *Wisdom* 7:17-21

Solomon's accomplishments receive further elaboration in Josephus' *Antiquities of the Jews*, where it is said of him,

> God allowed [Solomon] to learn the art of casting out demons[12] for the benefit and healing of men and the formulation of incantations[13] by which sicknesses are healed and he left behind the ways of performing exorcisms... [14]
>
> *Antiquities* 8.45

In this brief passage from the *Antiquities*, the ωδαι, *songs*, of the

Septuagint have become επωδαι, *incantations*, and Solomon's mastery of the demons is made explicit. It is from Josephus that we first hear of Solomon's signet ring which the exorcist Eleazar uses to expel a demon in the presence of no less a person than Vespasian, the future Caesar.[15] Solomon's fame is on a rising trajectory from the *Antiquities*, through the *Testament of Solomon* of late antiquity, to the well known grimoires of the present such as the 17th century *Clavicula Salomonis*.

When, *in the context of exorcisms*, the New Testament proclaims of Jesus, "Something greater than Solomon is here!"[16] an early tradition related to the control of demonic power, rather than kingship, is probably in sight and the title "Son of David" is a veiled reference to Jesus' success as an exorcist and healer. The identification of the title with the Messiah who comes from the line of David is a latter interpretive gloss which shifts the focus away from magical practice.

It is possibly for this reason that Mark, who also used the term, felt no need to concoct a story placing Jesus' birth in Bethlehem, the city of David. For the primitive tradition that Mark represented, "son of David" means simply "successor to Solomon" with all that implies.

Notes

1   As at Luke 1:32-33.

2   Mark 10:47-48, Matthew 9:27, 20:30, Luke 18:38-39.

3   Matthew 15:22.

4   Matthew 12:22-24.

5   Matthew 21:11.

6   Recently by David Duling, whose article "Solomon, Exorcism, and the Son of David" provides a thorough summation of the

evidence that *son of David* acknowledged Jesus' magical skills. *Harvard Theological Review* 68:235-252.

Roy Kotansky notes, "David, as an early Jewish exorcist himself anticipating Solomon of later lore, is able to ward off the spirit by singing and playing the kinnor." *Ancient Magic and Ritual Power*, 257.

7   Matthew 1:6.

8   Solomon's wisdom, extolled in 1 Kings 4:29-34, "surpassed…all the wisdom of Egypt," a land known in antiquity as the cradle of magic. Of Solomon the Septuagint reports, "and his songs were five thousand," a considerable improvement over the 1005 mentioned in the Hebrew bible. Regarding the possible purpose of these songs, it may be recalled that when Solomon's father David played the harp, the evil spirit sent from God left Saul (1 Samuel 16:14-23).

9   The Σοφια Σαλωμων, the *Wisdom of Solomon*, was included among the apocryphal books of the *Septuagint*, the Greek translation of the Hebrew bible made in Alexandria, Egypt, for the Greek-speaking Jews of the Diaspora. That *Wisdom* was known to the earliest Christians is virtually certain: Romans 9:21 is very likely a close paraphrase of Wisdom 15:7.

Solomon's magnificence is referred to by Jesus at Matthew 6:29.

10   συστασιν κοσμου και ενεργειαν **στοιχειων**: "the structure of the world and the operation of the **elemental spirits**…" "Conjuring of elemental spirits" is a possible alternative translation.

The term στοιχειον (stoicheion), *elements*, in reference to superhuman spirit powers occurs several times in the writings of Paul and his school (Galatians 4:3, 9, Colossians 2:8).

11   **πνευματων** βιας: "the **power** of spirits…" Demonic spirits, as at Mark 1:27.

Georg Luck: "Some translators obscure these facts; they write, e.g., 'the power of the winds', when the context shows that daemons are meant. Josephus certainly understood the passage in this way." *Witchcraft and Magic in Europe: Ancient Greece and Rome*, 117.

12 την κατα των δαιμωνιων **τεχνην**: "**the art** of casting out demons…" or literally, "the art against the demons…"

13 **επωδας** τε συνταξαμενος: "and the formulation of **incantations**…"

14 τροπους **εξορκωσεων** κατελιπεν: "he left behind the ways **of performing exorcisms**…"

15 *Antiquities* 8.46-49.

Morton Smith noted that "Solomon's control of demons was a matter of pride for Josephus…is often reported in Rabbinic literature, and is the subject of a romance preserved in several Greek versions, The Testament of Solomon." *Jesus the Magician*, 79.

16 Matthew 12:22-32, 42, Luke 11:14-23, 41.

Appendix B: Mary Magdalene

Although the fabulist tendency in Christianity appeared early, the improbable and mutually incompatible infancy narratives of Matthew and Luke pale before subsequent inventions. The *Infancy Gospel of Thomas* [1] has the child Jesus making sparrows out of mud and bringing them to life as well as striking his playmates dead and raising them. Other early apocryphal Gospels and Acts recount fictional lives of Jesus' mother and inflated exploits of Peter and Paul, to which are soon added the amazing deeds of the swelling roster of martyrs and saints.

Modern readers may see in these stories quaint notions of a credulous by-gone age, but these pious fictions are testimony to Christianity's genius for taking imaginary contructs —the divinity of Jesus and thus Jews as deicides,[2] to name but one— and turning them into social firestorms that consume millions of lives. The prudent reader therefore approaches any Christian document, regardless of its supposed authenticity, with skepticism.

That said, what are we to make of Mary Magdalene and her purported role in the life of Jesus?

The New Testament records as many as seven women named Mary: the mother of Jesus,[3] Mary Magdalene,[4] Mary the mother of James and Joses,[5] Mary the wife of Clopas,[6] Mary the sister of Martha and Lazarus,[7] Mary the mother of John Mark,[8] and yet another Mary mentioned in passing by Paul.[9]

According to Luke 8:2, Mary Magdalene, from whom seven demons had been exorcised, is mentioned in connection with other women who gave financial support to Jesus and "the twelve."[10] There have been several occasions to point out Luke's deficiencies as a historian; this reference is possibly derived from the same source as the spurious ending of Mark which also mentions the demons cast out of Mary Magdalene.[11] The identification of Mary Magdalene as the sinful woman of Luke 7:37-38 is characterized by Danker as no more than "later ecclesiastical gossip." [12]

The remaining canonical references are all embedded in the crucifixion stories. Matthew includes Mary Magdalene as one of the "many women" from Galilee who watched the event "from far away."[13] Mark, from which the accounts in Matthew[14] and Luke[15] are probably derived, agrees that she was one of the women who looked on from afar, and that she, Mary the mother of James, and Salome went to the tomb to anoint Jesus' body.[16]

John's gospel places Mary Magdalene in a group that stood at the foot of the cross, a detail that not only contradicts the other gospels, but is historically improbable.[17] John has her going to the tomb on the first day of the week,[18] but does not mention other women. She then returns to Peter and the beloved disciple, reports that the tomb is empty, and says "*we* do not know where they put him."[19] John claims the disciples saw the empty tomb but were unaware of its significance because "they did not understand the scripture"[20] that foretold Jesus would be raised from the dead. Accompanied by angels,[21] Jesus appears to Mary Magdalene who mistakes him for the gardener and does not recognize him until he speaks to her. Only then does she announce that she has seen the Lord.[22]

The story of Mary's encounter with the risen Jesus is almost certainly a pious fabrication in which the name of a particular woman who followed Jesus as one of a group is singled out to star in an apocryphal drama. If the accounts in Matthew and Luke rely heavily on Mark, then the appearance of Mary Magdalene in their gospels has a simple explanation: Matthew and Luke found her name mentioned in Mark and copied it.

Her role in the gospel of John does little to clarify the issue of her identity. To the contrary, both the grammatical inconcinnity and logical ambiguity of the passages raise questions about the authenticity of the story as a whole. At any rate, there is not the slightest hint in any of these accounts that Mary Magdalene was Jesus' *inammorata*.

A reference to Mary Magdalene which is often cited is found in a gnostic Christian document which forms part of the Nag Hammadi trove. Although called the *Gospel of Philip*, it is not a gospel in the commonly understood biographic sense. It is instead an anthology with virtually no narrative framework, consisting of around a hundred brief excerpts from other gnostic texts, none of which are known to have survived. Originally composed in Greek, it is known to us in a Coptic translation tentatively dated in the 3rd century.

The Mary Magdalene saying, besides being couched in the enigmatic language beloved of gnostic writers, is grossly defective:

> "And the companions of the [small gap in the manuscript] Mary Magdalene [small gap] her more than [small gap] the disciples [small gap] kiss her [small gap] on the [gap]" (*Gospel of Philip*, 55) Our curiosity notwithstanding, we simply cannot know what was in the gaps. [23]

Despite the fill-in-the-blanks state of preservation of the document, that it is almost certainly a translation from other sources of unknown provenance, and that it has no corroboration in the canonical gospels, it has been cited repeatedly to reveal the romantic life of the "real" Jesus and Mary Magdalene.

A second fragmentary document, a papyrus codex purchased in Cairo in 1896, is a gnostic text called the *Gospel of Mary*. It presents Mary Magdalene, to whom the gospel attributes superior spiritual insight based on visionary experience, in conflict with Peter. The gnostic preoccupation with the relationship between sin and matter and the nature of the soul is everywhere present in what remains of the text.

There is little doubt that this gospel reflects a contest between the gnostic Christians, who evidently created a Mary Magdalene who was a feminine prototype of sorts, and the emerging orthodox leaders who rejected women as teachers. Although it provides a narrow window

299

into the squabbles between 2nd century Christian sects, it is pretty doubtful that the gospel has anything of historical interest to say about Mary Magdalene.

It bears reiterating that gospels —*all gospels*— are theological tracts written to advance the agendas of various Christian factions. Be that as it may, the authors of recent books have read these fragmentary works as if they were straightforward historical evidence, unencumbered by competing theologies. My object is not to question what agendas the authors of such books on Mary Magdalene may be seeking to advance, but to point out that the Jesus myth is still very much in the process of elaboration nearly 2000 years after its beginning, *and that its relevance is still being manufactured.* To use a biological analogy, one might see in the mythic Jesus the ideological equivalent of a pleuripotent stem cell with the capacity to differentiate into any one of numerous forms as the situation demands. Or from a less elevated perspective, we might simply regard Jesus as the ultimate inflatable date.

Notes

1   Written in the early 2nd century. A *Gospel of the Nazarenes*, a *Gospel of Peter*, a *Gospel of the Ebionites*, a *Gospel of the Hebrews* are also known. The *Gospel Q*, has been reconstructed in part by subtracting Mark from Matthew and Luke, and another lost document which served as the basis for the passion material in Mark and John almost certainly existed. In total, some 21 gospels in various states of preservation are known, as well as the names of another 13 that did not survive. *Journal of Early Christian Studies* 11: 139.

2   From ecclesiastical Latin *deicida, god-killer.*

3   Mark 6:3.

4   Mark 15:40, 47.

5   Mark 15:40, 47.

6   John 19:25.

   This Mary may be the same person as Mary the mother of James.

7   John 11:19.

8   Acts 12:12.

9   Romans 16:6.

10 The number 12 is almost certainly a fiction reflecting early apocalyptic expectations (Matthew 10:5-7, 19:28).

   Burton Mack: "…the notion 'the twelve' was developed in the course of mythic elaborations with the purpose of laying claim to the concept of Israel." *Who Wrote the New Testament*, 201.

11 Mark 16:9.

12 *Greek-English Lexicon of the New Testament*, 617.

13 Matthew 27:55.

   According to the best manuscript evidence, Mary's name is also recorded as *Mariam* the Magdalene (Matthew 27:56, 28:1).

14 Matthew 27:56, 61, 28:1.

15 Luke places her with Mary the mother of James and Joanna, and "the other women with them" (Luke 24:10). This is Luke's only other mention of Mary Magdalene.

16 Mark 15:40, 47, 16:1.

17 John 19:25.

18 John 20:1.

19 John 20:2.

20 John 20:9.

This is a strange statement indeed in light of Mark 10:32-34 which has Jesus tell his disciples that he will be condemned to death, executed, and rise again after three days. In John's gospel the disciples as well as Jesus' enemies are often portrayed as astoundingly dull-witted (John 7:27, 42, 8:21-25, 12:16, 13:21-28). If Jesus expected that his confrontation with the temple authorities would somehow bring on the apocalyptic beginning of the kingdom, and his arrest and execution came as a surprise to his disciples, then it would make sense that those who did not abandon the movement would retroactively come to "understand" the significance of his death by examining "the scripture."

21   The two angels clothed in white (John 20:12) are an expansion on Mark's young man in a white robe (Mark 16:5).

22   John 20:15-16, 18.

23   *Lost Christianities: The Battles for Scripture and the Faiths We Never Knew*, 122.

References and Suggested Reading

Achtemeier, Paul J. "Clement of Alexandria and a Secret Gospel of Mark," *Journal of Biblical Literature* 93: 625-628.

Aland, Barbara and Kurt. *Novum Testamentum Graece*, 27th edition, 1993, Deutsche Bibel-gesellschaft.

Alter, Robert. *The World of Biblical Literature*, 1992, Basic Books.

Angus, Samuel. *The Mystery Religions: A Study in the Religious Background of Early Christianity*, Dover Publications, 1975 (a reprint of the 1928 edition).

Baddeley, Gavin. *Lucifer Rising: Sin, Devil Worship and Rock 'n 'Roll*, 1999, Plexus.

Bertram, Georg. "ενεργεω" in *Theological Dictionary of the New Testament*, 1964, Gerhard Kittel, editor, William B. Eerdmans.

Betz, Hans Dieter. "Magic and Mystery in the Greek Magical Papyri" in *Magika Hiera: Ancient Greek Magic and Religion*, Christopher A. Faraone & Dirk Obbink, editors, 1991, Oxford Univer-sity Press.

—. "Introduction to the Greek Magical Papyri," in *The Greek Magical Papyri in Translation: Including the Demotic Spells*, 2nd edition, 1992, University of Chicago Press.

Boardman, John. "The sixth-century potters and painters of Athens and their public," in *Looking at Greek Vases*, Tom Rasmussen & Nigel

Spivey, editors, 1991, Cambridge University Press.

Bonner, Campbell. "Traces of Thaumaturgic Technique in the Miracles," *Harvard Theological Re-view* 20: 171-181.

—. "The Technique of Exorcism," *Harvard Theological Review* 36: 39-49.

Boswell, John. *Same-Sex Unions in Premodern Europe*, 1994, Vintage Books.

Brenton, Lancelot C.L. *The Septuagint with Apocrypha: Greek and English*, 2003, Hendrickson Publishers.

Breyfogle, Todd. "Magic, Women, and Heresy in the Late Empire: The Case of the Priscillianists," in *Ancient Magic and Ritual Power*, Marvin Meyer & Paul Mirecki, editors, 2001, Brill Academic Publishers.

Brier, Bob. *Ancient Egyptian Magic*, 1981, Quill.

Brown, Scott G. "On the Composition History of the Longer ("Secret") Gospel of Mark," *Journal of Biblical Literature* 122: 89-110.

Büchsel, Friedrich. "δεω" in *Theological Dictionary of the New Testament*, Gerhard Kittel, editor, 1964, William B. Eerdmans.

Burkert, Walter. *Greek Religion*, 1985, Harvard University Press.

—. *Ancient Mystery Cults*, 1987, Harvard University Press.

Butterworth, G. W. *Clement of Alexandria: The Exhortation to the Greeks*, 1982 (reprint), Harvard University Press.

Carlson, Steven C. "Clement of Alexandria on the 'Order' of the Gospels," *New Testament Studies* 47: 118-125.

Chadwick, Henry. *Priscillian of Avila: The Occult and Charismatic in the Early Church*, 1976, Oxford University Press.

Ciraolo, Leda Jean. "Supernatural Assistants in the Greek Magical Papyri" in *Ancient Magic and Ritual Power*, Marvin Meyer & Paul Mirecki, editors, 1991, Brill Academic Publishers.

Comfort, Philip W. & David P. Barrett, editors. *The Text of the Earliest New Testament Greek Manuscripts*, corrected and enlarged edition, 2001, Tyndale House Publishers.

Conner, Randy P. *Blossom of Bone: Reclaiming the Connections between Homoeroticism and the Sacred*, 1993, Harper San Francisco.

Couliano, Ioan P. *Eros and Magic in the Renaissance*, 1987, University of Chicago Press.

Criddle, A. H. "On the Mar Saba Letter Attributed to Clement of Alexandria," *Journal of Early Christian Studies* 3: 215-220.

Crossan, John Dominic. *The Historical Jesus: The Life of a Mediterranean Jewish Peasant*, 1991, Harper San Francisco.

—. *Four Other Gospels: Shadows on the Contours of Canon*, 1992, Polebridge Press.

Cryer, Frederick H. "Magic in Ancient Syria-Palestine and in the Old Testament," in *Witchcraft and Magic in Europe: Biblical and Pagan Societies*, Bengt Ankarloo & Stuart Clark, editors, 2001, University of Pennsylvania Press.

Danker, Frederick William. *A Greek-English Lexicon of the New Testament and Early Christian Literature*, 3rd edition, 2000, University of Chicago Press.

Deissmann, Adolf. *Light from the Ancient East: The New Testament Illustrated by Recently Discovered Texts of the Graeco-Roman World*, 4th edition, 1922, Harper & Brothers.

de Quincey, Christian. *Radical Nature: Rediscovering the Soul of Matter*, 2002, Invisible Cities Press.

Dickie, Matthew W. *Magic and Magicians in the Greco-Roman World*, 2001, Routledge.

DiZerega, Gus. *Pagans & Christians: The Personal Spiritual Experience*, 2001, Llewellyn Publications.

Dodds, E.R. *The Greeks and the Irrational*, 1951, University of California Press.

Duling, Dennis C. "Solomon, Exorcism, and the Son of David," *Harvard Theological Review* 68:235-252.

Ehrman, Bart D. *The Orthodox Corruption of Scripture: The Effect of Early Christological Controversies on the Text of the New Testament*, 1993, Oxford University Press.

—. "The Neglect of the Firstborn in New Testament Studies," Presidential Lecture, Society of Biblical Literature, 1997.

—. *Jesus: Apocalyptic Prophet of the New Millennium*, 1999, Oxford University Press.

—. "Response to Charles Hedrick's Stalemate," *Journal of Early Christian Studies* 11:155-163.

—. *Lost Christianities: The Battles for Scripture and the Faiths We Never Knew*, 2003, Oxford Uni-versity Press.

—. *The New Testament: A Historical Introduction to the Early Christian Writings*, 3rd edition, 2004, Oxford University Press.

Eitrem, Samson. "Dreams and Divination in Magical Ritual," in *Magika Hiera: Ancient Greek Magic and Religion*, Christopher Faraone & Dirk Obbink, editors, 1991, Oxford University Press.

Eliade, Mircea. *Images and Symbols: Studies in Religious Symbolism*, 1969, Sheed and Ward.

Elkin, Adolphus P. *Aboriginal Men of High Degree: Initiation and Sorcery in the World's Oldest Tradition*, 1977, Inner Traditions International.

Eyer, Shawn. "The Strange Case of the Secret Gospel According to Mark: How Morton Smith's Discovery of a Lost Letter by Clement of Alexandria Scandalized Biblical Scholarship," *Alexandria: The Journal for the Western Cosmological Traditions* 3: 103-129.

Faraone, Christopher A. "The Agonistic Context of Early Greek Binding Spells" in *Magika Hiera: Ancient Greek Magic and Religion*, Christopher Faraone & Dirk Obbink, editors, 1991, Oxford University Press.

Felton, Debbie. *Haunted Greece and Rome: Ghost Stories from Classical Antiquity*, 1999, University of Texas Press.

Finucane, Ronald C. *Ghosts: Appearances of the Dead and Cultural Transformation*, 1996, Prometheus Books.

Flint, Valerie. "The Demonization of Magic and Sorcery in Late Antiquity: Christian Redefinitions of Pagan Religions" in *Witchcraft and Magic in Europe: Ancient Greece and Rome*, Bengt Ankarloo & Stuart Clark, editors, 1999, University of Pennsylvania Press.

Fowler, Miles. "Identification of the Bethany Youth in the Secret Gospel of Mark with Other Figures Found in Mark and John," *The*

Journal of Higher Criticism 5/1: 3-22.

Gager, John G. *Curse Tablets and Binding Spells from the Ancient World*, 1992, Oxford University Press.

Garrett, Susan R. *The Demise of the Devil: Magic and the Demonic in Luke's Writings*, 1989, Fortress Press.

—. "Light on a Dark Subject and Vice Versa: Magic and Magicians in the New Testament" in *Religion, Science, and Magic: In Concert and in Conflict*, Jacob Neusner, Ernest S. Frerichs & Paul Virgil McCracken Flesher, editors, 1989, Oxford University Press.

Geller, Markham J. "Jesus' Theurgic Powers: Parallels in the Talmud and Incantation Bowls," *Journal of Jewish Studies* 28: 141-155.

Girardet, Edward. "Afghanistan," *National Geographic* 204: 32-33.

Gordon, Richard. "Imagining Greek and Roman Magic" in *Witchcraft and Magic in Europe: Ancient Greece and Rome*, Bengt Ankarloo & Stuart Clark, editors, 1999, University of Pennsylvania Press.

Graf, Fritz. *Magic in the Ancient World*, 1997, Harvard University Press.

—. "How to Cope with a Difficult Life: A View of Ancient Magic" in *Envisioning Magic: A Princeton Seminar and Symposium*, 1997, Peter Schäfer & Hans G. Kippenberg, editors, Brill Academic Publishers.

—. "Excluding the Charming: The Development of the Greek Concept of Magic" in *Ancient Magic and Ritual Power*, Marvin Meyer & Paul Mirecki, editors, 2001, Brill Academic Publishers.

Grundman, Walter. "ἰσχυω" in *Theological Dictionary of the New Testament*, 1964, Gerhard Kittel, editor, William B. Eerdmans.

Hale, John R., et al. "Questioning the Delphic Oracle," *Scientific American* 289/2: 66-73.

Hanse, Hermann. "εχω" in *Theological Dictionary of the New Testament*, 1964, Gerhard Kittel, editor, William B. Eerdmans.

Haren, Michael J. "The Naked Young Man: A Historian's Hypothesis on Mark 14,51-52," *Biblica* 79: 525-531.

Hedrick, Charles W. "The Secret Gospel of Mark: Stalemate in the Academy," *Journal of Early Christian Studies* 11: 133-145.

Hoffman, R. Joseph. *Jesus Outside the Gospels*, 1984, Prometheus Books.

—. *Celsus: On The True Doctrine, A Discourse Against the Christians*, 1987, Oxford University Press.

—. *Julian's Against the Galileans*, 2004, Prometheus Books.

Holmes, Michael W. "Reasoned Eclecticism in New Testament Textual Criticism" in *The Text of the New Testament in Contemporary Research: Essays on the Status Quaestionis*, Bart D. Ehrman & Michael W. Holmes, editors, 1995, William B. Eerdmans.

Holzer, Hans. *Ghosts: True Encounters with the World Beyond*, 1997, Black Dog & Leventhat Publishers.

Hull, John M. *Hellenistic Magic and the Synoptic Tradition*, 1974, SCM Press Ltd.

Hutton, Ronald. "Modern Pagan Witchcraft" in *Witchcraft and Magic in Europe: The Twentieth Century*, Bengt Ankarloo & Stuart Clark, editors, 1999, University of Pennsylvania Press.

Janowitz, Naomi. *Magic in the Roman World: Pagans, Jews and Christians*, 2001, Routledge.

Jennings, Theodore W. Jr. *The Man Jesus Loved: Homoerotic Narratives from the New Testament*, 2003, Pilgrim Press.

Johnston, Sarah Iles. *Restless Dead: Encounters Between the Living and the Dead in Ancient Greece*, 1999, University of California Press.

Jones, Prudence and Nigel Pennick. *A History of Pagan Europe*, 1995, Routledge.

Kee, Howard Clark. "Magic and Messiah" in *Religion, Science, and Magic: In Concert and in Conflict*, Jacob Neusner, Ernst S. Frerichs & Paul Virgil McCracken Flesher, editors, 1989, Oxford University Press.

—. "The Terminology of Mark's Exorcism Stories," *New Testament Studies* 14: 232-246.

Kieckhefer, Richard. *Magic in the Middle Ages*, 1989, Cambridge University Press.

Kittel, Gerhard. "αγγελος" in *Theological Dictionary of the New Testament*, 1964, Gerhard Kittel, editor, William B. Eerdmans.

Kirby, Peter. "The Case Against the Empty Tomb," *The Journal of*

Higher Criticism 9: 175-202.

Klauck, Hans-Josef. *Magic and Paganism in Early Christianity: The World of the Acts of the Apostles*, 2003, Fortress Press.

Koester, Helmut. *Ancient Christian Gospels: Their History and Development*, 1990, Trinity Press International.

Kotansky, Roy. "Incantations and Prayers for Salvation on Inscribed Greek Amulets" in *Magika Hiera: Ancient Greek Magic and Religion*, Christopher Faraone & Dirk Obbink, editors, 1991, Ox-ford University Press.

—. "Greek Exorcistic Amulets" in *Ancient Magic and Ritual Power*, Marvin Meyer & Paul Mirecki, editors, 2001, Brill Academic Publishers.

Kraeling, Carl H. "Was Jesus Accused of Necromancy?" *Journal of Biblical Literature* 59: 147-157.

La Fontaine, Jean. "Satanic Abuse Mythology" in *Witchcraft and Magic in Europe: The Twentieth Century*, Bengt Ankarloo & Stuart Clark, editors, 1999, University of Pennsylvania Press.

Lake, Kirsopp. *Eusebius: The Ecclesiastical History*, Books I-V, 1926, Harvard University Press.

Lane Fox, Robin. *Pagans and Christians*, 1989, Alfred A. Knopf.

Larsson, Edvin. "εχω" in *Exegetical Dictionary of the New Testament*, Horst Balz & Gerhard Schneider, editors, 1991, William B. Eerdmans.

Luck, Georg. *Arcana Mundi: Magic and the Occult in the Greek and Roman Worlds*, 1985, Johns Hopkins University Press.

—. "Theurgy and Forms of Worship in Neoplatonism," in *Religion, Science, and Magic: In Concert and in Conflict*, Jacob Neusner, Ernest Frerichs & Paul Virgil McCracken Flesher, editors, 1989, Oxford University Press.

—. "Witches and Sorcerers in Classical Literature," in *Witchcraft and Magic in Europe: Ancient Greece and Rome*, Bengt Ankarloo & Stuart Clark, editors, 1999, University of Pennsylvania Press.

Mack, Burton L. *The Lost Gospel: The Book of Q and Christian Origins*, 1993, Harper San Fran-cisco.

—. *Who Wrote the New Testament? The Making of the Christian Myth*, 1995, Harper San Francisco.

MacMullen, Ramsay. *Christianizing the Roman Empire: A.D. 100-400*, 1984, Yale University Press.

Meyer, Marvin. *Secret Gospels: Essays on Thomas and the Secret Gospel of Mark*, 2003, Trinity Press International.

Meyer, Marvin and Richard Smith, editors. *Ancient Christian Magic: Coptic Texts of Ritual Power*, 1994, Harper San Francisco.

Marcovich, Miroslav. *Origenes: Contra Celsum Libri VIII*, 2001, Brill Academic Publishers.

Martinez, David. "'May She Neither Eat Nor Drink': Love Magic and Vows of Abstinence" in *Ancient Magic and Ritual Power*, Marvin Meyer & Paul Mirecki, editors, 2001, Brill Academic Publishers.

Michelet, Jules. *Witchcraft, Sorcery, and Superstition*, 1995, Citadel Press.

Metzger, Bruce M. *The New Testament: Its Background, Growth, and Content*, 2nd edition, enlarged, 1987, Abingdon Press.

Meyer, Marvin. *Secret Gospels: Essays on Thomas and the Secret Gospel of Mark*, 2003, Trinity Press International.

— and Richard Smith. "Introduction" in *Ancient Christian Magic: Coptic Texts of Ritual Power*, 1994, Harper San Francisco.

Munier, Charles. *Saint Justin: Apologie pour les Chrétiens*, 1995, Éditions Universitaires Fribourg Suisse.

Muñoz Delgado, Luis. *Léxico de magia y religión en los papiros mágicos griegos*, 2001, Consejo Superior de Investigaciones Científicas.

Neusner, Jacob. "Science and Magic, Miracle and Magic in Formative Judaism: The System and the Difference" in *Religion, Science, and Magic: In Concert and in Conflict*, Jacob Neusner, Ernest S. Frerichs & Paul Virgil McCracken Flesher, editors, 1989, Oxford University Press.

Nissinen, Martti. *Homoeroticism in the Biblical World*, 1998, Fortress Press.

Ogden, Daniel. "Binding Spells: Curse Tablets and Voodoo Dolls in the Greek and Roman Worlds" in *Witchcraft and Magic in Europe: Ancient Greece and Rome*, Bengt Ankarloo & Stuart Clark, editors, 1999, University of Pennsylvania Press.

—. *Greek and Roman Necromancy*, 2001, Princeton University Press.

—. *Magic, Witchcraft and Ghosts in the Greek and Roman Worlds*, 2002, Oxford University Press.

Osborn, Eric. "Clement of Alexandria: A Review of Research, 1958-1982," *The Second Century: A Journal of Early Christian Studies* 3: 219-244.

Otto, Walter F. *Dionysus: Myth and Cult*, 1965, Indiana University Press.

Oulton, J.E.L. Eusebius: *The Ecclesiastical History*, Books VI-X, 1932, Harvard University Press.

Pagels, Elaine. *The Gnostic Paul: Gnostic Exegesis of the Pauline Letters*, 1975, Trinity Press International.

—. *The Origin of Satan*, 1995, Random House.

Pearson, Birger A. *Gnosticism, Judaism, and Egyptian Christianity*, 1990, Fortress Press.

Pesce, M. and A. Dietro. "La lavanda dei piedi di Gv 13,1-20, il Romanzo de Esopo e I Saturnalia de Macrobio," *Biblica* 80: 240-249.

Peters, Edward. "Superstition and Magic from Augustine to Isidore of Seville" in *Witchcraft and Magic in Europe: The Middle Ages*, Bengt Ankarloo & Stuart Clark, editors, 2002, University of Pennsylvania Press.

Pinch, Geraldine. *Magic in Ancient Egypt*, 1994, University of Texas Press.

Powell, Mark Allen. "The Magi as Wise Men: Re-examining a Basic Supposition," *New Testament Studies* 46: 1-20.

Preisendanz, Karl. *Papyri Graecae Magicae: Die Griechischen Zauberpapyri*, 2001 (reprint), K.G. Saur.

Price, Robert. *Journal of Higher Criticism* 2/2: 69-99.

Quesnell, Quentin. "The Mar Saba Clementine: A Question of Evidence," *The Catholic Biblical Quarterly* 37: 48-67.

Rabinowitz, Jacob. *The Rotting Goddess: The Origin of the Witch in Classical Antiquity's Demonization of Fertility Religion*, 1998, Automedia.

Ricks, Steven D. "The Magician as Outsider in the Hebrew Bible and the New Testament" in *Ancient Magic and Ritual Power*, Marvin Meyer

& Paul Mirecki, editors, 2001, Brill Academic Publishers.

Ritner, Robert K. "Curses" in *Ancient Christian Magic: Coptic Texts of Ritual Power*, 1994, Harper San Francisco.

Robertson, A.T. *A Grammar of the Greek New Testament in the Light of Historical Research*, 3rd edition, 1934, Broadman Press.

Robinson, James M., Paul Hoffmann and John S. Kloppenborg. *The Sayings Gospel Q in Greek and English*, 2002, Fortress Press.

Rubenstein, Richard E. *When Jesus Became God: The Epic Fight over Christ's Divinity in the Last Days of Rome*, 1998, Harcourt Brace & Company.

Samain, P. "L'accusation de magie contre le Christ dans les évangiles," *Ephemerides Theologicae Lovanienses* 15: 449-490.

Sanders, Ed Parish. *The Historical Figure of Jesus*, 1993, The Penguin Press.

Selwyn, Edward Gordon. *The First Epistle of St. Peter: The Greek Text with Introduction, Notes and Essays*, 1952, Macmillan & Company.

Schlier, Heinrich. "δακτυλος" in *Theological Dictionary of the New Testament*, 1964, Gerhard Kittel, editor, William B. Eerdmans.

Schmidt, Brian B. "The 'Witch' of Endor, 1 Samuel 28, and Ancient Near Eastern Necromancy" in *Ancient Magic and Ritual Power*, Marvin Meyer & Paul Mirecki, editors, 2001, Brill Academic Publishers.

Scholem, Gershom G. *Major Trends in Jewish Mysticism*, 1941, Schocken Publishing House.

Schweitzer, Albert. *The Quest of the Historical Jesus*, 1910, Adam & Charles Black, Ltd.

Smith, Morton. *Clement of Alexandria and a Secret Gospel of Mark*, 1973, Harvard University Press.

—. *The Secret Gospel: The Discovery and Interpretation of the Secret Gospel According to Mark*, 1973, Harper & Row.

—. "On the Authenticity of the Mar Saba Letter of Clement," *The Catholic Biblical Quarterly* 38: 196-199.

—. *Jesus the Magician*, 1978, Harper & Row.

—. "Clement of Alexandria and Secret Mark: The Score at the End of the First Decade," *Harvard Theological Review* 75: 449-461.

Starr, Joshua. "The Meaning of Authority in Mark 1.22," *Harvard Theological Review* 23: 302-305.

Strelen, Rick. "Who Was Bar-Jesus (Acts 13,6-12)?" *Biblica* 85: 65-87.

Stroumsa, Guy G. "Comments on Charles Hedrick's Article: A Testimony," *Journal of Early Christian Studies* 11: 147-153.

Thomsen, Marie-Louise. "Witchcraft and Magic in Ancient Mesopotamia" in *Witchcraft and Magic in Europe: Biblical and Pagan Societies*, Bengt Ankarloo & Stuart Clark, editors, 2001, University of Pennsylvania Press.

Trachtenberg, Joshua. *Jewish Magic and Superstition: A Study in Folk Religion*, 1970, Atheneum.

Van Hoye, Albert. "La fuite du jeune homme nu (Mc 14,51-52)," *Biblica* 52: 401-406.

Van Voorst, Robert E. *Jesus Outside the New Testament: An Introduction to the Ancient Evidence*, 2000, William B. Eerdmans Publishing Company.

Wallace, Daniel B. "The Majority Text Theory: History, Methods, and Critique." In *The Text of the New Testament in Contemporary Research: Essays on the Status Quaestionis*, Bart Ehrman & Michael W. Holmes, editors, 1995, William B. Eerdmans.

—. *Greek Grammar Beyond the Basics: An Exegetical Syntax of the New Testament*, 1996, Zondervan Publishing House.

—. "7Q5: The Earliest NT Papyrus?" (2005) www.bible.org.

—. "The Synoptic Problem." (2005) www.bible.org.

Wenham, J.W. *The Elements of New Testament Greek*, 1991 edition, Cambridge University Press.

Winkler, John J. "The Constraints of Eros." In *Magika Hiera: Ancient Greek Magic and Religion*, Christopher Faraone & Dirk Obbink, editors, 1991, Oxford University Press.

Young, Richard A. *Intermediate New Testament Greek: A Linguistic and Exegetical Approach*, 1994, Broadman & Holman Publishers.

Index

JSM - Journal for the Academic Study of Magick ISSN 1479-0750

A multidisciplinary, peer-reviewed print publication, covering all areas of magic, witchcraft, paganism etc; all geographical regions and all historical periods.

Issue 1 £13.99, airmail $25, ISBN 1869928 679, 200pp
Beyond Attribution: The Importance of Barrett's Magus/Alison Butler * Shadow over Philistia: A review of the Cult of Dagon/John C. Day * A History of Otherness:Tarot and Playing Cards from Early Modern Europe/ Joyce Goggin * Opposites Attract: magical identity and social uncertainty/Dave Green * 'Memories of a sorcerer': notes on Gilles Deleuze-Felix Guattari, Austin Osman Spare and Anomalous Sorceries./Matt Lee * Le Streghe Son Tornate: The Reappearance of Streghe in Italian American Queer Writings/Ilaria Serra * Controlling Chance, Creating Chance: Magical Thinking in Religious Pilgrimage/Deana Weibel

Issue 2 £19.99, ISBN 1869928 725, , 420pp
Alien Selves: Modernity and the Social Diagnostics of the Demonic in 'Lovecraftian Magick': Woodman/Wishful Thinking Notes towards a psychoanalytic sociology of Pagan magic: Green/A Shell with my Name on it: The Reliance on the Supernatural During the WW1. Chambers/The Metaphysical Relationship between Magic and Miracles: Morgan Luck/Demonic Possession, and Spiritual Healing in Nineteenth-Century Devon: Semmens/ Human Body in Southern Slavic Folk Sorcery: Filipovic & Rader/Four Glasses Of Water: Snell/The Land Near the Dark Cornish Sea:. Hale/Kenneth Grant and the Magickal revival: Evans/Magic through the Linguistic Lenses of Greek mágos, Indo-European *mag(h)-, Sanskrit màyà and Pharaonic Egyptian ¡eka: Cheak/The symbolism of the pierced heart: Froome/Nicholas Roerich: McCannon/Book Review, etc.

Issue 3 £19.99, ISBN 1869928962, 300pp
Contents: Hannah Sanders - Buffy and Beyond: Language and Resistance in Contemporary Teenage Witchcraft / Amy Lee - A Language of Her Own: Witchery as a New Language of Female Identity/ Dave Green - Creative Revolution: Bergsonisms and Modern Magic / Mary Hayes - Discovering the Witch's Teat: Magical Practices, Medical Superstitions in The Witch of Edmonton / Penny Lowery - The Re-enchantment of the Medical: An examination of magical elements in healing. / Jonathan Marshall - Apparitions, Ghosts, Fairies, Demons and Wild Events: Virtuality in Early Modern Britain / Kate Laity - Living the Mystery: Sacred Drama Today / David Geall - 'A half-choked meep of cosmic fear' Is there esoteric symbolism in H.P.Lovecraft's The Dream-Quest of Unknown Kadath? / Susan Gorman - Becoming a Sorcerer: Jean-Pierre Bekolo's Quartier Mozart and the Magic of Deleuzian and Guattarian Becoming / Book Reviews

Visit our website: www.mandrake.uk.net
or call for a catalogue on +44 (0)1865 243671
email mandrake@mandrake.uk.net
write to: PO Box 250, Oxford, OX1 1AP (UK)

outrageous claim P   he could well
have been a homosexual quote alike
Beutel he was d too high a
records on the other & every two seated   distortion?
gays lesbians are a   natural quote.
by humanity throughout its history.

Printed in the United Kingdom
by Lightning Source UK Ltd.
110963UKS00001B/388